Multicultural Awareness in the Health Care Professions

María C. Juliá

Contributing Authors:
Hilda Burgos-Ocasio
Elizabeth L. Chung
Karen V. Harper
Anahid DerVartanian Kulwicki
Shary Scott Ratliff
María J. Robbins
Daryle Spero
Gretchen H. Waltman
Greta Berry Winbush

Allyn and Bacon
Boston • London • Toronto • Sydney • Tokyo • Singapore

Executive Editor: Karen Hanson
Managing Editor, Social Work: Judy Fifer
Vice-President, Publisher: Susan Badger
Editorial Assistant: Jennifer Normandin
Executive Marketing Manager: Joyce Nilsen
Production Administrator: Annette Joseph
Production Coordinator: Holly Crawford
Editorial-Production Service: Ann Mohan,
    WordCrafters Editorial Services, Inc.
Composition Buyer: Linda Cox
Manufacturing Buyer: Aloka Rathnam
Cover Administrator: Suzanne Harbison
Cover Designer: Jennifer Burns

Printed on Recycled Paper

Library of Congress Cataloging-in-Publication Data
Multicultural awareness in the health care professions: María C.
    Juliá; contributing authors, Hilda Burgos-Ocasio . . . [et al.]
        p.   cm.
    Includes bibliographical references and index.
    ISBN 0-13-142234-0 (pbk.)
    1. Transcultural medical care—United States.   2. Health behavior—
United States—Cross-cultural studies.   3. Ethnic groups—Medical
care—United States.   4. Minorities—Medical care—United States.
I. Julia, Maria C.
RA418.5.T73M85   1995
362.1'08'693—dc20
                                                                     95-13345
                                                                        CIP

Printed in the United States of America

10 9 8 7 6 5 4 3 2   00 99 98 97 96

Contents

Preface

> *To my parents, with love,*
> *MCJ*

The continuing demographic changes in the United States are forcing those who work in the helping professions to recognize that they must become not only more culturally sensitive but also culturally competent. Helping professionals are confronting the fact that they must deal with different ethnic groups in their daily work, and they are recognizing that cultural proficiency has become a necessity if they are to meet the needs and challenges presented by these groups. Competent practice with ethnic groups involves attending to people's cultural values and sociocultural reality (Chau, 1991). Competent practice implies ethnocultural knowledge and acceptance of the cultural values, beliefs, and uniqueness of the groups being served. This book responds to the need for a desk reference for health care professionals that will assist them in understanding different ethnic groups with whom they interact in their daily practice.

The book is designed with two audiences in mind: students and practitioners of the helping professions, particularly the health care professions. The structure and content of the book make it useful both as a classroom primary text and as a professional desk reference. Each chapter provides concrete and practical information on health-related ethnic variables that will help readers gain cultural awareness, knowledge, sensitivity, and understanding and, consequently, the foundation for competent practice in working with a variety of ethnic groups. The book is also intended as a secondary textbook in courses dealing with cultural diversity and ethnicity in professional education in areas such as education, law, medicine, nursing, social work, and theology. It provides information that will enable teachers to introduce approaches to multiculturalism in the helping professions. It encourages an approach that is *multicultural*, that puts the emphasis on the culture, not the professional.

The chapters address the history, characteristics, and culture of different ethnic groups, focusing on understanding the health beliefs and practices of each group. Because culturally diverse individuals "should be the primary source of information about their situation, condition or direction, [and] any efforts directed at identifying, developing, or evaluating information related to the culturally diverse should involve individuals from the specific populations" (Locke, 1992, p. 159), the book was conceived and written with ethnic and gender strategies in mind. Each chapter was written by a woman experienced in the helping professions who, in all but one case, is indigenous to the ethnic group about which she writes. As Locke wrote, "We must ask the culturally different to write their own stories" (1992, p. xii), and these women's descriptions and analyses of their experiences and understanding of their culture give students and health care professionals the opportunity to obtain firsthand knowledge about different ethnic groups with whom they will be interacting in their professional practice.

An anonymous reviewer pointed out that the majority of information for the human and medical services fields has been written by men. We need female perspectives to provide new understandings. Since this book provides mainly maternal and child health examples, female representatives of each culture are particularly suited to discuss the woman-centered themes and practices characteristic of their culture, as well as cultural barriers to health services delivery. Each writer, however, addresses the heterogeneity of her ethnic group and within-group differences and discloses her subgroup identity as a potential bias. The authors also bring to the work orientations from a variety of health care professions—nursing, social work, nutrition, home economics, and medicine—adding a multidisciplinary perspective to this multicultural study.

To provide a model for examining ethnic diversity and to ensure consistency in the content of the chapters, each author followed an organizational and conceptual framework established in a detailed outline. The outline guided the authors in making sure that relevant ethnic variables were given consideration. The emphasis that the individual authors have placed on selected elements of the culture and their differing approaches to the common framework reflects the cultural significance and cultural relevance of topics to the individual ethnic groups. Unevenness in the elements highlighted in different chapters reflects the uniqueness of each group.

We cannot expect health care professionals to be knowledgeable about every ethnic group or about all cultural aspects of a given group. But what is core and important knowledge from the perspective of indigenous authors can contribute to the understanding of the priorities and basic cultural elements of each ethnic group.

The chapters are structured to include (a) major themes of history and an overview of the ethnic group, (b) patterns of acculturation and assimilation, (c) the cultural group's conception of health and illness, (d) cultural beliefs, (e) illustrations of maternal and child health practices, and (e) potential barriers to the formal health care delivery system. The chapters also include glossaries and lists of suggested readings. The following list of cultural themes introduces the concepts covered in each of these major areas:

History and Overview of the Culture

- Geographic location
- Immigration patterns
- Current and historical political patterns
- Group composition

Acculturation and Assimilation

- Assimilation and acculturation patterns
- Language usage
- Philosophical and religious belief systems

Cultural Concepts of Health, Illness, and Death

- Views and beliefs
- Coping strategies

Cultural Concepts of Health and the Family

- Definition of family (immediate, extended, and kinship networks)
- Function and structure of the family
- Roles

Cultural Beliefs

- Folk medicine
- Illness causation
- Healing practices
- Cultural roles related to the practice of folk medicine
- Perception of medical practice and health care providers

Maternal and Child Health Practices: Cultural Illustrations

- Presence or absence of rites of passage
- Cultural view of pregnancy and prenatal care
- Genetic predispositions in regard to prenatal care and birth defects
- Medical interventions during pregnancy
- Acceptance of high-technology and life support systems
- Adolescent pregnancy
- Infertility
- Labor and childbirth
- Perceptions of breastfeeding and circumcision
- Childrearing practices
- Infant care
- Nutrition

Potential Barriers to the Health Care Delivery System

- Cultural factors in gaining access to health care
- Attitudes toward health care personnel
- Ability to communicate
- Other factors that may affect access to care

The book is not intended to be a comprehensive description of all cultures present in the United States, nor does it attempt to address every aspect of the cultures presented here. The treatment of the various ethnic groups introduces health care providers to the values, beliefs, and practices of different people in order to sensitize them to the presence of differences among ethnic groups. The book seeks to expand our understanding of cultural differences and to encourage a building on cultural strengths based on differences and similarities. The authors explore the concept of contemporary health care delivery for women and children to bridge gaps in communication and relationships between ethnic groups. We hope to promote and facilitate competency in our daily encounters with ethnic minorities in the health care system and to create a level of understanding that will lead to the road to good health for everyone.

Acquiring multicultural knowledge and skills should be a top priority of health care professionals. By educating ourselves in multiculturalism, we are acting on our commitment to the needs and issues of ethnic groups: "To do less will only serve to keep ethnic groups in the position of victims of racism and ourselves in the role of oppressors" (Jones, 1990, p. 70). The Introduction and Chapter 1 address the basic concepts of culture, ethnicity, and health and their relevance to the thrust and goal of the book.

ACKNOWLEDGMENTS

We would like to express our appreciation to Professors John D. Bower, of Bethel College; Aida M. Bruns, of Bridgewater State College; Jane Isaacs Lowe, of the University of Pennsylvania; Deborah H. Siegel, of Rhode Island College; and Oliver J. Williams, of the University of Minnesota, for their helpful reviews of the original manuscript. Thanks also to Nancy Roberts, Karen Hanson, and Judy Fifer at Allyn and Bacon and Ann Mohan at WordCrafters for their continuing practical assistance. Most of all, to Jim, my appreciation for always being there with support and encouragement. Thank you for helping me in shaping many of my ideas.

REFERENCES

Chau, K. (1991). Social work with ethnic minorities: Practice issues and potentials. *Journal of Multicultural Social Work, 1*(1), 23–39.

Jones, W. T. (1990). Perspectives on ethnicity. *New Directions for Student Services, 51*, 59–72.

Locke, D. (1992). *Increasing multicultural understanding: A comprehensive model.* Newbury Park, CA: Sage.

Introduction

The editor of this book has been practicing in the health field for many years in various capacities—as a frontline health care provider, administrator of health services, policymaker, planner, researcher, and educator. In each of these professional positions, she has experienced one of today's most critical crises in health care: a lack of cultural awareness, understanding, sensitivity, and competency in dealing with the variety of ethnic subcultures present in the United States. Early in her career, she saw that both the conventional models of providing health care and, as research indicates, the traditional approaches to health care delivery are inappropriate and unacceptable for an ethnically heterogeneous population (Rathwell & Phillips, 1986).

Three basic assumptions set the framework for the book. First, culture exerts its most fundamental and far-reaching influence through the methods we employ to understand and respond to illness (Kleinman, 1978). Second, neither Zangivill's (1911) "melting-pot" conceptualization of U.S. society nor Hodgkinson's (1987) "rainbow coalition" approach does justice to or reflects the multiethnic reality of this country. Rather, the multiethnic society is a mosaic in which every part contributes to the whole without losing its uniqueness and particular values. Third, health care providers often are unaware of and lack knowledge and understanding of the cultural or ethnic differences of the people with whom they work.

Three areas in which the health needs of ethnic groups need to be taken into account and where substantial changes need to take place are (1) better planning of services, (2) greater inclusion of ethnic minority professionals, and (3) improved multicultural training of existing health service providers. In fact, in his discussion about multiculturalism, Axelson (1993) stressed the need for professionals to become knowledgeable and understanding of the cultures that make up U.S. society. We believe this book will contribute to achieving these goals.

Health care providers from all disciplines usually participate in conferences, workshops, and other educational activities that address the issues of culture and ethnicity. Although these activities are valuable, issues are not always addressed comprehensively. Quality time for discussion may be limited, coverage of cultural subgroups may be either too superficial or overwhelming, or the information about groups may begin to merge and confuse listeners. Consequently, at the end of what should be an enlightening experience, health care professionals may not be sure whether the healing practice of *espiritismo* is used by Hispanics or Asians, whether yen medicine is practiced by Hispanics, or whether *Hakins* is the author of a book they should read. As a result of personal and professional interactions with health professionals involved in working with ethnic subgroups, the authors of this book believe strongly that there is a need for more and better mechanisms for developing cultural awareness, sensitivity, and competency in working with various ethnic subgroups. We strongly agree with Axelson (1993) that the key to understanding an individual is based on an appreciation of "the uniqueness of each person in the context of that person's group experience" (p. 21)—that is, the person's ethnic background.

Recognizing the importance of these ideas led to the development of this book. Determining its format was another task. Over too many cups of coffee for conscientious health professionals, we decided to work on a resource to help health professionals deal with multicultural issues. As the idea took shape, it became clear to us that what was needed was a desk reference with discrete chapters summarizing some of the most prevalent historical and acculturation background characteristics, values, and beliefs of ethnic subgroups in the United States and the groups' views, approaches, and practices concerning illness and health. We wanted the work to be a valuable reference in health care professionals' libraries, a source they could refer to for better understanding when they encountered a member of a different ethnic group who needed health care.

The book covers a number of the different ethnic groups residing in the United States, including not only the larger, more acknowledged groups, but also groups that are rapidly increasing in size. Together, these include African Americans, Amish, Appalachians, Arabs, Asians, Hispanics, Jews, and Native Americans. Some groups, such as African Americans and Hispanics, were obvious choices based on their large population. Other groups, such as persons from the Arabic nations, were included based on recent political developments that are expected to have an impact on immigration. The rationales for inclusion of other small groups are presented by the authors in their individual chapters.

The criteria for selecting authors to contribute chapters to the book included (a) education and experience as a health professional, (b) involvement as an indigenous person within one of the selected subgroups, and (c) experience with and commitment to the provision of services to a particular ethnic community.

Providing health care that meets the needs of ethnic groups requires the health care professional to consider cultural, social, religious, and linguistic differences. Health care professionals "cannot effectively understand the clients' problems without having some understanding of the problems peculiar to the clients' . . . background" (Montalvo, Lasater, & Valdez, 1982, p. 342). As Rathwell and Phillips (1986) have indicated, these ethnic variables include cultural differences and attitudes toward illness, health, and health care; unfamiliarity with, poor understanding of, and distrust of health care professionals, service models, and facilities, as well as other perceived and real barriers to care such as stigma attached to particular diseases; differences in personal life-style patterns and family hierarchy; and language difficulties. Hardships associated with distinct cultural differences, the stresses of immigration, and the presence of prejudices and discrimination are other particularly important factors that inhibit people from seeking health care. All of these environmental barriers and social hardships are associated with the disproportionate incidence of health problems found among the various ethnic subgroups in U.S. society.

Professionals organize health care services for people, but it is the people who decide when to use them. Although the United States has attempted to develop service delivery models for specific cultural groups, many ethnic groups are chronically underserved and many service providers continue to ask, "Why don't they come to the clinic?" (Boyle & Andrews, 1989). As an alternative, we need to develop national policies and procedures that are responsive to the specific needs and problems of ethnic minorities. The current Westernized model of health care in this multiethnic society does not work because it does not reach many of those it intends to serve. Providing health care to ethnic minorities is "frequently ineffective because providers of services do not understand the culture of the ethnic group they are [serving]" (Thoma, 1977, p. 124). If proposed health care reforms are to be successful in reaching underserved ethnic groups, cultural differences and ethnic realities need to be taken into consideration in the organization, planning, and implementation of health services.

Designing services and planning for the workforce to implement them will have to include adaptations to diversity. Ethnic diversity also will have to be considered in selecting and using treatment modalities and approaches and in targeting staff skills. Otherwise, many services will continue to "be incomplete, inappropriate and unresponsive to the needs and interests of minority populations" (Montalvo et al., 1982, p. 342).

Responses to health and illness are social phenomena; they are not guided solely by physiological processes (Schlesinger, 1985). Each culture has its own explanatory model of illness (causes, onset, course, and treatment), and it is very likely different from that of the health professionals and health care organizations involved in the helping process (Germain, 1984). Many times these perceptions of health and illness depart dramatically from and are seemingly incongruous with the prevailing approaches to health (Schlesinger, 1985). Under these circumstances, the attitudes of the individuals providing care are of utmost importance. Utilization of health services will occur when there is a "goodness of fit" between the services provided and the sociocultural reality of the individual(s) being served (Chau, 1991, p. 23).

Practitioners who aspire to work in a cross-cultural context need to cultivate an awareness of their own cultural values, beliefs, and feelings and how these influence their attitudes and behaviors toward clients. Client and practitioner both bring role expectations and stereotypes from their own cultural reference groups that can cause cultural conflicts (Leininger, 1988). As well as bringing their own ethnic influences to the health care setting, health care practitioners are also socialized into the subculture of their own profession. In health care institutions, a special language is spoken, rituals are practiced, and a set of beliefs is maintained within a system that in itself is ethnocentric (Spector, 1985).

The predominant health care system in this country is a medical model based on the belief that physiological processes can be manipulated through biochemical and technological means. Many of these practices must seem strange and illogical to individuals from other cultures. Medical facilities may be far removed from a client's orientation to a more holistic, spiritual, and family-based context for healing. The goal of a culturally appropriate and competent program is to bridge the gap by making service relevant to cultural patterns.

The authors did not want to limit their efforts only to sensitizing helping professionals to cultural diversity; they also wanted to introduce the knowledge and understanding needed for development of competencies. To develop competency and empowerment, however, practitioners must first start by identifying and sensitizing themselves to the problems faced by various ethnic groups before they can develop the ability to act with relevance in working with people who are different from themselves. In his model of multicultural understanding, Locke (1992) discussed a set of principles of multicultural practice. Among the guidelines presented for enhancing multicultural understanding, he stressed learning "as much as possible about different cultures and [sharing] what you learn with others" (p. 161). Knowledge and understanding of cultural values, attitudes, beliefs, and behaviors are critical, and they lead to an increased capability to work with people from different cultures. Knowledge about traditional health-related practices of the cultural group, folk medicine, remedies common to the cultural group, and the cultural definition of care is essential to the health care professional (Kavanagh & Kennedy, 1992). Culturally sensitive care encourages effective interaction, a step toward improving health care services. This is the ultimate goal of this book.

REFERENCES

Axelson, J. (1993). *Counseling and development in a multicultural society.* Pacific Grove, CA: Brooks/Cole.

Boyle, J. S., & Andrews, M. M. (1989). *Transcultural concepts in nursing care.* Glenview, IL: Scott Foresman.

Chau, K. (1991). Social work with ethnic minorities: Practice issues and potentials. *Journal of Multicultural Social Work, 1*(1), 23–39.

Germain, C. (1984). *Social work practice in health care: An ecological perspective.* New York: The Free Press.

Hodgkinson, H. (1987). The demographic picture and what it means for higher education: Special report. *Black Issues in Higher Education, 3*(22), 2–3.

Kavanagh, K., & Kennedy, P. (1992). *Promoting cultural diversity: Strategies for health care professions.* Newbury Park, CA: Sage.

Kleinman, A. (1978). Clinical relevance of anthropological and cross-cultural research: Concepts and strategies. *American Journal of Psychiatry, 135*(4), 427–431.

Leininger, M. (1988). Leininger's theory of nursing: Cultural care diversity and universality. *Nursing Science Quarterly, 1*(4), 152–160.

Locke, D. (1992). *Increasing multicultural understanding: A comprehensive model.* Newbury Park, CA: Sage.

Montalvo, F., Lasater, T., & Valdez, N. (1982). Training child welfare workers for cultural awareness: The culture simulator technique. *Child Welfare, 61*(6), 341–352.

Rathwell, T., & Phillips, D. (1986). *Health, race, and ethnicity.* London & Dover, NH: Croom Helm.

Schlesinger, E. (1985). *Health care social work practice: Concepts and strategies.* St. Louis: Times Mirror/Mosby.

Spector, R. E. (1985). *Cultural diversity in health and illness* (2nd ed.). Norwalk, CT: Appleton-Century-Crofts.

Thoma, M. (1977). The effects of a cultural awareness program on the delivery of health care. *Health and Social Work, 2*(3), 123–136.

Zangivill, I. (1911). *The melting pot: Drama in four acts.* New York: Macmillan.

▶ 1

Understanding
the Concepts

The United States is made up of people of diverse national origins, races, religions, histories, and cultures. The dynamic interplay of old, recent, and new immigrants has had and continues to have a significant impact on the national identity and ethnicity of the country. Some theorists (e.g., Katz & Ivey, 1977) argue that the melting pot is an antiquated concept. Others assert that Whites who "hold the melting pot view and do not see themselves belonging to any race or ethnic group have denied their ethnocentricity" (Jones, 1990, p. 65). In place of the blended image of cultures, the present reality of nonassimilation makes pluralism a strong and significant characteristic of U.S. society. Thus, multiculturalists advocate a nation in which "the goal . . . is unity in diversity, [where] the dominant culture benefits from coexistence and interaction with the cultures of adjunct groups" (Axelson, 1993, p. 14).

According to Jones (1990), by the year 2010 one third of the U.S. population will be regarded as minority. U.S. citizens will trace their descent to Africa, Asia, the Hispanic world, the Pacific Islands, and Arabia, rather than to White Europe. This increasing ethnic diversity raises numerous and important challenges for U.S. society. What will be the relations among persons of different ethnic backgrounds, and how will the concerns and sociopolitical actions of the United States as a nation be altered?

RELATING DIVERSITY TO HEALTH CARE CONCERNS

A critical area of concern within this environment of ethnic diversity is health. How healthy will the people who are born into and/or reared in an ethnocentric culture within a multicultural society be? Is the soaring infant morbidity and mortality rate in specific ethnic groups a reflection of those groups' inability to assimilate into the predominant Anglo-Saxon culture, the result of the economic and political structures of society, or the effect of a health care system oblivious to ethnic differences? These questions have implications for how we increase our awareness, knowledge, and appreciation of cultural differences, because "when we want to understand people['s] . . . [problems and needs], we need to know about their culture" (Jones, 1990, p. 60).

If one subscribes to a holistic view of health and ethnicity as a gestalt of interrelated parts in the life of an individual, culture becomes a primary consideration. Culture is the fabric of meaning through which humans interpret their experiences and guide their actions. It provides the external sources of information the individual needs in giving meaningful cues to the larger environment and social system. Culture is most commonly defined as a set of beliefs, assumptions, and values widely shared by a group that serves to structure the behavior of the individuals of the group throughout the course of their life (Rizk, 1991). Some theorists suggest that there is no such thing as human nature independent of culture (Geertz, 1973). Becoming humanized is becoming an individual, and people become individuals under the guidance of the cultural patterns of their families and communities. Culture provides a link to other members of the group, provides meaningful rituals throughout life, and directs individual behavior. All humans must face life's challenges and crucial events, such as birth, growth, disease, death, conflict, and communication (Berreman et al., 1971), and culture provides the medium through which negotiation of these life events may be understood, shared, and communicated.

According to Wood (1989), ethnic groups are "distinguished on the basis of race, religion, or national origin" (p. 351). She establishes the distinction between ethnicity and culture, with the definition of one concept inclusive of the other: *Culture* refers to socially transmitted beliefs, institutions, and behavior patterns, while *ethnicity* "connotes a common history, a shared culture, a sense of peoplehood" (Wood, 1989, p. 351). Axelson (1993) conceptualizes ethnicity as derived from national or geographical place of origin, while Harwood (1981) defines it as a collectivity on the basis of common origin and shared culture. The individual's perception of the world and view of human nature are defined and views of self or identity are determined, valued, and respected within the ethnic group. The culture can be seen as an instrument for satisfying individual needs for problem solving, relieving stress, and adjusting to the external realities of life.

Broadly conceived, culture can be described as "the totality of learned, socially transmitted behavior of a group" (Axelson, 1993, p. 3). Culturally sensitive and knowledgeable professionals should be able to understand not only core interrelated concepts such as rules, status, roles, and values, but also the important considerations of any group of people, such as gender identities, family structure, parenthood, religious practices, and folk medicine. By acknowledging these influences of culture on personal identities and the role culture plays in people's lives, we begin to understand the implications of culture for the health care professions and helping processes.

IMPORTANCE OF CULTURAL CONGRUENCE IN HEALTH CARE

All ideology attempts to explain the why of things (Berreman et al., 1971). Religion provides rules of conduct that prescribe how a person should act in relation to the sacred, and it accounts for many facets of behavior and rituals of a society. Like language, religion serves as another important mechanism for cultural identity: satisfying the believer's need to be strengthened and reaffirmed at regular intervals. A religion identifies individuals as members of a group who ascribe to practices that assume and protect their role in the universe (Durkheim, 1915).

From these beliefs often emerges folk medicine, an important consideration when examining health care. Folk medicine is used by virtually all ethnic groups, all age groups, both sexes, and by most people regardless of financial status. Over time, folk medicine has been relinquished to the rigors and standards of the scientific methods of medicine. Instead of extracting truth, meaning, and practicality from folk practices, scientific medical practice has belittled and dismissed them, creating a schism between medicine as we know it in "establishment" health care and medicine as it is known to people from various ethnic groups. As a result, large pieces of the human experience are ignored by modern medicine because they do not fit into the edifice created by current medical scientific philosophy, and this alienates ethnic groups from the mainstream culture.

Ethnicity is "often a determinant of social inequality" (Wood, 1989, p. 352) as ethnic groups are relegated to minority status—that is, they are disadvantaged in terms of political, social, and economic opportunities. In health care, minority status is reflected in issues related to discrimination (i.e., barriers to access and availability of services) (Wood, 1989, p. 392), while ethnicity is particularly relevant in considering the factors that determine attitudes and beliefs about health as well as health-related behaviors (Harwood, 1981). Affirmation of diversity involves recognizing the effects of cultural differences on the definition and interpretation of illness and wellness. To address these perceptions accurately, the cultural meaning of healing also needs to be examined from the experience of the group. Since it is culture, not nature, that influences an individual's perception of health or disease, the system of healers and healing emerges directly from the prevalent world view of a culture (Boyle & Andrews, 1989). *Healing*—the alleviation of illness as culturally experienced by an individual—needs to be placed within the context of the traditional systems of health care to be understood. This is also the case with *care*, another health-related concept bound by cultural expectations. Essential for human growth, well-being, coping, curing, and survival (Leininger, 1988), care must be culturally congruent to be acceptable to the recipient.

The effectiveness of health care providers in reaching and working with multicultural populations rests heavily upon the sensitivity, respect, and understanding paid to ethnic diversity. The barriers to providing appropriate services to ethnic populations are a lack of appropriate informational materials concerning resources, rights, and responsibilities for multiethnic groups, compounded by a shortage of trained bilingual, multiculturally educated personnel among health care provider organizations (Chan, 1990). The subsequent lack of culturally responsive service affects client behavior, access, and outcome.

ETHNOCENTRISM, ACCULTURATION, AND ASSIMILATION

Since health professionals are generally members of the dominant culture as well as their own ethnic subgroup, it is imperative that they become aware of the values, beliefs, and traditions associated with their own ethnicity. We have been acculturated and socialized to our own value systems, and these processes include setting standards for judgment and deciding what is good and what is bad. It becomes easy to tune others out, and this ethnocentrism, or an individual's preoccupation and identification with his or her own culture, sometimes leads to inaccurate judgments about all other groups (Berreman et al., 1971).

Ethnocentrism can be a socially useful psychological consequence of learned culture, but it often leads to failures in understanding and accepting other people that may produce sharp conflicts between groups (Berreman et al., 1971). The assimilation of an individual from a cultural minority into the dominant culture occurs by mutual consent: "For some, the dominant culture resists assimilation. For others, the immigrant group [or individual(s)] itself elects to remain outside the main cultural group" (Locke, 1992, p. 5). Either way, individuals from ethnic subgroups are affected by both the issues of their individual ethnic group and those of the dominant culture.

Acculturation, the intermeshing of various cultural threads of ethnic and mainstream groups, ameliorates the friction between groups through an often implied or acknowledged acceptance of another culture's ways of thinking and doing things. Acculturation entails a dynamic process of rearranging experiences, selecting appropriate functional elements that provide for the individual or group easy transition through a life event in the mainstream culture (Rizk, 1991). Due to its adaptive function, acculturation is usually considered to be positive, and the underlying assumption is that the greater the acculturation the better the outcome (Rizk, 1991). However, this is not always the case. A study published recently suggested that infant mortality rates for Mexican Americans may be getting worse as the members of this culture become "Americanized" (Rizk, 1991). As learned behaviors in the Hispanic culture change (e.g., support for the pregnant woman by her community and low incidence of smoking and drinking during pregnancy), the outcome of pregnancy worsens.

Acculturation is adaptation. Assimilation is change. Assimilation implies a gradual process over time wherein one set of cultural traits is relinquished and a new set is acquired through communication with and participation in the dominant culture. For example, English-speaking immigrants assimilate more easily into society than do immigrants who do not speak English. The latter soon discover the desirability of learning the new language for gaining acceptance into the mainstream culture.

The degree of acculturation of the individual varies according to age, generation, social support, socioeconomic opportunities, length of residence in the United States, and, most important, personality characteristics and life experiences. In the process of adapting to the mainstream culture, the individual selects which values of his or her ethnic culture to retain and which of the new culture to incorporate. From the mainstream cultural perspective, retained remnants of the ethnic culture explain such phenomena as folk medicine and voodoo, practices and beliefs that stand out as markedly different from the dominant culture (Kumabe, Nishida, & Hepworth, 1985).

CHALLENGE TO HEALTH CARE PROFESSIONALS

Individuals retain or relinquish their ethnicity according to the meaning they find in it. Since the degree to which individuals display behaviors associated with their culture varies, the challenge is to be sensitive without stereotyping (Randall-David, 1989). In order to personalize care, culture must be considered in addition to the wide variety of other forces that affect how a person behaves (Roberts, n.d., cited in Rizk, 1991). Understanding begins at the most basic level of concern and respect for the individual and is "learned best by meeting the people themselves and letting them describe who they are from their own perspective" (Spector, 1985, p. 244). It is important to identify the strengths present within cultural differences and collaborate with those strengths. Practitioners and health care planners need to approach the community to describe how care can best be delivered and the individual to define how care can best be received. For this, clients become the best source of information. Respecting a person's cultural inheritance shows a respect for the person. This book is about respect and appreciation of ethnic diversity.

REFERENCES

Axelson, J. (1993). *Counseling and development in a multicultural society*. Pacific Grove, CA: Brooks/Cole.

Berreman, G. D., & contributing consultants. (1971). *Anthropology today*. CA: CRM Books.

Boyle, J. S., & Andrews, M. M. (1989). *Transcultural concepts in nursing care*. Glenview, IL: Scott Foresman.

Chan, S. (1990). Early intervention of culturally diverse families of infants and toddlers with disabilities. *Infants and Young Children: An Interdisciplinary Journal of Special Care Practices, 3*(2), 78–87.

Durkheim, E. (1915). *The elementary forms of religious life*. New York: Free Press.

Geertz, C. (1973). *The interpretation of culture*. New York: Basic Books.

Harwood, A. (1981). *Ethnicity and medical care*. Cambridge, MA: Harvard University Press.

Jones, W. T. (1990). Perspectives on ethnicity. *New Directions for Student Services, 51*, 59–72.

Katz, J., & Ivey, A. (1977). White awareness: The frontier of racism awareness training. *Personnel and Guidance Journal, 55*, 485–487.

Kumabe, K., Nishida, C. & Hepworth, D. (1985). *Bridging ethnocultural diversity in social work and health*. Honolulu: University of Hawaii.

Leininger, M. (1988). Leininger's theory of nursing: Cultural care diversity and universality. *Nursing Science Quarterly, 1*(4), 152–160.

Locke, D. (1992). *Increasing multicultural understanding: A comprehensive model*. Newbury Park, CA: Sage.

Rizk, M. (1991). *An introduction to cultural differences*. Unpublished manuscript. Cleveland, OH: Cleveland Regional Perinatal Network.

Spector, R. E. (1985). *Cultural diversity in health and illness* (2nd ed.). Norwalk, CT: Appleton-Century-Crofts.

Wood, J. (1989). Communicating with older adults in health care settings: Cultural and ethnic considerations. *Educational Gerontology, 15*, 351–362.

SUGGESTED READINGS

Brazelton, B. (1990). *Zero to three.* Washington, DC: National Center for Clinical Infant Programs.

Denis, R. (1985). Health beliefs and practices of ethnic and religious groups. In E. Watkins & A. Johnson (Eds.), *Removing cultural and ethnic barriers to health care* (pp. 12–28). Chapel Hill: University of North Carolina.

Pedersen, P. (1990). The multicultural perspective as a fourth force in counseling. *Journal of Mental Health Counseling, 12*(1), 93–95.

Pedersen, P. (1988). *Handbook for developing multicultural awareness.* Alexandria, VA: American Association for Counseling and Development.

Randall-David, E. (1989). *Strategies for working with culturally diverse communities and clients.* Washington, DC: Association for the Care of Children's Health.

Rautenberg, E. (1990). *Ethnicity and health: The pluralist papers.* New York: Institute on Pluralism and Group Identity, American Jewish Committee.

Watkins, E., & Johnson, A. (1985). *Removing cultural and ethnic barriers to health care,* (pp. 12–28). Chapel Hill: University of North Carolina.

▶ 2

African-American
Health Care:
Beliefs, Practices,
and Service Issues

GRETA BERRY WINBUSH

When clients or patients come into your office or agency, they represent not only individuals but also a family, a group of people, or a segment of society. To best meet their needs, it is important to understand their past and current circumstances. Maximizing service delivery to minority populations, and particularly to African Americans, requires sensitivity to the following information:

Historical background.
Health beliefs and practices.
Major health-related concerns.
Patterns of response to major health-related needs.

OVERVIEW OF AFRICAN AMERICANS

Entry into the United States

African Americans vary by time lived in the United States, country of origin, and immigration patterns. The majority of African Americans did not come to the United States voluntarily; they were brought here as slaves. Even though they have been here as long as the first European settlers, they still find themselves discriminated against and often unwelcomed in many facets of everyday life (e.g., education, occupation, health care, law).

Not all of the original African Americans were slaves. Some were free during the slavery period, but they were still treated slightly worse than White slaves (Pinkney, 1993). More recent immigrants have included economic and political refugees from the Caribbean, who unfortunately are subjected to similar or greater discrimination.

Sociodemographic Information

African Americans comprise the largest minority population in the United States, and their numbers are increasing at a faster rate than the numbers of European Americans (Feagin & Feagin, 1993; Pinkney, 1993). African Americans are younger and have proportionately more older adults than any other minority group. The women outnumber the men. Although African Americans as a group have gained some advantage, by almost all aggregate socioeconomic measures of well-being (e.g., income, living standards, health and life expectancy, occupation, residential opportunities, and political and social participation), they have fared worse than European Americans (Pinkney, 1993). In fact, some consistently remain in disadvantaged circumstances (Wilson, 1987), and their plight is a growing concern among African-American communities. This group includes individuals who remain at the lower socioeconomic level of society across generations. They are unemployed and receive public assistance for finances, housing, food, and health care.

African-American Families and Churches

The primary social institutions of African Americans are the family and the church, followed by social and political organizations. The family and the church have the most influence on the everyday lives of African Americans whether one focuses on their strengths or their weaknesses. Despite historical factors undermining African-American families (slavery; matriarchal myths; economic, social, and legal inequalities; and the changing role of the church), these social institutions have prevailed. Contrary to popular belief, not all African-American families live in poverty and not all are father-absent. Indeed there are undesirable gaps on the economic front, but the number of African Americans represented in the middle to upper socioeconomic classes has increased. Moreover, two-parent households are much more prevalent among African-American families than is popularly believed. African-American families vary by type of marriage, household pattern, family functioning, and degree of stability, just as other population groups vary. These families have strong kinship bonds, a strong work orientation, a strong religious orientation, and adaptability of family roles (Hill, 1972; Russell & Jewell, 1992).

Churches play an important role in African-American communities. Religion among African Americans can be traced back to African traditions in which religion filtered through all aspects of family and community life—work, education, health, and recreation (Mbiti, 1989). For example, Roberson (1985) found religion to be linked to health beliefs. Prayer is often a common method of treating health-related concerns for African Americans (Spector, 1985), particularly among the middle class and older adults (Gibson, 1982). To some, the church is considered the most important factor in family life, providing a sense of identity, community, ministry, education, socialization, and advocacy (Feagin & Feagin, 1993; Pinkney, 1993). In fact, many African-American political leaders have been ministers.

However, just as there is diversity in types of family among African Americans, there are also diversities in church life and its impact. The collective "Black church" that is frequently referred to actually represents a number of churches within African-American communities that vary in religious beliefs, organization, and activities. This diversity is often reflective of denominational or nondenominational philosophies (i.e., Christians, Hebrew denominations, Islamic groups, Seventh-Day Adventists, and Jehovah's Witnesses) (Pinkney, 1993). Although there is diversity in African-American church and family life, some common threads include the strengths generated by support networks, religious organizations, and informal health care systems. Unfortunately, each of these areas is currently striving to maintain or redefine its role given the social, economic, and health challenges confronting African-American communities today (e.g., teen pregnancy, an aging population, AIDS). For example, interest is growing in the capacity of the church to meet the needs of its members with respect to caring for older adults (Walls, 1993), preventing drug use and violence among youth (Issacs, 1992), and lessening family instability (Pinkney, 1993).

CONCEPTS OF HEALTH AND HEALTH CARE PRACTICES

Views of Health, Illness, and Death

According to Jackson (1981), "the presence of standardized cultural rituals of marriage, birth, and death applicable to African Americans as an ethnic group, have yet to be identified" (p. 116). However, assumptions have been made about each of these areas. Bailey (1991) and others have suggested that African Americans primarily have their roots in West Africa and therefore reflect some of the cultural beliefs and patterns common to West Africans, such as extended family networks and a strong belief in spiritualism (Hines & Boyd-Franklin, 1982; Pinderhughes, 1982). For example, West Africans traditionally have perceived health as a dynamic process of the mind, body, and spirit (Jacques, 1976), and they have attributed illness to naturalistic and personalistic causative agents (e.g., demons, evil spirits, a spell) or disharmony with God (Jacques, 1976; Powers, 1982; Spector, 1985). Similarly, Russell and Jewell (1992) have noted that African Americans characterize health as a continuum evolving around mind, body, and soul, not as a dichotomy between mind and body. It also has been noted that African Americans' views on health vary in that some hold themselves responsible for their own health, some hold others responsible, some see poor health as a part of aging, and some see poor health as a result of spells (Jackson, 1981). These varied views might explain the paucity of empirical information on the preference for and prevalence of use of either mainstream or nonmainstream medical health care systems among African Americans. However, both systems are used by African Americans, and health care providers need to sensitize themselves to one another's strengths in the common goal of improving their clients' health status.

Health Beliefs and Health Practices

Health belief models attempt to explain why people engage in healthy behavior, their use of health care services, and how they follow medical recommendations. Family health behaviors (e.g., service use) are based on beliefs—a set of assumptions about the costs and benefits of the behaviors—and these in turn are based upon cultural and personal histories, previous experience with the "helping professions," and any other experiences (Thompson, 1992). For some African Americans, perceived costs (whether financial, psychological, or social) related to help seeking are often insurmountable.

Bailey (1991) examined help-seeking behavior among a group of urban African Americans using Chrisman's (1977) health-seeking model. He viewed help-seeking behavior as the sick person's actions and the steps taken to resolve the health problem. Chrisman saw this process as consisting of five major steps, which are not necessarily sequential but are important relative to an individual's particular sociocultural setting. African Americans in Bailey's (1991) study fit Chrisman's model:

1. For African Americans, sociocultural and psychological factors prevent personal and public recognition of illness symptoms.
2. The illness-related shifts in role behavior prove conflicting for African Americans given their reluctance to accept rights and obligations due the "sick role" and their ever pressing familial obligations (particularly for African American women).
3. For African Americans, lay consultation and referral outside the household consisted mostly of friends and/or other relatives, not formal health care professionals.

Susceptibility to a disease and motivation often are associated with African Americans' decision to seek care (Berkanovic & Telesky, 1985). They are more likely to see a physician if it is easy to do so, if there is continuity of care, and if they feel they are unusually susceptible to disease. African Americans need far more explicit evidence than is presently available for claims of illness and a friendlier source of care in order to seek medical attention.

4. Treatment actions vary according to class, region, and degree of assimilation including self-help, alternative or native health practitioners, and formal health professionals (Bailey, 1991).

African Americans' responses to poor health are diverse; they include self-help remedies, folk medicine, mainstream services, or no treatment at all. No one particular strategy can be associated with African Americans as a group. According to Jackson (1981), health care responses fall into two general modes of action: self-treatment or treatment by others. This model of symptom management can be used regardless of ethnic identity or geographic location.

Self-help strategies often consist of home remedies such as those used for colds, coughs, sore throats, fever, stomach and intestinal problems, rashes, and aches (Kronenfield & Wasner, 1982; Powers, 1982; Scott, 1974). Specifically, these remedies include teas, syrups, castor oil, roots, wine poultices, special diets, vitamins, jewelry, and topical ointments. However, a particular person's favorite remedy depends on family tradition and prior experience (Roberson, 1987).

Help from others is provided predominantly by the family, and particularly by women in the family (i.e., mother, wife, daughter), followed by friends or relatives outside the home (Jackson, 1981). Use of nonmainstream health strategies does occur among African Americans, but the use of mainstream health strategies is more prevalent (Kronenfield & Wasner, 1982).

Some elements of folk medicine continue to be favored by segments of the U.S. population. The unorthodox healers include, among others, homeopaths, chiropractors, and faith healers (Kronenfield & Wasner, 1982). Healers, fortune tellers, root doctors, and herb doctors, to name a few, are found in African-American folk culture (Powers, 1982). Traditionally, these paraprofessionals were sanctioned in a variety of ways: through a calling from God, training from a family member, or years of practice. Their functions included treatment of serious and nonserious illnesses, counseling, and removal of hexes (spells). Referrals usually came from family members, and client satisfaction was reportedly high (Powers, 1982).

African Americans may regard traditional folk healers more highly than those associated with modern medicine (Capers, 1991), and they are more likely to seek significant blood relatives or others for health care than traditional health and human service agencies in times of stress (Lassiter, 1987) and in dealing with personal health problems (Neighbors, 1985). This is particularly evident among African-American women (Baker & Cook, 1983) and among inner-city women seeking health advice during pregnancy (St. Clair & Anderson, 1989). However, studies of health and healing practices of five ethnic groups have revealed serial or simultaneous use of both orthodox and folk systems of care (Kronenfield & Wasner, 1982; Powers, 1982; Scott, 1974).

5. Adherence to treatment is a problem regardless of race; however, [the problem] is noticeably high among African Americans (Bailey, 1991).

Although Jackson (1981) stressed the scarcity of hard data on patient compliance for African Americans, data have shown that there are both attitudinal (e.g., willingness or lack of) and behavioral (e.g., carrying out or ignoring doctor's orders) responses to treatment recommendations (Davis, 1968). Models for examining compliance behavior might shed further light on these behaviors among particular ethnic and nonethnic groups in the United States.

In sum, just as there is diversity in health beliefs and practices in general, there are intragroup differences among African Americans relative to particular beliefs and practices. Undoubtedly, these issues are not unique to African Americans, but African Americans have been found to possess stronger, more deep-seated contemporary health beliefs than Hispanics and Asian Americans (O'Hair, O'Hair, & Southward, 1987), and they show a greater concern about their health (Weissfeld, Kirscht, & Brock, 1990). African Americans also tend to hold more positive and confident beliefs about health care providers and the delivery system than do Hispanic and Asian Americans (O'Hair et al., 1987).

MAJOR HEALTH-RELATED CONCERNS

Health Care Status

In comparison to White Americans, African Americans are in dispropor-
tionately poor health and have been so since the days of slavery (Bryd &
Clayton, 1992). They have higher prevalence rates for major chronic diseases (e.g., cancer, diabetes, heart disease, and stroke). Moreover, they have
significantly higher morbidity and mortality rates than White Americans
and, in some cases, other minority groups (Holloway & Yam, 1992; U.S.
Department of Health and Human Services, 1990). The rates for African-
American women are slightly higher than those for White women
(Pinkney, 1993; Reed, 1992). There are gender differentials as well; Black
men most often show higher rates than White men and White women
(Holloway & Yam, 1992).

Areas of troubling health statistics in African-American communities
include infant and maternal mortality; pregnancy among unmarried teens;
impoverished living conditions of Black children; homicide among young
African-American males; chemical dependency of adults, children, and,
increasingly, newborns; and AIDs among teens and infants (Edelman,
1990; Emanuel, Hale, & Berg, 1989; Issacs, 1992; Kessel, Kleinman, Koontz,
Hogue, & Berendes, 1988; McBride, 1991; Pinkney, 1993; Reed, 1992;
Thompson, 1992).

Infant and Maternal Mortality

Although infant mortality rates have declined, the large disparity between
African Americans and nonminority groups is still troubling (Kessel et al.,
1988). African-American women are less likely to have adequate prenatal
care and more likely to have late or no prenatal care (Reed, 1992). A profile
of the women who receive little or no prenatal care revealed that these
women are poor, uneducated, and unmarried; have no health insurance or
regular health provider; and often have experienced feelings of depression
and negative attitudes toward health care and prenatal care in general
(Reed, 1992).

Low birth weight is the most significant factor in neonatal deaths,
including Black infant mortality (Reed, 1992). Speculation about causes
includes the high number of African-American mothers who are unmarried, teenagers, of high parity, and less educated—factors strongly associated with low birth weight (Emanuel et al., 1989). These authors preclude
race alone as the predominating factor.

Further inquiry into the causes of infant mortality has generated the
possibility of nongenetic factors such as the mother's childhood environ-

ment (e.g., her mother's interuterine life, her mother's adult stature) and her pregnancy environment (e.g., weight, urban lifestyle, lead poisoning) as contributing factors (Emanuel et al., 1989, Kessel et al., 1988; Reed, 1992). These findings suggest that health care policymakers should go beyond universal care during the nine months of pregnancy and delivery and look toward improving the childhood environments of Black women. In short, society must be sensitive to the care of its children. More important, it must understand that the lack of such sensitivity is a long-term detriment to its communities.

Some researchers have concluded that low access to and utilization of obstetric care by African-American women and other minority group women are factors in their high rates of maternal mortality (Hughes, Johnson, Rosenbaum, Butler, & Simons, 1988; Reed, 1992). Hughes and others (1988) have concluded that a history of poor access to medical care has impacted both prenatal and postnatal care of both mothers and infants. Adverse birth outcomes for African Americans are related to low socioeconomic status, inadequate prenatal care, lack of access to maternal and child health programs, and lead poisoning (Reed, 1992). Preventive measures to date have been directed toward nutrition and education in healthy lifestyles for parents and children.

Adolescent Pregnancy

The pregnancy rate for non-White teenagers is twice that for White teenagers. African-American mothers are younger, they are more likely to have premarital births, and they are less likely to place their babies for adoption (Mech, 1986; Pinkney, 1993; Zelnick & Kantner, 1974).

Some see the high rate of teen pregnancy in African-American communities as alarming due to its economic consequences. Children living below the poverty level in substandard housing face increased health and social risks (Pinkney, 1993). Although studies have shown that young African-American mothers are less responsive to their infants than White mothers (Engelke & Engelke, 1992; Luster & Rhoades, 1989), it has also been found that those who believe that their behavior will make a difference tend to engage in behavior that stimulates development in their infants (Engelke & Engelke, 1992).

African-American Children Living in Poverty

African-American children are more likely now than they were in 1980 to be born into poverty, lack early prenatal care, have single mothers or unemployed parents, be unemployed as teenagers, and not go to college after high school graduation (Edelman, 1990). For some of these factors, the likelihood is two to five times greater for African-American children than for white children.

Ghetto life associated with poverty is also characterized by debilitating health practices and debilitated health. As early as the 1840s, the impact of ghetto conditions on health was clear with regard to tuberculosis and high infant mortality (Foner, 1970). Economics and health status go hand in hand.

Homicide

Homicide and family violence (e.g., child abuse, wife abuse, elder abuse) are a growing public health concern. Homicide, in particular, is a growing concern in African-American communities, where it is the leading cause of death for young men and women (Reed, 1992). For an African-American male aged 15 to 24, homicide is now the most likely cause of death (Reed, 1992). The risk of death by homicide for African-American male youths is greater than that for young African-American females, young White males, and young White females (Pinkney, 1993).

AIDS

African-American communities have a disproportionate share of conditions conducive to the spread of AIDS (e.g., lack of knowledge about transmission and prevention, low socioeconomic status) (Reed, 1992). African Americans are at a greater risk of getting AIDS, and this risk is a growing reality in AIDS-related infant and child mortality.

Chemical Dependency

Although reports of African-American involvement with drugs are exaggerated and often contradictory, there is some merit to the reports of growing use among African Americans, and, most important, to the detriments associated with drug use (e.g., homicide, crack-cocaine-addicted babies, homelessness) (Pinkney, 1993; Reed, 1992). According to Pinkney (1993), explanations for this problem in African-American communities can be traced back to issues of poverty and racism. More specifically, standards of behavior are set forth by society for all persons, but options for achieving them are limited for minority persons such as African Americans.

PATTERNS OF RESPONSE TO HEALTH CARE NEEDS

African Americans' Response to Health Needs

African Americans' use of health care services varies depending on the problem and the type of service (Jackson, 1981). For example, in a study of indicators of use such as office and hospital visits, the rates for African Americans were low for the former and high for the latter in comparison to European Americans (National Center for Health Statistics, 1990). African Americans were most likely to seek health care in hospital outpatient departments, emergency rooms, and health centers. However, income, more than race, was the prevailing factor in these use patterns (National Center for Health Services Research, 1982). African Americans are less likely to have a regular family doctor, and use of health care services is typically episodic (Reed, 1992).

More specifically, despite the increased availability of services for maternal and child health care, these services are not being used or are underused by many mothers, particularly minority and poor women and children (Reed, 1982). Although there has been some research supporting the association of health beliefs and health behavior in this area, research has shown that this relationship could possibly change over time and during the course of treatment (Kviz, Dawkins, & Ervin, 1985).

There is a growing thrust toward self-help—that is, African Americans identifying resources within their own communities to address their concerns. African-American self-help is important, but the task of resolving their problems is not only that of African-American communities, but also that of society at large. Solutions are couched not only in self-help strategies, but also in policy and program efforts at the federal, state, and local levels.

System Response to Health-Related Concerns of African Americans

For African Americans, cultural beliefs and health practices have a significant impact on the use of health care services, and these beliefs and practices vary across age, socioeconomic status, geographic location, and degree of assimilation into the larger society (Russell & Jewell, 1992). To say the least, the current health care regimes fail to incorporate the cultural health beliefs and practices of African Americans. This is particularly sad, given that studies show that although these beliefs do affect adherence to treatment regimes (Berg & Berg, 1989), poor health is not a consequence of fundamental beliefs about health (Weissfeld et al., 1990).

As with their health status, African Americans fare worse than nonminorities in access to and delivery of health care (Bryd & Clayton, 1992; Council on Ethical and Judicial Affairs, 1990). It is felt that slavery and racial segregation in the early socioeconomic and political development of the United States planted a deeply rooted racial divide in the areas of hospitals, medical education and professions, and allocation of health care services (Bryd & Clayton, 1992; McBride, 1991). Although an early twentieth century Black health movement provided the seed for community-based or indigenous Black community health mobilization, it, too, was ineffective in reducing major infectious diseases and other health problems of African Americans, primarily due to the inadequacy of Black hospitals (McBride, 1991).

More specifically, at a time when African-American women, infants, and adolescents are experiencing high AIDS rates, programs to control the spread of AIDS have not been as successful in African-American communities as in nonminority communities (McBride, 1991). And often those programs that do offer some help in addressing health-related concerns in African-American communities are threatened by budget cuts or elimination.

Removing Barriers to Service Use

Disparities in health care are due in part to barriers stemming from both the client and the system (Russell & Jewell, 1992). More specifically, barriers for African Americans include inability to pay, lack of transportation or child care, decreased understanding of treatment plans, and inability to incorporate prescribed health plans into daily living patterns (Russell & Jewell, 1992).

System barriers involve policies, administration, and the development and delivery of appropriate treatment models. Bailey (1991) has suggested that clinicians expand their biopsychosocial service delivery models to include specific sociocultural information concerning African Americans' patterns of seeking health care. Cultural patterns do make a difference in patient care, and this concept will facilitate development of practical and culturally relevant programs. Bryd and Clayton (1992) have suggested that the African-American medical profession rise to the challenge of the continuing health care crisis in their communities. According to these authors, "Health care is evolving into the next civil right in question for African Americans" (p. 197).

REFERENCES

Bailey, E. (1991). *Urban African American health care.* Lanham, MD: University Press of America.

Baker, A., & Cook, G. (1983). Stress, adaptation and the black individual. *Journal of Nursing Education, 22,* 237–242.

Berg, J., & Berg, B. L. (1989). Compliance, diet and cultural factors among Black Americans with end-stage renal disease. *Journal of National Black Nurses' Association, 3,* 16–28.

Berkanovic, E., & Telesky, C. (1985). Mexican-American, African-American, and White-American differences in reporting illnesses, disability, and physician visits for illness. *Social Science and Medicine, 20*(6), 567–577.

Bryd, W., & Clayton, L. (1992). An American health dilemma: A history of Blacks in the health system. *Journal of the National Medical Association, 84*(2), 189–200.

Capers, C. (1991). Nurses' and lay African Americans' views about health behavior. *Western Journal of Nursing Research, 13*(1), 123–135.

Chrisman, N. (1977). The help-seeking process: An approach to the natural history of illness. *Culture and Medical Psychiatry, 1,* 351–377.

Council on Ethical and Judicial Affairs. (1990). Black-White disparities in health care. *Journal of the American Medical Association, 263*(17), 2344–2346.

Davis, M. (1968). Physiologic, psychological and demographic factors in patient compliance with doctors' orders. *Medical Care, 6,* 115–122.

Edelman, M. W. (1990). The Black family in America. In E. C. White (Ed.), *The Black women's health book: Speaking for ourselves.* New York: Seal Press.

Emanuel, I., Hale, C., & Berg, C. (1989, Autumn). Poor birth outcomes of American Black women. *Journal of Public Health Policy,* pp. 299–308.

Engelke, M., & Engelke, S. (1992). Predictors of the home environment of high risk infants. *Journal of Community Health Nursing, 9*(3), 171–181.

Feagin, J., & Feagin, C. (1993). *Racial and ethnic relations.* Englewood Cliffs, NJ: Prentice Hall.

Foner, E. (1970). *America's Black past: A reader in Afro-American history.* New York: Harper & Row.

Gibson, R. (1982). Blacks at middle and late life. *American Academy of Political and Social Science, 464,* 79–90.

Hill, R. (1972). *The strengths of Black families.* New York: Emerson Hall.

Hines, P., & Boyd-Franklin, N. (1982). Black families. In M. McGoldrich & J. Pearce (Eds.), *Ethnicity and family therapy* (pp. 84–107). New York: Guilford.

Holloway, M., & Yam, P. (1992). Reflecting differences: Health care begins to address the needs of women and minorities. *Scientific American, 266,* 13.

Hughes, D., Johnson, K., Rosenbaum, S., Butler, E., & Simons, J. (1988). *The health of America's children.* Washington, DC: Children's Defense Fund.

Issacs, M. (1992). *Violence: The impact of community violence on African American children and families.* Arlington, VA: National Center for Education in Maternal and Child Health.

Jackson, J. (1981). Urban Black Americans. In A. Hardwood (Ed.), *Ethnicity in medical care* (pp. 37–129). Cambridge, MA: Harvard University Press.

Jacques, G. (1976). Cultural health traditions: A Black perspective. In M. Branch & P. Paxton (Eds.), In *providing safe nursing care for ethnic people of color* (pp. 115–123). New York: Appleton-Century-Crofts.

Kessel, S., Kleinman, J., Koontz, A., Hogue, C., & Berendes, H. (1988). Racial differences in pregnancy outcomes. *Clinics in Perinatology, 54*(4), 745–754.

Kronenfield, J., & Wasner, C. (1982). The use of unorthodox therapies and magical practitioners. *Social Science and Medicine, 16,* 1119–1125.

Kviz, F., Dawkins, C., & Ervin, N. (1985). Mothers' health beliefs and use of well-being services among high-risk populations. *Research in Nursing and Health, 8*(4), 381–387.

Lassiter, S. M. (1987). Coping as a function of culture and socioeconomic status for Afro-Americans and Afro-West Indians. *Journal of the New York State Nurses Association, 18,* 18–30.

Luster, T., & Rhoades, K. (1989). The relation between child-rearing beliefs and the home environment of a sample of adolescent mothers. *Family Relations, 38,* 317–322.

Mbiti, J. (1989). *African religions and philosophy* (2nd ed.). Oxford, England: Heineman.

McBride, D. (1991). *From TB to AIDS: Epidemics among urban Blacks.* Albany: State University of New York.

Mech, E. (1986). Pregnant adolescents. *Child Welfare, 65,* 555–567.

National Center for Health Services Research. (1982). *Unusual sources of medical care and their characteristics:* (DHHS Publication No. [PHS] 82-3324). Washington, DC: U.S. Government Printing Office.

National Center for Health Statistics. (1990). *Health United States, 1989.* Hyattsville, MD: U.S. Public Health Service.

Neighbors, H. (1985). Seeking professional help for personal problems. *Community Mental Health Journal, 21,* 156–166.

O'Hair, D., O'Hair, M., & Southward, G. (1987). Physician communication and patient compliance. *The Journal of Compliance in Health Care, 2*(2), 125–129.

Pinderhughes, E. (1992). Legacy of slavery: The experience of Black families in America. In M. Mirkin (Ed.), *The social and political contexts of family therapy* (pp. 289–306). Boston: Allyn and Bacon.

Pinkney, A. (1993). *Black Americans* (4th ed.). Englewood Cliffs, NJ: Prentice Hall.

Powers, B. (1982). The use of orthodox and Black American folk medicine. *Advances in Nursing Science, 4*(3), 35–48.

Reed, W. (1992). *Health and medical care of African-Americans.* Boston: William Monroe Trotter Institute, University of Massachusetts at Boston.

Roberson, M. (1985). The influence of religious beliefs on health practices of Afro-Americans. *Topics in Clinical Nursing, 7,* 57–63.

Roberson, M. (1987). Home remedies: A cultural study. *Home Healthcare Nurse, 5*(1), 35–40.

Russell, K., & Jewell, N. (1992). The cultural impact of health-care access: Challenge for improving the health of African Americans. *Journal of Community Health Nursing, 9*(3), 161–169.

Scott, C. (1974). Health and healing practices among five ethnic groups in Miami, Florida. *Public Health Reports, 89,* 524–532.

Spector, R. (1985). *Cultural diversity in health and illness* (2nd ed.). Norwalk, CT: Appleton-Century-Crofts.

St. Clair, P., & Anderson, N. (1989). Social network advice during pregnancy. *Birth, 16,* 103–108.

Thompson, L. (Ed.). 1992. *Health care of black male children and adolescents.* Washington, DC: National Center for Education in Maternal and Child Health.

U.S. Department of Health and Human Services. (1990). *Health status of the disadvantaged—Chartbook, 1990.* (DHHS Pub. No. [HRSA] HRS-P-DV90-1). Washington, DC: U.S. Government Printing Office.

Walls, C. (1993). The role of church and family support in the lives of older African Americans. In L. Burton (Ed.), *Families and aging* (pp. 67–78). Amityville, NY: Baywood.

Weissfeld, J., Kirscht, J., & Brock, B. (1990). Health beliefs in a population: The Michigan blood pressure survey. *Health Education Quarterly, 17*(2), 141–155.

Wilson, W. (1987). *The truly disadvantaged.* Chicago and London: University of Chicago Press.

Zelnick, M., & Kantner, J. (1974). The resolution of teenage first pregnancies. *Family Planning Perspectives, 6,* 74–80.

SUGGESTED READINGS

Ambrose, J. (1977). The Black church as a mental health resource. In D. Jones & W. Matthews (Eds.), *The Black church: A community resource* (pp. 105–113). Washington, DC: Institute for Urban Affairs, Howard University.

Apt, N. A. (1992). Family support to the elderly people in Ghana. In H. Kendig, A. Hasimoto, & L. Coppard (Eds.), *Family support for the elderly* (pp. 203–212). New York: Oxford University Press.

Council on Ethical and Judicial Affairs. (1990). Black-White disparities in health care. *Journal of the American Medical Association, 263,* 2344–2346.

Davis, M. (1986). How the church can help the chemically sensitive. *Christ Century, 103,* 325–327.

Gumede, M. V. (1990), *Traditional healers.* Braamfontein, South Africa: Skotaville.

Haber, D. (1984). Church-based programs for Black caregivers of noninstitutionalized elders. *Journal of Gerontological Social Work, 7,* 43–49.

Johnston, M. (1977). Folk beliefs and ethnocultural behavior in pediatrics. *Nursing Clinics of North America, 12,* 77–84.

McAdoo, H. (1981). *Black families.* Beverly Hills, CA: Sage.

McAdoo, H., & Crawford, V. (1991). The Black church and family support programs. *Prevention in Human Services, 9*(1), 193–203.

Northup, D., & Hamrick, K. (1990). *Weapons and minority youth violence.* Newton, MA: Education Development Center.

Poole, T. (1990). Black families and the Black church: A sociological perspective. In H. E. Cheatham & J. Stewart (Eds.), *Black families: Interdisciplinary perspectives* (pp. 33–48). London: Transaction.

Randall-David, E. (1989). *Strategies for working with culturally diverse communities and clients.* New York: The Association for the Care of Children's Health.

Snow, L. (1974). Folk medical beliefs and their implications for care of patients: A review based on studies among Black Americans. *Annals of Internal Medicine, 81,* 82–96.

Stewart, H. (1971). Kindling of hope in the disadvantaged: A study of the Afro-American healer. *Mental Hygiene, 55,* 96–100.

Wilson, L., & Stith, S. (1991). Culturally sensitive therapy with Black clients. *Journal of Multicultural Counseling and Development, 19*(1), 32–43.

► **3**

Amish Health Care Beliefs and Practices

GRETCHEN H. WALTMAN

This chapter was not written by a member of the Amish culture, because it is unlikely that an individual Amish person would be willing to be recognized as the author. Amish society emphasizes the importance of community life and that one's accomplishments are as a member of that community, not as an individual. Furthermore, no Amish health care professionals were available as authors because an Amish person would have to leave the Amish church and community to obtain higher education. Therefore, the sources of information for this chapter included (a) the author's lifelong experience of living among and having business and personal relationships with Amish people, (b) appropriate literature references, (c) interviews with key informants such as health care professionals who provide services to the Amish community, and (d) Amish informants and reviewers.

The term *Amish* as used in this chapter refers to Old Order Amish, the most prevalent group in Ohio, where the largest Amish settlement is located (Hostetler, 1993, p. 91). There are other groups, such as the ultraconservative Swartzentruber Amish, the less conservative New Order Amish, and the more liberal Beachy Amish, that vary from the Old Order Amish in lifestyle practices and community norms and expectations. Health care professionals must clearly identify which group an Amish person is affiliated with, as that information will affect health care decisions. In general, the more conservative Amish groups are less likely than others to use modern health care facilities and technology.

As with any other culture, the Amish cannot be characterized by any particular set of absolute beliefs or life-style practices. This chapter provides general information about the Amish and raises issues that are important for health care professionals to consider regarding family and individual health care, with an emphasis on maternal and child health.

THE AMISH COMMUNITY

The Amish, or "plain people," are a socioreligious group who resist assimilation into modern society. Their simple life-style is based on European peasant culture, and they practice numerous social controls to avoid modernization. However, interaction with the outside world often occurs in the health care arena when an Amish person requires hospitalization for mental or physical illness or consults a local physician for medical care.

History and Overview

The Amish trace their roots to the Anabaptist movement during the sixteenth-century European Reformation. The Anabaptists, meaning "rebaptizers," advocated adult baptism, separation of church and state, and literal obedience to the teachings of Christ. They also espoused the ideals of peace and nonresistance and mutual helping. Being neither Catholic nor Reformation Protestants, the Anabaptists were rejected and persecuted for their beliefs and customs. This heritage of martyrdom is important to today's Amish people, who are willing to be jailed when their beliefs conflict with secular laws. For instance, a Minnesota court sentenced an Amish man to seven days in jail for failing to display a slow-moving vehicle sign on his buggy; the Amish objected to using the sign because its bright orange color was too "worldly" (McAuliffe, 1988). The resulting court case, which found in favor of the Amish, is described by Zook (1993).

The Amish arrived in America in the early 1700s from Germany, Switzerland, and the Alsace area of France, settling first in Pennsylvania (Hostetler, 1993). Currently, approximately 145,000 Old Order Amish live in twenty-three of the United States and one Canadian province (Hostetler, 1993). The largest Amish settlement is located in East Central Ohio in Holmes, Wayne, Coshocton, Stark, and Tuscarawas counties. There are no longer any Amish living in Europe, but the Amish in the United States and Canada do migrate to less populated areas in search of farmland far away from urban areas.

Amish Life-Style

The Amish attempt to be visibly separate from the outside world, based on their interpretation of the biblical text "Be not conformed to this world" (Rom. 12:2). Hostetler (1982) explains that "the Amish believe they must be separate from the world in order to attain eternal life" (p. 5). They wear plain, dark-colored clothing, home made in a distinctive style. They avoid the use of electricity and telephones in their homes and do not own automobiles, trucks, or modern farm implements. They use horses for farm work and for horse-and-buggy transportation. Worship services are held in homes in the winter and barns in the summer. Formal education for an Amish child ends with the completion of the eighth grade in Amish parochial or public school, affirmed by the Supreme Court decision on *Wisconsin* v. *Yoder et al.* (Hostetler, 1989; Lindholm, 1993). Although they must conform to minimum state educational requirements, Amish parochial schools are usually one or two rooms containing all eight grades. Amish life-style and religious practices are governed by the Ordnung, an unwritten set of laws for each community.

At home and in their community, the Amish speak a language that is often called "Pennsylvania Dutch," primarily an oral language derived from German dialects, Swiss, and English. Amish children learn English in school, and adults use it in contacts with the outside world. Language is not a communication barrier for adults, but preschool children may not yet understand English. Because English is not the primary language, an Amish person may not be very articulate, and some language constructions in English may sound awkward to a non-Amish person. The Amish value face-to-face communication.

Variations do exist among different settlements and church districts. For example, some church districts permit use of power lawnmowers; others require use of old-fashioned push mowers. Most Amish are permitted to ride in an automobile or use a non-Amish neighbor's telephone, but they may not own these modern items.

Amish Mutual Aid

The Amish community has a strong network of mutual support and assistance for its members. One outstanding example is an Amish barnraising, where several hundred men from many church districts gather to build a new barn, completing the main construction in one day. The Amish women plan and prepare the noon meal for the workers. Smaller mutual aid projects, called *frolics*, involve several neighbors and friends gathering to help build, for example, a small shed or corn crib. Harvesting of crops is often a group activity. A sudden death, serious illness, or accident brings an immediate response of emotional support and assistance with daily home maintenance and farm chores. Waltman (1992) observes that "there is a prescribed, ritualistic response to human tragedy and common disaster" (p. 104).

Because they object to participation in governmental assistance or commercial insurance plans, the Amish communities have their own system of property and health insurance involving regular financial assessments from families. The monetary amount of the assessment is based on the family's net worth. However, the health insurance fund can quickly be exhausted by a serious illness or lengthy hospitalization due to the rising costs of health care. Additional voluntary donations may be sought from Amish and non-Amish sources. In the Holmes County, Ohio, area, a cooperative effort by Amish and non-Amish people resulted in the formation of the Rainbow of Hope Foundation, which assists all families in the area with health care costs resulting from catastrophic illnesses affecting infants and children. Funds are raised through benefit auctions, bake sales, and private donations.

Health Care

The Amish are generally a healthy people because they are well nourished; get adequate amounts of exercise; and do not usually use alcohol, tobacco, or drugs other than for medicinal purposes. A study of health behaviors of four hundred Amish adults in Holmes County, Ohio, using the Behavioral Risk Factor Survey, found that patterns of positive health behavior, such as less consumption of alcohol and tobacco, reflect characteristics of Amish culture and may be responsible for certain favorable mortality rates among the Amish (Levinson, Fuchs, Stoddard, Jones, & Mullet, 1989; Fuchs, Levinson, Stoddard, Mullet, & Jones, 1990).

Hostetler (1993) explains, "The Amish emphasize hard work, and for them, a healthy person is one who has a good appetite, looks physically well, and can do rigorous physical labor" (p. 322). Conversely, illness is defined not by symptoms but by inability to perform daily functions or work. This may partially explain why many Amish seem to delay consulting medical doctors until they are really uncomfortable or sick.

Concern about health and illness is illustrated by the many reports in *The Budget*, a weekly newspaper published for the Amish, about accidents, injuries, contagious diseases, and illnesses (Yoder, 1990). The initial response to illness and symptoms is to try home remedies and patent medicines as cures. *The Budget* contains advertisements for mail-order remedies for arthritis, rheumatism, fatigue, constipation, and many other ailments. *Budget* readers exchange home remedies through a column called

"Information Please." For boils, suggestions are to drink black walnut leaf tea, eat raisins, or add burdock root to drinking water ("Information please," 1991, p. 19). An Amish person may consult a non-Amish licensed chiropractor; a massage therapist; a reflexologist; or an Amish "pow-wow" folk practitioner who uses words, charms, or physical manipulation to treat symptoms of illness. These responses to illness reflect a desire for a specific cause-and-effect relationship between symptoms and cure, as the Amish may lack scientific knowledge about the complexities of diagnosis and treatment of illness.

Because there are no Amish physicians, dentists, nurses, or social workers, the Amish seek medical care from trained non-Amish physicians and other health care professionals. These professionals need to be tolerant of the Amish person's health care choices—such as home remedies and folk medicine practitioners—if the treatment does not harm the patient. A trustworthy health professional is one who will take time to talk with patients and families and accept an informal form of address, such as "Dr. Dan." Speaking Pennsylvania Dutch is an added asset for establishing a relationship with Amish patients.

The Amish are permitted to use modern health care facilities and services including surgery, hospitalization, anesthesia, blood transfusions, and dental work. However, distance, lack of transportation, and cost can serve as barriers to accessing the health care delivery system. For example, traveling by horse and buggy to a physician or hospital can take a full day. Furthermore, the Amish person may resist having to pay for extensive laboratory or diagnostic procedures. The medical community can accommodate the Amish community by taking medical services to accessible sites. For example, a physician/specialist can use a mobile office to see Amish patients in their local area one day a week or give children immunizations at a local livestock auction.

Death and Dying

Within the Amish culture, death is accepted as a natural occurrence in the progression of life, a belief buoyed by a religious system that embraces the concept of eternal life. Because the Amish prefer to care for terminally ill family members at home, the patient is surrounded by loved ones. The caretakers are able to experience some anticipatory grief as they tend to the needs of the patient. When death occurs, the family of the deceased person receives immediate emotional support and concrete help from other relatives, neighbors, and friends. A sudden or tragic death of an adult or child is accepted as "God's will." An Amish acquaintance of the author's whose wife died suddenly from a heart attack commented, "I guess it was just her time." Amish society was using hospice care for terminal illness and mutual support during bereavement long before our contemporary society began advocating these concepts. Bryer (1979) observes that "the real power in the Amish way of death is that they do not ignore it, thereby allaying the anxieties created by events they cannot fully understand or control" (p. 259).

THE AMISH FAMILY

The family is the center of Amish life. According to Hostetler (1993), "procreation, nurture, and socialization are the major functions of the Amish family" (p. 145). Children are welcomed into the family and considered to be blessings—even those with congenital mental or physical defects who may require special care. Family members work, play, and worship together, and that is how the Amish life-style, religion, and values are passed on from one generation to another.

Family Structure

The father is the head of the family and must be consulted regarding major decisions such as initiating sophisticated medical treatment for a child. He may discuss a problem or issue with his wife or other family members, but the father will then communicate the decision to health care professionals.

Amish children are reared in a close-knit family environment of parents, siblings, grandparents, and other relatives. Three generations of the family live on a farm, with the grandparents living in a separate house called the *daadi haus*. The grandparents continue to assist with family activities and farm work as long as they are able, and they are cared for by children and grandchildren when they become aged or ill. Family members are treated with respect, and those with disabilities are not considered a burden.

Family Roles

Amish culture assigns men and women definite and rigid roles, and they must follow traditional rituals for courtship, marriage, childbearing and rearing, death, and burial. Kraybill (1989) explains that "age and sex roles are essential building blocks in Amish society. . . . Amish families are organized around traditional sex roles" (p. 71).

The Amish father is responsible for providing for his family through his farm or a job in the local community. The declining availability of farmland has forced many Amish men to work away from home, usually as carpenters, masons, or laborers in factories and businesses. Other enterprising Amish men have home-based businesses such as furniture making or harness repair. This trend toward nonfarm employment is an example of economic acculturation, as reported by Foster (1984) and Savells (1988). Attending a weekly livestock auction serves both a social and a business purpose for an Amish farmer: He can buy or sell animals and visit other Amish farmers attending the auction. He may take one or two children with him, but usually not his wife.

Kraybill (1989) further explains that "the Amish husband is seen as the spiritual head of the home. He is responsible for its religious welfare and has the final word on matters related to the church and the outside world" (p. 71). In the Amish church, only men serve as bishops, ministers, and deacons.

Amish culture teaches girls to serve and please others: their husbands, children, parents, relatives, and other Amish brethren. The Amish wife is expected to willingly submit herself to her husband and be his helper. The patriarchal character of Amish society is exemplified in the practice of identifying an Amish wife by using her husband's name: "Eli Katie" means Eli's wife, Katie. She manages the household, takes care of the yard and garden, and helps with milking. Ericksen and Klein (1981) describe the economic importance of Amish women as they are involved in household production of food and clothing. Social life for an Amish woman is centered around church, weddings, funerals, quilting bees, home products parties, and barnraisings.

Amish families usually have many children, including multiple births, one or two years apart. According to Erickson and Klein (1981), Amish women produce an average of seven children. Both parents care for and discipline children; older children may help to care for younger children. Amish children are taught to suppress their feelings and emotions other than pleasure. For example, an Amish child will usually not complain about pain following a surgery.

Children are an economic asset to the family, as they assist their parents with housework and farm chores, gardening, food preservation, or work in a small family business. Involving young children in family work and activities strengthens family ties and promotes survival of the Amish life-style. However, this childrearing practice can also result in untimely accidents and deaths. Jones (1990) reports on a study of Amish persons admitted to a hospital with trauma-related injuries, including an unusual number of incidents involving young children—ages two, four, five, and six—being kicked by horses. Reports in *The Budget* describe an eight-year-old boy who was trampled by a buggy horse (May 23, 1990, p. 18) and a thirteen-year-old boy whose foot was almost severed by a hay mower cutting bar (July 4, 1990, p. 14). The practice of involving children in work may present a dilemma for child welfare and health care workers, who might consider these accidents preventable. Wright, Saleebey, Watts, and Lecca (1983) caution that "many cases of abuse and neglect are difficult to define. When the agency suspects pathology and maltreatment, it may ignore the possibility that it is witness to culturally different standards of child-rearing" (p. 130).

MATERNAL AND CHILD HEALTH PRACTICES

Maternal and child health practices among the Amish are affected by cultural traditions and religious beliefs. Decisions regarding birth control, prenatal care, delivery, infant care, and childhood immunizations are either predetermined by the Amish church or made with final approval by the husband/father.

Conception and Prenatal Care

Amish couples do not use birth control to limit family size, as this would be interfering with God's will. Amniocentesis and therapeutic abortion are also not acceptable. Folk wisdom is woven into prenatal care practices, such as cautions that walking under a clothesline will result in a stillbirth or crawling through a window will cause the umbilical cord to be wrapped around the baby's neck.

Prenatal care will usually be sought early in the first pregnancy, but much later—third trimester—for subsequent pregnancies if the mother feels well. Complications such as toxemia and diabetes may be reduced due to the mother's well-nourished state. Distance to the doctor or clinic, lack of transportation, and cost of care could encourage pregnant mothers to delay the initial visit to the physician. One accommodation made by a physician for Amish maternity patients is to schedule prenatal visits every eight weeks instead of every month during the first two trimesters, thereby reducing the expenditures of time, energy, and money for prenatal care. Another accommodation is conducting Lamaze classes in a church close to the Amish community, easing transportation barriers and creating a comfortable atmosphere for the classes.

Labor, Birth, and Delivery

Most Amish women receive information from their mothers about labor and delivery; they are unlikely to complain about the pain and discomfort involved. Delivery may be at home, at a midwife's home, or at a hospital.

Heikes (1985) conducted a survey among Wayne County, Ohio, Amish and found that "first deliveries and those with predictable medical complications were the childbirths most likely to occur in a hospital" (p. 54).

To accommodate the Amish preference for a culturally compatible home atmosphere for delivery, a freestanding birthing center, the Mount Eaton Care Center, approved by the Ohio Department of Health, was opened in 1985 close to the Amish community. Used for low-risk normal deliveries, the center features a plain decor, has no telephones or television in the rooms, and has no separate nursery or delivery room. Labor, delivery, and postpartum care are accomplished in the patient's room; newborn babies stay in the room with the mothers. Overnight accommodations are available for the father or other relatives to stay at the center, and there is a barn for the Amish horses. A similar birthing center was recently opened in Geauga County, Ohio.

Local hospitals serving the Amish, offering a range of services for normal and high-risk deliveries, have developed cost-effective birthing centers by reducing the number of hospitalization days for a delivery and postpartum care. Joel Pomerene Memorial Hospital in Millersburg, Ohio, was one of the first hospitals in the area to adopt the birthing center concept for maternity patients.

Infant Care

Almost all Amish babies are breastfed unless there is a medical reason not to breastfeed; some babies may receive supplemental bottle feedings. Circumcision is not universally accepted, and the decision regarding circumcision needs to be discussed with the baby's father on a case-by-case basis. The procedure should be carefully explained to both parents so they can make an informed decision.

A baby who is critically ill or has serious congenital malfunctions will not necessarily receive "heroic" or "high-tech" treatment to prolong life if there is not a reasonable chance that the baby will survive. The Amish parents may request to take the baby home and wait for "God's will" regarding a life or death outcome. Health care professionals need to respect the parents' wishes in these cases.

Babies with special needs, such as a special feeding formula or treatment for hemophilia, may be enrolled in a government program such as Women, Infants and Children (WIC) for nutrition supplements or Bureau for Children with Medical Handicaps (BCMH) subsidies for medical treatment. Amish parents need to be informed about these programs, and then they can make a decision about participation, perhaps in consultation with their bishop.

Immunization

Immunization for communicable diseases is accepted in varying degrees by different Amish groups. For example, Heikes (1985) reports that 58 percent of the Main Body Old Order Amish had their children ten years of age and younger immunized, while none of the more conservative Swartzentruber Amish children received immunizations. Although most states permit a religious-grounds waiver from required school-age childhood vaccinations, Amish children attending public school are still more likely to be immunized than children attending Amish parochial schools.

Although the Amish church has no rule forbidding immunizations, some parents object, perhaps because they feel the immunizations are too modern or that immunizations are similar to insurance. Guyther (1979) suggests that the objection to immunizations is based on the belief that "one may be lacking in the faith that God will protect, and consequently is hedging his bet that the child will not contract a serious communicable disease" (p. 40). The infrequent but inevitable negative physical reactions to immunizations tend to reinforce the Amish person's doubts about their value. For example, Guyther (1979) reports on a case of community-contact, vaccine-associated poliomyelitis, in which a young unvaccinated Amish mother contracted paralytic polio after contact with four infants who received oral trivalent polio vaccine.

An outbreak of a communicable disease such as measles or whooping cough in an Amish community, with some serious complications in a few patients, will prompt a renewed interest in preventive vaccinations. Local public health officials can encourage mass immunizations by offering them at no or low cost and by holding clinics at locations easily accessible to the Amish, such as an Amish school or the community livestock auction. Both parents will probably present their children for the immunizations and should sign consent forms, because this is a very serious decision.

Infertility

Cross and McKusick (1970) conducted an extensive demographic survey of the Holmes County Amish community and found that 3.8 percent of the Amish women who lived with their husbands until at least forty-five years of age had never been pregnant. Hostetler (1993) estimates the rate of childlessness for the Amish at 4.4 percent, compared to 7.5 percent for the U.S. population as a whole. He comments that this is not surprising, "since among the Amish there is no divorce and children are wanted" (p. 100).

With the strong emphasis on family life in Amish culture, childless couples evoke some sympathy from their Amish brethren with families.

However, close ties with extended families and interactions with many nieces and nephews provide the childless couple with opportunities to interact with children. Adoption of a child is acceptable and usually occurs informally within the local Amish community. Problems confronting childless couples include the lack of support with the labor-intensive farming practices and concern about who will assume responsibility for the farm when the Amish man wishes to retire. One childless couple known to the author participates in a national support group for childless couples. They travel by hired van to attend meetings at various Amish settlements (*The Budget*, July 18, 1990, p. 23) and communicate with other childless couples through a circle letter (*The Budget*, July 18, 1990, p. 2).

Genetics

Intermarriage among the Amish results in a couple sharing one or two common ancestors; many couples are as closely related as second cousins. This inbreeding does not inevitably result in hereditary defects, but, as Hostetler (1993) explains, "if the gene pool of a group of people contains certain recessive tendencies, the probability that a child will be born with a birth defect is greater when the members intermarry and the gene is carried by both father and mother" (p. 331).

Amish communities are a valuable resource for conducting genetic studies for several reasons, as explained by Francomano (in press):

(1) *The high degree of inbreeding has resulted in the presence of a large number of recessive disorders, many of which were unrecognized outside of the Amish population;*

(2) *The community is a closed community; members may leave, but outsiders join the community extremely rarely;*

(3) *The Amish genealogies are extensive and meticulously maintained.*

The standard of living is fairly high and consistent, reducing variables such as alcohol and drug abuse or malnutrition.

The birth of a child with a hereditary defect does not deter an Amish couple from having more children. An abnormal child is referred to as a "special child" and is accepted as "God's will." For example, one family may have several siblings with cystic fibrosis. Genetic counseling is inappropriate for Amish couples, and sterilization would be considered only for a legitimate medical reason such as the mother's health. Sterilization would not be considered as an option to avoid genetic problems or to limit family size for convenience.

Several hereditary diseases and conditions occur in Amish populations, such as hemophilia, cystic fibrosis, dwarfism, neurologic disorders, and Down syndrome. McKusick (1978) has assembled many separate genetic studies on the Amish and continues to conduct field studies in the Lancaster, Pennsylvania, and Holmes County, Ohio, Amish settlements. This research is sponsored by The Johns Hopkins Hospital and The Johns Hopkins University, Baltimore, Maryland.

McKusick (1978) reported on the high incidence of Ellis-van Creveld syndrome dwarfism in the Lancaster County settlement. A second type of dwarfism, cartilage-hair hypoplasia, is found among Amish throughout the country, including the Holmes County settlement (McKusick, 1978). Two neurologic disorders, Mast syndrome and Troyer syndrome, are found in the Holmes County Amish (Cross & McKusick, 1978a,b). The genetic risk for Down syndrome is not thought to be higher in the Amish than in the general population, but children with Down syndrome may seem to occur more frequently in Amish families due to large families and the longer reproductive life of Amish women, who may bear several children after age thirty-five.

Recent genetic and demographic studies on the Amish have focused on mental illness. Egeland and colleagues (1987) conducted research with Lancaster County Amish families and reported on a possible genetic predisposition to manic-depressive illness. A community-based survey was conducted by Coblentz (1991) in Holmes County to assess the types and frequencies of mental disorders among the Amish, comparing the number of psychological problems in the Amish sample with a nationwide sample. Results of this study indicate that the Amish have higher frequencies of total disorders, phobias, schizophrenia, affective disorders, and psychosexual dysfunctions; noticeably absent were manic episodes or bipolar disorders.

Health care professionals may wonder why the Amish cooperate with genetic studies when they will not benefit directly from the findings. A sense of altruism prompts the Amish to participate in these studies, to advance knowledge of genetics and hereditary conditions that will benefit society as a whole. Also, the Johns Hopkins researchers are very sensitive to Amish culture and have a genuine concern for Amish persons with physical and mental disabilities, offering health care resources to help them.

Health Education

Health promotion and disease prevention are not priorities among the Amish. Amish people are generally reactive, rather than proactive, regarding knowledge of disease transmission. Medical advice is sought for symptoms that interfere with daily work and activities, not for prevention of underlying causes.

Any health education programs directed at the Amish must be culturally compatible with their needs and values. For example, health care professionals should not use videotapes and a television monitor to show health education programs; posters and flipcharts are more appropriate. Informal one-on-one approaches to discussion of health promotion and disease prevention would probably be most comfortable for most Amish persons. Mixing Amish with non-Amish persons in any health education group is probably not advisable. Wiggins (1983) suggests using *The Budget* to disseminate health information to the Amish, possibly as paid advertisements by national health organizations.

IMPLICATIONS FOR HEALTH CARE PROFESSIONALS

It is important for health care professionals to understand and appreciate Amish culture, especially health care beliefs and practices, in order to work effectively with this population. Suggested guidelines for working with Amish patients and families include the following:

1. Determine, by asking, which Amish group the patient or family belongs to, because this influences health care decisions.
2. Tolerate and try to understand parallel medical care practices such as use of home remedies and folk medicine practitioners.
3. Recognize the patriarchal nature of Amish society: Approach the Amish community through a bishop, an Amish family through the father.
4. Evaluate alleged child abuse and neglect within the cultural context of Amish childrearing practices.
5. Avoid, or approach with caution, discussion of birth control or genetic screening.
6. Establish face-to-face relationships with Amish patients. Be genuine in approach, use basic language, and avoid the use of technical language or jargon.
7. Take time to explain the medical problem, suggested approach, or solution, and be patient while decisions regarding medical care are made, perhaps in consultation with other family members or the bishop.
8. Allow a reasonable amount of physical space when talking with an Amish person; avoid touching, especially between genders, unless appropriate for a physical examination.

9. Respect the wishes of the family regarding medical care, even if they are not in agreement with medical staff recommendations.
10. Avoid aggressive legal action, such as gaining custody of a child to force heroic medical care, because this will alienate the Amish family and community from the local medical care system.

Following these guidelines will result in an improved relationship between health care professionals and the Amish population, with mutual benefits as they learn from each other. Hostetler (1993) suggests that the Amish may provide models of survival for modern people:

Amish communities have preserved some of the qualities the larger American society once had, and now seeks to regain: intimate family and community relationships, respect for children and grandparents, religion as a way of life, mutual help in times of crisis, the use of restraints to control the influence of technology, and a dignified way of dying without going broke. (p. 397)

ACKNOWLEDGMENTS

The author gratefully acknowledges the following key informants, who contributed their knowledge about and experiences with the Amish for this article.

Carole Burkey, R.N., B.S.N.
Director, Personal Health Services
Deputy Health Commissioner
Holmes County General Health District
Millersburg, Ohio

Clair A. Francomano, M.D.
Assistant Professor, Medicine and Pediatrics
The Johns Hopkins Hospital
Baltimore, Maryland

Katherine A. Hopkins, R.N., M.P.H.
Assistant in Medicine
Immunogenetics Laboratory
The Johns Hopkins University
Baltimore, Maryland

Elton Lehman, D.O.
Medical Director
Mount Eaton Care Center
Mount Eaton, Ohio

Daniel J. Miller, M.D.
Family Practitioner
Walnut Creek, Ohio

Rebecca L. Mutschelknaus, ACSW, LISW
Director of Social Services
Joel Pomerene Memorial Hospital
Millersburg, Ohio

Donald A. Waltman, D.V.M.
Veterinarian
Baltic, Ohio

Numerous Amish informants who wish to remain anonymous.

GLOSSARY

Amish (*ah*-mish) Also called "plain people," a religious and social group who aspire to live separately from the modern world through manner of dress, language, family life, and avoiding the use of modern conveniences or higher education.

Anabaptist A name, meaning "rebaptizer," given to a religious group during the Protestant Reformation who advocated adult baptism, separation of church and state, and literal obedience to the teachings of Christ. Historical parent group of the Amish.

Bishop The leader and chief authority of an Amish congregation. Administers religious rites such as communion, baptism, and marriage, and shares preaching responsibilities with ministers.

Barnraising A gathering of several hundred Amish men and women to build a new barn for an Amish (rarely non-Amish) farmer, with the main construction being completed in one day. The men build the barn, and the women prepare and serve food for all attending. Outstanding example of Amish mutual aid and a major social (and tourist) event in Amish communities.

The Budget An English-language newspaper that serves Amish and Mennonite communities throughout the Americas. Published weekly by Sugarcreek Budget Publishers, Inc., 134 North Factory Street, P. O. Box 249, Sugarcreek, OH 44681. Telephone: (216) 852-4421.

Church district A congregation of Amish designated by a geographic location within the larger settlement (e.g., "New Bedford East"). Size is usually about twenty-five to thirty-five families, or the number of people who can be accommodated for church service in a home or barn. A complete list of church districts, bishops, deacons, and ministers is given in the *Almanac* published by Ben Raber, Raber's Book Store, 2467 County Road 600, Baltic, OH 43804.

Daadi (doh-dee) house, grossdaadi (grandfather) house A smaller house built near or attached to the main Amish farmhouse. When a married child takes over the farm, the parents move into the "daadi house" and the young, growing family occupies the larger original home.

English "Outsider," the name given by Amish to non-Amish people.

Frolic A "working bee" involving any number of men, usually neighbors or relatives who gather at an Amish farm to build a small building such as a shed or corn crib. Example of Amish mutual aid.

Go high, or jump over Phrase meaning leaving the Amish church (e.g., "Andy Miller is planning to go high").

Mennonite A religious group that shares a common Anabaptist heritage with the Amish but is more liberal in life-style practices. Mennonites usually drive cars, have electricity and telephones in their homes, and dress less conservatively than the Amish. There are many variations of Mennonites, ranging from very conservative to liberal.

Ordnung Unwritten set of rules that governs the life-style and religious practices of an Amish community. Some of the rules have direct biblical support; others are based on tradition (i.e., "That's just our way"). Each church district has its own Ordnung, which promotes separation from the outside world and unity within the group.

Pennsylvania Dutch Primarily an oral language used by Amish at home and in the Amish community. Derived from German dialects, Swiss, and English. Conversational Pennsylvania Dutch may be offered as an adult education course in a public school near an Amish community for non-Amish persons wishing to learn the language.

Pow-wow Amish folk medicine practitioner who uses words, charms, or physical manipulation to treat symptoms of illness. Evidence of healing by a pow-wow practitioner is supported mainly by oral testimonies. The pow-wow practitioner does not charge fees but may accept "contributions" for services.

Reflexologist Practitioner who manipulates the feet to cure human ills.

Scribe Person who writes weekly letters to *The Budget* describing events in a local Amish or Mennonite community. Scribes usually report on weather conditions, progress of crops, marriage, births, deaths, illnesses, church services, visitors, and social gatherings.

Wisconsin v. *Yoder et al.* Case brought before the United States Supreme Court resulting in the 1972 decision, with no dissenting votes, granting the Amish release from compulsory education beyond the eighth grade. The opinion of the Court was written by Chief Justice Warren E. Burger.

REFERENCES

Bryer, K. B. (1979). The Amish way of death. *American Psychologist, 34*(3), 255–261.

Coblentz, E. B. (1991). *Epidemiology of mental disorders and help seeking behavior among the Amish.* Unpublished doctoral dissertation, The University of Akron, Ohio.

Cross, H. E., & McKusick, V. A. (1970). Amish demography. *Social Biology, 17*(2), 83–101.

Cross, H. E., & McKusick, V. A. (1978a). The Mast syndrome: A recessively inherited form of presenile dementia with motor disturbances. In V. A. McKusick (Ed.), *Medical genetic studies of the Amish* (pp. 294–306). Baltimore: The Johns Hopkins University Press.

Cross, H. E., & McKusick, V. A. (1978b). The Troyer syndrome: A recessive form of spastic paraplegia with distal muscle wasting. In V. A. McKusick (Ed.), *Medical genetic studies of the Amish* (pp. 281–293). Baltimore: The Johns Hopkins University Press.

Egeland, J. A., Gerhard, D. S., Pauls, D. L., Sussex, J. N., Kidd, K. K., Allen, C. R., Hostetter, A. M., & Houseman, D. E. (1987). Bipolar affective disorders linked to DNA markers on chromosome 11. *Nature, 325,* 783–787.

Erickson, J., & Klein, G. (1981). Women's roles and family production among the Old Order Amish. *Rural Sociology, 46*(2), 282–296.

Foster, T. W. (1984). Separation and survival in Amish society. *Sociological Focus, 17*(1), 1–15.

Francomano, C. A. (In press). Cultural and religious factors affecting the provision of genetic services to the Amish. In N. Fisher (Ed.), *Handbook on medical genetics and ethnocultural diversity.* Baltimore: The Johns Hopkins University Press.

Fuchs, J. A., Levinson, R. M., Stoddard, R. R., Mullet, M. E., & Jones, D. H. (1990). Health risk factors among the Amish: Results of a survey. *Health Education Quarterly, 17*(2), 197–211.

Guyther, J. R. (1979, October). Medical attitudes of the Amish. *Maryland State Medical Journal*, pp. 40–41.

Heikes, J. K. (1985). *Differences among the Old Order Amish of Wayne County, Ohio and their use of health care services.* Unpublished master's thesis, The Ohio State University, Columbus.

Hostetler, J. A. (1982). *The Amish.* Scottdale, PA: Herald Press.

Hostetler, J. A. (1989). *Amish roots.* Baltimore: The Johns Hopkins University Press.

Hostetler, J. A. (1993). *Amish society* (4th ed.). Baltimore: The Johns Hopkins University Press.

Information please. (1991, February 27). *The Budget,* p. 19.

Jones, M. W. (1990). A study of trauma in an Amish community. *The Journal of Trauma, 30*(7), 899–902.

Kraybill, D. B. (1989). *The riddle of Amish culture.* Baltimore: The Johns Hopkins University Press.

Levinson, R. M., Fuchs, J. A., Stoddard, R. R., Jones, D. H., & Mullet, M. E. (1989). Behavioral risk factors in an Amish community. *American Journal of Preventive Medicine, 5*(3), 150–156.

Lindholm, W. C. (1993). The national committee for Amish religious freedom. In D. B. Kraybill (Ed.), *The Amish and the state* (pp. 109–123). Baltimore: The Johns Hopkins University Press.

McAuliffe, B. (1988, July 3). Amish man takes on law, goes to jail. New Philadelphia, OH: *The Times-Reporter*, p. A-8.

McKusick, V. A. (Ed.). (1978). *Medical genetic studies of the Amish.* Baltimore: The Johns Hopkins University Press.

Savells, J. (1988). Economic and social acculturation among the Old Order Amish in select communities: Surviving in a high-tech society. *Journal of Comparative Family Studies, 19*(1), 123–135.

Waltman, G. H. (1992). Clinical issues with Amish and formerly-Amish clients. In J. Borner, H. Doueck, & M. Jacobsen (Eds.), *Emerging from the shadows: Selected papers from the Fifteenth National Institute on Social Work and Human Services in Rural Areas* (pp. 98–110). Mayville, NY: Chautauqua County Department of Social Services.

Wiggins, L. R. (1983). Health and illness beliefs and practices among the Old Order Amish. *Health Values, 7*(6), 24–29.

Wright, R. Jr., Saleebey, D., Watts, T. D., & Lecca, P. J. (1983). *Transcultural perspectives in the human services.* Springfield, IL: Charles C. Thomas.

Yoder, E. S. (1990). *I saw it in* The Budget. Hartville, OH: Diakonia Ministries.

Zook, L. J. (1993). Slow-moving vehicles. In D. B. Kraybill (Ed.), *The Amish and the state* (pp. 145–160). Baltimore: The Johns Hopkins University Press.

SUGGESTED READINGS AND RESOURCES

Books

Armstrong, P., & Feldman, S. (1986). *A midwife's story.* New York: Arbor House.

Hostetler, J. A., & Huntington, G. E. (1992). *Amish children: Education in the family, school, and community* (2nd ed.). New York: Harcourt Brace Jovanovich.

Kaiser, G. H. (1986). *Dr. Frau: A woman doctor among the Amish.* Intercourse, PA: Good Books.

Kraybill, D. B. (1990). *The puzzles of Amish life.* Intercourse, PA: Good Books.

Miller, L. (1989). *Ben's Wayne.* Intercourse, PA: Good Books.

Miller, L. (1992). *Our people: The Amish and Mennonites of Ohio.* Scottdale, PA: Herald Press.

Schreiber, W. I. (1962). *Our Amish neighbors.* Chicago: The University of Chicago Press.

Randall-David, E. (1989). *Strategies for working with culturally diverse communities and clients.* Bethesda, MD: Association for the Care of Children's Health.

Zielinski, J. M. (1983). *The Amish across America.* Dubuque, IA: Kendall/Hunt.

Articles

Campanella, K., Korbin, J. E., & Acheson, L. (1993). Pregnancy and childbirth among the Amish. *Social Science & Medicine, 36*(3), 333–342.

Foster, T. M. (1981, December). Amish society: A relic of the past could become a model for the future. *Futurist*, pp. 33–40.

Huntington, G. E. (1988). The Amish family. In C. H. Mindel, R. W. Habenstein, & R. Wright Jr. (Eds.),

Ethnic families in America: Patterns and variations (3rd ed.). New York: Elsevier.

Huntington, G. E. (1993). Health care. In D. B. Kraybill (Ed.), *The Amish and the state.* Baltimore: The Johns Hopkins University Press.

Miller, S. R., & Schwartz, R. H. (1992). Attitudes toward genetic testing of Amish, Mennonite, and Hutterite families with cystic fibrosis. *American Journal of Public Health, 82*(2), 236–242.

Palmer, C. V. (1992). The health beliefs and practices of an Old Order Amish family. *Journal of the American Academy of Nurse Practitioners, 4*(3), 117–122.

Wenger, A. F. (1991). The culture care theory and the Old Order Amish. In M. M. Leininger (Ed.), *Culture care diversity and universality: A theory of nursing* (pp. 147–177). New York: National League for Nursing Press.

Wenger, A. F. (1991). Culture-specific care and the Old Order Amish. In *NSNA/Imprint, 38*(2), 80–82, 84, 87.

Zook, L. (1989). The Amish in America: Conflicts between cultures. *Journal of American Culture, 12*(4), 29–33.

Videos

Ruth, J. L. (Producer & Director). (1991). *The Amish: A people of preservation.* Harleysville, PA: Heritage Productions, 1191 Sumneytown Pike, Harleysville, PA 19438. Telephone: (610) 287–8888.

Dauwalder-Troyer, L. (Producer), & Bowers, R. F. (Director). (1993). *The Amish: Between two worlds.* Millersburg, OH: Amish Heartland Productions, 6005 County Road 77, Millersburg, OH 44654. Telephone: (216) 893–2596.

Other

The Young Center for the Study of Anabaptist and Pietist Groups, Elizabethtown College, One Alpha Drive, Elizabethtown, PA 17022-2298. Telephone: (717) 367-1151, Donald B. Kraybill, Ph.D., Director. The Center fosters scholarly research related to a variety of Anabaptist and Pietist groups, with access to Elizabethtown College library and archives, which include resources on the Amish and Mennonites. Seminars, lectures, and conferences organized by the Center disseminate research findings and interpret the religious heritage of Anabaptist and Pietist groups. The Center sponsored an international conference, *Three Hundred Years of Persistence and Change: Amish Society 1693–1993,* July 22–25, 1993.

▶ 4

Culturally Relevant Health Care Service Delivery for Appalachia

KAREN V. HARPER

Recognized as a special population caught in grinding poverty and isolated by subcultural practices, the Appalachian poor gained the attention of the nation as a targeted area in the midst of political and economic changes of the 1960s. Three decades later the region continues to suffer extreme poverty and generally lags behind urban areas in social and educational opportunities for its people. Not far from metropolitan centers and the nation's capital, this region has preserved its folk heritage. Racially and religiously similar to the dominant culture, the people in the region have been the victims of stereotypical labels. Despite these negative labels, this population has evidenced a strong will to preserve traditional life-styles in the familiar mountains that have been home for generations of families.

The challenge of delivering health and human services to people living in the region and to those Appalachians who may live and work in urban areas outside the region is not insurmountable. Such delivery requires a broader understanding of the region, the life-style, and the struggle to survive in rugged, isolated terrain that paints much of the historical, geographic, and economic backdrop of the region.

The plight of those living in the Appalachian mountains became known when Appalachia became politically constructed as a region suffering serious socioeconomic deprivation in the 1960s. Flicker and Graves (1971) portrayed the life-style and hardship of the region that caught national media attention in the mid-1960s and early 1970s as a place where:

> . . . more than a third of the population is unemployed, where the government check—social security, welfare, aid to dependent children—is the prime source of income, and where some men are so far from their last job that it cannot properly be said that they have a trade at all. Here the average adult has a sixth-grade education, three-fourths of the children who start school drop-out before they complete the 12th grade, and the statistics of human pathology—tuberculosis, silicosis, infant mortality—are so high that they do not belong in the Western world at all. (p. 41)

The Appalachian region lags the nation in employment. West Virginia's unemployment rate in April, 1994, was 8.9 percent, as compared to the nation's rate of 6.4 percent ("Payroll Employment," 1994). After decades of socioeconomic hardship, the 1980s and 1990s have been years of growth even though lagging statistics suggest that much is yet to be achieved. Another example of progress is that 99 percent of West Virginia's preschool children were immunized in 1994 ("Immunizing West Virginia's Preschool Children," 1994). As many as 30.1 percent of West Virginia's children were living in poverty in 1985, as compared to 25.9 percent in 1989 (Kids Count, 1993).

The following discussion of the Appalachian region and the cultural beliefs and practices of Appalachian families offers information for health care professionals who wish to provide culturally relevant health care to people of the region. Although health problems and resources in rural Appalachia have long been targeted for change by various providers and funding streams, health care providers outside the region know little about the unique blend of Appalachia's heritage and health service system. Despite advancing research and knowledge about health needs of the U.S. population in general, the lack of consistent health care consumption and the challenge of delivering competent health care in remote and often economically depressed areas continue to perplex many providers. Moreover, many Appalachians have migrated to urban areas, where they have experienced cultural confusion and have often avoided using human services, including health care. This chapter addresses barriers to providing health care to Appalachian people in the region and applies to many who have migrated from the region and live in urban areas today.

THE APPALACHIAN REGION

Parts of twelve states and all of West Virginia, 397 counties in total, lie along the Appalachian mountain range and have been identified as Appalachia (Burlage, 1970). Extending from Alabama to New York, this region was mostly settled in the 1700s. Isolated by treacherous mountains and rivers, without roads and transportation, early settlers scattered throughout the hollows and hills, establishing a rural life-style reflective of agrarian, fundamentalist, and traditionalist practices. English-Welsh, Scots-Irish, and German customs are evident in the rural life-style and are part of the Appalachian subculture. Historically, the people were characterized by strong values of individualism and personalism; traditional and fundamental religious sects; arts, crafts, and music unique to the region; language variation that has dialectal qualities; a strong extended family system; and a fierce sense of personal independence (Caudill, 1963; Coles, 1971; Harper, 1970; Looff, 1971). These subcultural traits contribute to the multiple sources that define health, wellness, and health care, especially for those experiencing cultural and technological lags, geographic isolation, and too few resources (Hansen & Resick, 1990.) The region is adjacent to major urban areas and is widely diverse. There are university and college towns, working class towns, farming areas, upper-income suburbs, areas of extreme poverty, isolated homes, and friendly small towns. Many Appalachians continue to share values reflective of their traditional belief systems, and much of the area maintains a regional identity despite the changing world around its geographic borders.

Located close to the metropolitan spread of the nation's eastern seaboard, the region has vast mountains that are home to those with the courage to live in remote and rugged areas. Severity of isolation and poverty and intensity of subcultural beliefs and practices vary within this vast rural region. Within the thirteen-state Appalachian region, Southern Appalachia has about 190 counties, or about 80,000 square miles. It is this targeted area that has the most intense need for resources in social, economic, health, and education service delivery within the Appalachian region. Parts of Alabama, Georgia, Kentucky, North Carolina, Tennessee, Virginia, and West Virginia comprise the area identified as Southern Appalachia (Photiadis & Schwartzweller, 1971). Exploited by extractive industries for its coal and timber, the region has lost natural resources, been deforested, and experienced devastating flooding and soil erosion.

Poverty throughout Appalachia has been targeted for federal initiatives for decades by agencies such as the Appalachian Regional Commission, which has brought a wide range of progress to the region including major highways, educational development, expanded human services, and a wide range of economic development to small towns and communities. Even with intensive effort, economic progress is not uniform across the region. It is impacted by numerous economic changes, technology, transportation access, and disasters such as flood and forest fires in some sections. For example, the twenty eight counties in the state of Ohio that belong to the Appalachian region have lost earlier gains. In the 1970s, Appalachia's poverty declined, but in the 1980s it increased beyond its earlier level (*Ohio Poverty Indicators*, 1987).

Urban Appalachians: Subcultural Influence Outside the Region

The Appalachian region is not homogeneous. Cross-fertilization of rural and urban life-styles has occurred, with out-migration linking Appalachians within the region with relatives who have relocated in urban centers. The mass exodus of millions from the Appalachian region who left in search of employment and a better life ended in flight from rural to urban poverty for many (Obermiller & Oldendick, 1986). As many as two million Appalachian people left the region by 1971. It is estimated that at least seven million people eventually migrated from Appalachia (Obermiller, 1989; Stekert, 1971). Cities such as Cincinnati, Cleveland, Columbus, Baltimore, Detroit, Akron, and Chicago are geographically close to the Appalachian region and for many years have received migrating families—many of whom have been identified as needing extensive social services to ameliorate poverty, illiteracy, social disadvantages, physical and mental health problems, and problems of teen pregnancy and high school dropout rates (Friedl, 1980; Obermiller & Olendick, 1986).

Known as "urban Appalachians" or "Appalachian migrants," many of the region's best educated sons and daughters left behind extended kinship networks and moved to urban centers in search of employment and opportunity. Some families who migrated to urban centers clung to traditional Appalachian beliefs and practices and never accommodated to urban living. Today, some migrants maintain strong family bonds while others have moved home to retire among familiar faces and places that held meaning for them in their youth.

Relocated Appalachians who migrated to Appalachian ghettos in urban centers gained attention from professionals who were unfamiliar with their subcultural values and practices (Lantz & Harper, 1989). Stereotypical labels were rapidly applied in the face of unrelenting problems of poverty, poor school attendance, crowded and run-down housing, unfamiliarity with health and welfare systems, family feuding, an orientation to person rather than time, language differences, and social skills deficits.

Philliber (1983) notes that the exception to this resettlement struggle was the smooth transition of the region's college-educated young adults who moved into jobs in the urban centers.

Lantz and Harper (1989) have noted that the Appalachian flight from rural to urban poverty was often accompanied by the absence of extended family support and familiar community and religious networks that provided a sense of belonging and meaning. The seriousness of loss of identity and self-esteem is often buried in common descriptions of homesickness or feelings of loneliness. Relocation elicits a deep sense of loss of perceived meaning that is likely to be accompanied by existential depression. This disruption in meaning and ensuing depression may be accompanied by thoughts of suicide, violence toward others, alcoholism, and general reduction of energy (Lantz, 1986).

Appalachian Lifestyle: Subcultural Images

The Appalachian population is an ethnic minority group that is indistinguishable by race from the dominant population and ill-defined by education and income. All social classes can be found in the population, even within extended family networks in which individuals may have widely different income and social status. Although sometimes labeled as "forgotten" and described as an "invisible minority" (Harper, 1986), the Appalachian population in the southeastern United States has maintained unique qualities of its regional life-style. Language, art, music, and personal characteristics—similar to but different from the mainstream population—perpetuate a subculture reflected in the life-style of many in the region.

Appalachians have been victims of stereotyping (e.g., "hillbilly," "country bumpkin," "briar," "hick," "ridge runner," "barefoot and pregnant") (Friedl, 1980; Plaut, 1988). Some mountain people carry on a folk tradition that is reflected in stereotypical images of the region that are especially detrimental to the region and are discriminatory.

Strong family and kinship ties, fatalism, and religious fundamentalism are prevalent throughout Appalachia (Ford, 1962; Jones, 1983; Photiadis & Schwarzweller, 1971; Walls & Billings, 1977). Individualism, independence, and traditionalism characterize many Appalachians. Traditional Appalachians often are present oriented, looking to the past for strength to deal with the present and fatalistically viewing the future as a predetermined voyage. Given to action rather than dialog, Appalachian natives are fiercely impulsive in protecting self and kin. Traditional values call for a mistrust of strangers and acute awareness of body language. Stoic, nonverbal, and able to tolerate long periods of silence, they value their privacy and take verbal promises very seriously.

Need for Culturally Relevant Health Service Delivery in Appalachia

Urban social service and health care professionals have been quick to identify the problems of social adjustment and service utilization evidenced by Appalachian migrants in urban centers but slow to gain an understanding of their cultural heritage or to develop relevant practices. Many professionals and urban community systems label these migrants as backward and ignorant. A study of 106 Appalachian families in Columbus, Ohio, uncovered differences in expectations between Appalachian patients and urban doctors. According to Obermiller (1989), Friedl's earlier study found that migrants expected personal interests similar to those known in their earlier face-to-face environment and were confused by impersonal care, expensive health services, inflexible payment expectations, and difficulty in traveling to and locating urban clinics. Conducting a more recent study of 512 Cincinnati residents, Obermiller (1989) reported that Appalachians were concerned about their health, particularly regarding heart disease, accidents, and injuries. Moreover, they had about the same knowledge as non-Appalachian respondents concerning smoking, exercise, and nutrition.

Influenced by their heritage, fundamentalism, and fatalism, Appalachian migrants approach urban human services and health care from a culturally relevant position that often conflicts with perceptions of urban providers. Some relocated Appalachian families have not learned to be active consumers in an impersonal system; instead, they have participated in a familiar caregiving system of extended family support and home remedies. Confusion ensuing from the lack of articulation between subcultural practices and the professional health care delivery system is further compounded by problems of poverty including a lack of money, insurance, and transportation. Among many poor Appalachian families, professional health care service is sought only in episodes of health crisis.

According to Harper and Lantz (1995), professionals who aspire to work in a cross-cultural context must accept and respect human differences and similarities. Every culture and subculture has ways of coping, helping, and defining that must be understood by those who intervene cross culturally to achieve positive outcomes in clinical or administrative service. Unless the delivery of health care and social services is carried out in a culturally relevant context, the professional may create a potentially damaging situation for the minority person and may risk oppressing the already oppressed by expecting compliance with cultural majority standards (Harper & Lantz, 1995; Torrey, 1986).

Much remains to be learned about the Appalachian subculture and the standards by which it has been judged to be not only different but also inferior. Ethnographic studies have identified cultural differences among countries that lead to the interpretation of everyday beliefs or practices as deviant when viewed in a different cultural context (Torrey, 1986). Instead of gaining clarity and understanding of subcultural variations, anger, hatred, discrimination, and even indifference are evident and appreciation of any difference is lost. Cultural diversity is reflected in the U.S. population, a culture in which racial, ethnic, religious, and other minority groups have been expected to assimilate. Assimilation certainly is not uniform, and some groups have maintained their life-styles and beliefs alongside mainstream U.S. culture for generations. Minority groups whose race, language, religion, and beliefs are similar to those of the majority tend to be ignored and to have little organized voice. Being similar but different, members of the nearly invisible minority population in the Appalachian mountains have experienced great socioeconomic disadvantage and continue to need accessible, expert, and affordable services.

CULTURALLY BOUND HEALTH BELIEFS AND PRACTICES

Folk Healers and Folk Medicine

Every society has healers for its ill, therapists for its confused, and medicines to ease pain and prolong life. Torrey (1986) and Dennis (1985) point out that whether witchdoctor or psychiatrist, the culturally prescribed healer has a shared world view of culture and speaks a common language. Faith in healing ultimately reflects the human need to avoid pain and to survive. Some religious and folk practices found in the Appalachian region reflect belief systems based in fundamentalist or Pentecostal practices, which include visions, repentance, laying on hands, faith healing, and predetermination or a strong fatalistic belief that God's will is supreme (Coles, 1983). Folk practices related to the moon inform planting, harvesting, and onset of labor in childbirth. Fear of water and exclusion from heaven have produced mountain-top cemeteries and prevented graves from being relocated (Lewis, Messner, & McDowell, 1985, p. 22). Folk medicine defines application of home remedies and prayer for recovery. For the Appalachian prone to seeking modern medical care only in health crises, folk remedies ease the irritations of routine health problems. Appalachian oral traditions and intergenerational teaching have preserved folk medicine to treat the frequent ailments that pester people.

Examples of folk remedies include erasing wrinkles by wiping one's face with a baby's wet diaper, chewing the root of horseradish to cure sore throat, easing earache by inserting a clove of garlic in the ear, and reducing inflammation by placing a poultice of cow manure on it ("Health Advice," 1989).

As recently as the mid-1980s, there was evidence that folk medicine continued to be practiced. In a door-to-door survey of every twelfth house ($N = 82$) in rural Tennessee, 43 percent of the individuals reported that they used some form of folk remedy while 20 percent reported that they had stopped using such remedies (Lang, Thompson, Summers, Hanson, & Hood, 1988). The remedies used in this area include kerosene for croup, wormafuge weed for worms, wild cherry tree bark for cough, yellow root for diabetes, garlic for high blood pressure, burnt whiskey for diarrhea and vomiting, and motor oil for athlete's foot (Lang et al., 1988).

Patterns of folk solutions for somatic disorders have emerged among the traditional practices that are more than two hundred years old. Appalachian folk healers, the "granny women," "herb doctors," and other root workers or spirit doctors have provided considerable help to Appalachian families (Lantz & Harper, 1989; Lewis et al., 1985). These helpers share a world view of birth, life, and death that has meaning for many within Appalachia. Among southern Appalachian Black families, researchers have found that some people follow spiritualists and faith healers in addition to using a variety of natural materials in self-treatment (Dennis, 1985).

Friedl (1980) questions literature that suggests that those who avoid using modern-day health services depend on folk medicine. Instead, he suggests that using available health care involves barriers. For example, barriers such as a lack of money and transportation limit access to medical facilities and may contribute to the use of home remedies. Friedl notes that many Appalachian people lack knowledge of the importance of preventive care and of ways in which physicians can refer patients to specialists and hospital facilities. Many are confused about entry to major hospitals for scheduled, nonemergency treatment and often view emergency rooms as the portal to hospitalization. These barriers may be strong enough that some patients find self-treatment less stressful.

Health Beliefs and Current Health Care

Regardless of the comfort and availability of centuries-old remedies, modern medicine has surpassed folk medicine throughout the region. For most Appalachians, information from media sources and increased education in general have reduced dependence on home remedies and old practices. Although some may find comfort in thoughts of old family remedies and remember stories of cures and symptom relief, most Appalachians use modern-day health care services. In many ways, the region's tradition of folk medicine has uniquely linked body and environment and has given meaning to being in the world with nature. This sense of meaning held by those who share a common world view is reflective of the Appalachian subculture (Lantz & Harper, 1989).

For many people, the health beliefs of a particular cultural group coexist with scientific medicine, and some choose to use both systems while others avoid professional health care. Health care clinics can be found throughout Appalachia, even in many remote areas (Reul, 1985).

For the most part, traditional remedies have little meaning for young Appalachian families who have been influenced by mainstream culture and who have not internalized folk remedies as their major cure system (Hansen & Resnick, 1990). On the other hand, these same families have not learned to use modern health care and are caught in a cultural or informational lag that creates confusion in their view of health and illness. Appalachian families who do not have a systemic way of finding relief from illnesses are particularly vulnerable.

Maternal and Child Health Care

Appalachia's children suffer perhaps the most of any age group in this population. The rate of infant mortality within a population is one measure of unmet needs experienced by that population. Despite funding and program development efforts, infant mortality continues to be a problem. Infant mortality rates vary by county throughout the region. While some counties approximate the 1990 goal of United States Public Health Service of no more than twelve infant deaths per one thousand annually (Mabry, 1988), other estimates suggest that the infant mortality rate in Appalachia is higher than the rest of the nation. For example, in thirty two Appalachian counties in Kentucky, the infant mortality rate is 50 percent higher than the national average (Flannery, 1982). Infant mortality occurred in 11.3 of every 1,000 births in Kentucky's central Appalachian counties between 1980 and 1984 (Bagby et al., 1986). The infant mortality rate of babies born to West Virginia teenage mothers in 1989 was 11.2 per 1,000 live births (Dye & Holmes, 1990). The rate for 1990 averaged 9.9 per 1,000 live births, while the national average for the same year was 9.2 per 1,000 live births (*Kids Count*, 1993). Mabry (1988) emphasizes that counties where infant mortality has been reduced may have more primary care health centers, but specialized practitioners are not available.

Due to expense and distance, many rural Appalachian families do not use health services other than those available at primary care clinics that are easily accessible. In addition to infant mortality, many babies have low birth weights and physical disabilities. Many are born to mothers who have not had prenatal health care. In 1990, 9.7 percent of all births in West Virginia were to unmarried teens, 1.0 percent above the national average (*Kids Count*, 1993).

For Appalachian mothers who give little personal attention to health care for themselves and their infants, the family and fundamental religion are major support systems. Being part of an extended family system, the new baby is welcomed by a variety of relatives and friends. Strong religious beliefs credit an infant's arrival, or even early mortality, as one more sign of "God's will" that is to be accepted (Harper, 1970). Few children are placed for adoption by their Appalachian mothers; instead, they are protected by the extended family if the biological mother or father is unable to provide adequate care. Fewer babies are being born at home or delivered by lay midwives today than in the past. Instead, childbirth generally occurs in hospitals scattered throughout the region and is often attended by nurse-midwives. The extended family will encourage the new mother to breast-feed her infant, and about 50 percent will do so. Cultural traditions in Appalachia sometimes interfere with both prenatal and postnatal health care utilization, but for the most part, cultural practices are relatively harmless. They often include a variety of myths that are more "old wives' tales" than common practice. Examples of such myths include the following:

1. Hanging up clothes on a clothesline with the hands above the head will cause the umbilical cord to wrap around the baby's neck.
2. If the pregnant woman puts away (freezes or cans) strawberries while pregnant, the baby will have a strawberry mark at birth.
3. If the pregnant woman has a lot of heartburn during her pregnancy, the baby will be born with a lot of hair.
4. Eating hot peppers while pregnant will purify the blood (preventing toxemia or pre-eclampsia).
5. If the baby is carried high, it will be a girl; if carried low, it will be a boy.
6. If one's wedding ring is tied on a string and the ring turns in a circle [while held over the wrist], the baby will be a girl, but if it swings back and forth, the baby will be a boy.
7. An ax under the bed will cut the pains of labor.
8. If the placenta and cord are planted behind the house, the soul of the baby will stay close to home. (Day, 1983, p. 6)

For those who are socioeconomically disadvantaged by the severe poverty of the Appalachian region, birth of a new child brings hope for a better future. Historically, the region has had high birth rates; however, family planning services have been effective in educating the Appalachian population to practice contraception and control the size of their families. A recent study of one central Appalachian county confirmed that contraceptive practices in the county were similar to national practices. Families were informed and willing to utilize contraceptives. Interestingly, for about 50 percent of families, the contraceptive method of choice was female sterilization (Gairola, Hochstrasser, & Garkovich, 1986; Hochstrasser & Gairola, 1991). There is little literature comparing the extent of informed consent by the family to views of the value of female fertility in the region and the opinion of professionals working with the family. Determining the role of male and female responsibility for preventing pregnancy is also an area that needs further study.

AVAILABILITY OF HEALTH CARE SERVICES FOR APPALACHIAN FAMILIES

Lack of health care, untreated illnesses, and infant mortality rates that were twice as high as those of the nation brought attention to Appalachia's rural poor in the 1960s. For most of the past three decades, health care development and service delivery have been major objectives of the Appalachian Regional Commission. The Commission has spent over $552,000,000 establishing numerous primary care centers to bring health care within a thirty-mile radius of most Appalachian families, and it has been instrumental in helping primary care clinics become essential providers throughout the region (Bagby et al., 1986). These clinics link most Appalachian families to hospitals in the region—a secondary layer of care—and provide access to research centers as well.

One example is the Goodlark Rural Health Care System in central Tennessee. This geographically dispersed health care service delivery system serves eleven counties. Operating four satellite clinics staffed by physicians, nurse practitioners, and a broad range of ancillary medical staff, the Goodlark system provides a wide range of primary health care services in this depressed rural area. Program evaluation revealed that of the four clinics, those with the most comprehensive services retained patients longer and had fewer patients seeking hospitalization or comprehensive care at larger, more distant facilities. Nurse practitioners were seen as perhaps the most cost-effective staff members. In an assessment of factors that determine use of health care facilities, Goodlark's patients reported convenience or accessibility of the facility, courteous attention, and competent care as factors influencing their decision to use the facility (Powers, 1983).

Similar to the geographically dispersed model of the Goodlark clinics, numerous small facilities can be found throughout the Appalachian region where primary care is provided to families experiencing a range of health problems including high infant mortality, iron deficiencies, lack of transportation to access health care, and general denial of health needs except in cases of acute, life-threatening episodes (Flannery, 1982).

Named as the Outstanding Rural Practice by the National Health Association, the Lincoln County Primary Care Center in rural West Virginia is evidence of a successful primary care center that has been in operation for about twenty years. The Center operates with a sliding fee scale and turns nobody away. (Having a doctor/patient ratio of 1/4,000, West Virginia was ranked forty-ninth of fifty states in 1990 in access to health care [Casto, 1992]).

BARRIERS TO THE HEALTH CARE INTERCHANGE OF APPALACHIAN FAMILIES AND HEALTH PROVIDERS

The Appalachian population faces barriers of geographic accessibility, affordability, and education for preventive service utilization, as well as lack of information about the importance of preventing, rather than just curing, illness. Delivering health care services to Appalachia's population is a political and multidisciplinary concern. The challenge of comprehensive health care delivery for this group has been the focus of numerous articles, research, and conferences shared by disciplines including social work, nursing, medicine, psychology, theology, education, law, anthropology, and sociology. An ecological approach to barriers to health care delivery and service utilization can best occur when professional support systems, political funding streams, and system deficits that link the Appalachian person with the health care system are identified and evaluated. The environment in Appalachia suggests that the transactions between health consumers and providers are central to effective and efficient service delivery and utilization. The ecological configuration of health consumers and health professionals in Appalachia calls for cooperation and collaboration among health and human service professionals so that community networks can develop.

IMPLICATIONS FOR HEALTH CARE PRACTICE

Cultural Competence

It is essential that health care service delivery be accomplished in a culturally competent manner and that an understanding and appreciation of the subculture in the Appalachian region inform this delivery process. Practitioners from the variety of professions involved in providing comprehensive health and human services must learn about health care beliefs, folk remedies, and the colorful history of the region. Minority groups' practices and beliefs impact their members' world view of wellness and utilization of physical treatment, whether it be modern medicine or folk medicine. Beyond understanding, practitioners must listen carefully, convey respect, individualize their approach to patients, and enter into the world view of the patient as much as possible so that health and wellness fit into a culturally consistent definition.

Strengths Model

Approaching any interactive process from only a deficit position is generally shortsighted. The strengths of the Appalachian population in overcoming major health care deficits need to be given equal attention. At one time the region was far above the national average in untreated chronic disease, infant mortality, birth rate, dental caries, malnutrition, untreated allergies, eye disease, heart disease, and respiratory disorders. In the 1990s, status in the Appalachian region is approaching that of much of the nation at large, despite broad gaps in ease of accessibility to clinics and easy access to expert providers. The Appalachian population is very responsive to internal control over preventing illness. The independent and self-sufficient nature of Appalachian people supports the practice of good nutrition, exercise, and fluids to keep a strong body. Traditional personal and religious values have given way to widespread contraceptive usage, family planning, and professional care instead of folk healers and folk cures. In general, use of folk remedies has decreased among young families in the region. The majority of residents in Appalachia are utilizing professional services for most of their pressing health care needs.

Spirituality and Values

Consistent with this population's traditional orientation to living in balance with God and nature, professional health care is sometimes viewed as necessary only to stop suffering. Human service professionals, including health care providers and social workers, must gain a culturally competent perspective that includes recognition and acceptance of both common human needs and cultural diversity. Culturally competent practice is essential for professionals who want to provide life-enhancing services to Appalachian families. In the early stages of care, providers must nurture trust. Respect for extended family members' opinions and advice is also part of the process of accepting health care recommendations and treatments. Many people have a trusted doctor, nurse, or relative whom they may wish to consult for reassurance even though they are not involved in the problem assessment or treatment plan. Appalachian patients need to be granted respect and patience as they make health care choices that may threaten their independence and self-sufficiency at times. Furthermore, the sophistication and level of knowledge held by many quiet-spoken and sometimes reluctant patients should never be underestimated. It is especially important that the person seeking health care be given consideration and respect at all times.

Diversity

Working with Appalachian clients and patients requires recognition of the similarities and differences in the traditional life-styles and values of those who live alongside the mainstream U.S. culture while clinging to regional values and practices. The region has people of all religions, all professions, and all levels of education and sophistication. There is diversity in age, gender, race, life-style, and socioeconomic class. Simply living in the region does not instill traditional life-style patterns. The range of human and cultural diversity requires competent professionals to have a broad world view.

Education

The challenge to deliver high-quality services in a culturally relevant manner continues. Authorities such as Bagby and colleagues (1986), Powers (1983), and Flannery (1982) have raised issues concerning providing health care in the region from a culturally competent perspective. Clearly, such care must be culturally relevant, accessible, and affordable, and it must include education of the people.

Education can raise awareness of the importance of primary care in preventing serious and sometimes irreversible health problems, and can address ways to access affordable, if not free, primary care providers and facilities. In rural areas, the possibilities for extending primary care into homes and small communities or delivering service through mobile vans have considerable merit. The cost of educating people to use primary care will be offset by the benefits of the care itself (Kelleher, 1991). There should be no more instances of removing a child's orthodontic braces because the family could no longer afford to pay (Greenlee & Lantz, 1993).

Economic and Program Development

To develop a perspective of health care in the Appalachian region, it is essential to begin with an understanding of health care in the nation. Solving the financial burden of health care provision in Appalachia's vast socioeconomically depressed region is linked to the overall economy of the nation. According to Couto (1989), the core of health care in Appalachia is "the political economy of health care and health" (p. 5). The problems of lack of power and accompanying lack of health and mental health care recognized in the region in the 1960s were addressed by commitments to eradicate poverty and suffering in the War on Poverty and by funds from numerous federal grants, private foundations such as the Robert Wood Johnson Foundation and Kellogg Foundation, and the Appalachian Regional Commission. In the 1990s, there is continued support for health care development, including community health centers. There are multiple providers such as local public health departments, United Mine Workers clinics, and private facilities where reimbursement includes Medicaid, Medicare, private pay, and private insurance. However, these sources cannot fund total health care for this rural population, nor can funds be used to provide enough of the latest equipment or attract an adequate number of competent providers for rural clinics. It is estimated that in West Virginia, 250,000 to 350,000 people have no insurance and that 70,000 of these are children (West Virginia Health Care Planning Commission, 1991).

The challenge of funding health care for the poor is a hurdle for the Appalachian region to overcome (Galen, 1993). A model of managed care, if done through interdisciplinary efforts at the community level, may be one economically feasible solution for many who seek culturally competent health care in this region.

Moving beyond a singular view, Tripp-Reimer (1982) defines health care as an interactive process interpreted by both the provider and the patient. From an ethnocentric perspective, professionals with different cultural backgrounds use their own experiences and standards as a base from which to interpret Appalachian health care needs and services. On the other hand, Tripp-Reimer proposes that from a "cultural relativist perspective the caregiver attempts to understand the behavior of clients within the context of the client's culture" (1982, p. 180). Perhaps the cultural lag or information gap in using professional health care referred to by Hansen and Resnick (1990) and discussed earlier in this chapter can be bridged if ethnocentric and culturally relevant perspectives can be incorporated into all levels of health care. From such a position, effective health care professionals will be better able to approach the Appalachian patient as a person of strength and to appreciate the colorful and rich heritage of this stoic and resourceful population.

REFERENCES

Bagby, J. W., Carpenter, C., Eller, R., Holman, G., Hoskins, M. S., & Tichamyer, C. (1986). *The status of health care in Appalachian Kentucky.* Lexington: The Appalachian Center, University of Kentucky.

Burlage, R. (1970). ARC's first six-year plan: A critical interpretation. *People's Appalachia, 1,* 4.

Casto, J. E. (1992). Primary care center. *Appalachia, 25*(3), 13–18.

Caudill, H. (1961). *Night comes to the Cumberlands.* Boston: Little, Brown.

Coles, R. (1971). *Children of crisis, Vol. 2. Migrants, sharecroppers, mountaineers.* Boston: Little, Brown.

Coles, R. (1983). God and the rural poor. In B. Ergood & B. Kuhre (Eds.), *Appalachia: Social context past and present* (pp. 322–329). Dubuque, IA: Kendall/Hunt.

Couto, R. A. (1989). The political economy of Appalachian health. In *Health in Appalachia: Proceedings from the 1988 Conference on Appalachia* (pp. 5–16). Lexington: Appalachian Center, University of Kentucky.

Day, A. Y. (1983). Childbearing practices in the Appalachian culture. *Frontier Nursing Service Quarterly Bulletin, 59*(1), 1–7.

Dennis, R. E. (1985). Health beliefs and practices of ethnic and religious groups. In E. Watkins & A. Johnson (Eds.), *Removing cultural and ethnic barriers to health care* (pp. 12–18). Chapel Hill: The University of North Carolina.

Dye, T. O., & Holmes, A. P. (1990, November). *Recent trends in adolescent pregnancy in West Virginia.* Paper presented at the Fifth Annual University of Kentucky Conference on Appalachia, Lexington.

Flannery, M. (1982, March–April) Appalachian health care: The struggle to reach remote areas. *Appalachia,* pp. 17–24.

Flicker, V. B., & Graves, H. S. (1971). *Deprivation in America.* Beverly Hills, CA: Glencoe.

Ford, T. R. (1962). *The southern Appalachian region: A survey.* Lexington: The University Press of Kentucky.

Friedl, J. (1980, September) What happens when Appalachia goes urban? *Urban Health,* pp. 35–37.

Galen, M. (1993). Can the poor afford health care reform? *Business Week, 3339,* 31–33.

Gairola, G. A., Hochstrasser, D. L., & Garkovich, L. E. (1986). Modern contraceptive practice in rural Appalachia. *American Journal of Public Health, 76*(8), 1004–1008.

Greenlee, R., & Lantz, J. (1993). Family coping strategies and the rural Appalachian working poor. *Contemporary Family Therapy, 15*(2), 121–137.

Hansen, M. M., & Resick, L. K. (1990). Health beliefs, health care, and rural Appalachian subcultures from an ethnographic perspective. *Family Community Health, 13*(1), 1–10.

Harper, K. (1970). Appalachia: A way of life. *Social Welfare in Appalachia, 11,* 26–32.

Harper, K. V. (1986, July). *The impact of regional development on rural poverty: An analysis of continuing human need.* Paper presented at the 11th National Institute on Social Work in Rural Areas, James Madison University, Harrisonburg, Virginia.

Harper, K. V., & Lantz, J. (1995). *Cross-cultural social work: An existentialist approach.* Chicago: Lyceum.

Health advice. (1989). From The poor man's medicine bag (Home remedies and helpful hints) by Tim Wager, 1984. *Now and Then, 6*(1), 9.

Hochstrasser, D. L. & Gairola, G. A. (1991). Family planning and fertility in southern Appalachia: A community study. *Human Organization, 50*(4), 393–416.

Immunizing West Virginia's preschool children. (1994). *Families First, 3*(1), 5.

Jones, L. (1983). Appalachian values. In B. Ergood & B. Kuhre (Eds.), *Appalachia: Social context, past and present* (pp. 125–129). Dubuque, IA: Kendall/Hunt.

Kelleher, K. C. (1991). Free clinics: A solution that can work . . . now! *The Journal of the American Medical Association, 266*(6), 838–841.

Kids count. (1993). Washington, DC: Center for the Study of Social Policy.

Lang, F., Thompson, D., Summers, B., Hanson, W., & Hood, M. (1988). A profile of health beliefs and practices in a rural East Tennessee community. *Journal of the Tennessee Medical Association, 81*(4), 229–233.

Lantz, J. (1986). Family logo therapy. *Contemporary Family Therapy, 8*(2), 124–135.

Lantz, J., & Harper, K. V. (1989). Network intervention: Existential depression and the relocated Appalachian family. *Contemporary Family Therapy, 11*(3), 213–223.

Lewis, S., Messner, R., & McDowell, W. A. (1985). An unchanging culture. *Journal of Gerontological Nursing, 11*(8), 21–26.

Looff, D. (1971). *Appalachia's children.* Lexington: University Press of Kentucky.

Mabry, C. C. (1988). Children: The vulnerable population of Appalachia. In *Health in Appalachia: Proceedings from the 1988 Conference on Appalachia* (pp. 163–170). Lexington: Appalachian Center, University of Kentucky.

Obermiller, P. (1989). Rx: Stumpwater and streptomycin: Urban Appalachian health. *Now and Then, 6*(1), 26–27.

Obermiller, P. J., & Oldendick, R. (1986). Moving on: Recent patterns of Appalachian migration. In J. Lloyd & A. G. Campbell (Eds.), *The impact of institution in Appalachia* (pp. 148–165). Boone, NC: Appalachian Consortium Press.

Ohio poverty indicators (Vol. 2 Trends: 1970–1987) (1987). Cleveland, OH: Department of Planning and Program Development, Council for Economic Opportunities in Greater Cleveland.

Payroll employment, unemployment, and hours and earnings in West Virginia. (1994, June). *Economic Summary,* p. 2.

Philliber, W. W. (1983). Correlates of Appalachian identification among Appalachian migrants. In B. Y. Braxton, M. L. Crutchfield, W. E. Lightfoot, & J. R. Steward (Eds.), *The Appalachian experience: Proceedings of the sixth annual Appalachian Studies Conference* (pp. 10–14). Boone, NC: Appalachian Consortium Press.

Photiadis, J. D., & Schwarzweller, H. (1971). *Change in rural Appalachia: Implications for action programs.* Philadelphia: University of Pennsylvania Press.

Plaut, T. (1983). Cross-cultural conflict between providers and clients and staff members. In S. Keefe (Ed.), *Appalachian mental health* (pp. 161–174). Lexington: The University Press of Kentucky.

Powers, J. S. (1983). Primary care in an underserved rural area: The Goodlark experience in middle Tennessee. *Public Health Reports, 98*(4), 390–396.

Reul, M. R. (1985). Environmental, cultural, and ethnic barriers to rural health care. In E. Watkins & A. Johnson (Eds.), *Removing cultural and ethnic barriers to health care* (pp. 12–18). Chapel Hill: The University of North Carolina.

Stekert, E. J. (1971). Forces for conflict: Southern mountain medical beliefs in Detroit. In A. Paredes & E. J. Stekert (Eds.), *The urban experiences and folk tradition* (pp. 95–136), Austin: University of Texas Press.

Torrey, E. F. (1986). *Witchdoctors and psychiatrists.* New York: Harper & Row.

Tripp-Reimer, T. (1982). Barriers to health care: Variations in interpretation of Appalachian client behavior by Appalachian and non-Appalachian health professionals. *Western Journal of Nursing Research, 4*(2), 179–191.

Walls, D. S., & Billings, D. B. (1977). The sociology of southern Appalachia. *Appalachian Journal, 5,* 131–144.

West Virginia Health Care Planning Commission. (1991). *For the health of West Virginia: A report to the governor and the legislature.* Charleston, WV: Author.

SUGGESTED READINGS

Coles, R. (1990). *The spiritual life of children.* Boston: Houghton-Mifflin.

Ergood, B., & Kuhre, B. (Eds.). (1983). *Appalachia: Social context past and present.* Dubuque, IA: Kendall/Hunt.

Flora, C. B., Flora, J. L., Spears, J. D., & Swanson, L. E. (1992). *Rural communities.* Boulder, CO: Westview.

Harper, K. V. (1992). Intervention in cultural confusion of relocated children. In B. Locke & M. Egan, (Eds.), *Fulfilling our mission: Rural social work in the 1990s* (pp. 60–67). Morgantown: West Virginia University.

Hill, I. T. (1992). The role of medicaid and other government programs in providing medical care for children and pregnant women. *U.S. Health Care for Children, 2*(2), 134–153.

Keefe, S. E. (Ed.). (1988). *Appalachian mental health.* Lexington: The University Press of Kentucky.

Starfield, B. (1992). Child and adolescent health status measures. *U.S. Health Care for Children, 2*(2), 25–39.

West Virginia Hospital Association. (1991). *The picture of health care in West Virginia.* South Charleston: Author.

West Virginia Health Care Planning Commission. (1992). *Health care reform in West Virginia: A shared responsibility.* Charleston: Author.

Richmond, R. E., Richabaugh, J., Huffman, J., & Epperly, N. (1987). Colorectal cancer mortality and incidence in Campbell County, Kentucky. *Southern Medical Journal, 80*(8), 953–957.

Simon, J. M. (1987). Health care of the elderly in Appalachia. *Journal of Gerontological Nursing, 13*(7), 32–35.

Tucker, T. C. (1988). *Cancer mortality in rural Appalachian Kentucky* (Appalachian Data Bank Report No. 6). Lexington: Appalachian Center, University of Kentucky.

▶ 5

Arab Americans

ANAHID DERVARTANIAN KULWICKI

For several decades, many health care professionals in the United States have focused on Western values when providing care to their clients. This has resulted in neglect and alienation of clients of diverse cultural backgrounds with specific health care needs and expectations. The current crisis in the health care delivery system and the increasing morbidity and mortality rates among ethnic populations have raised serious concerns about the quality of health care in the United States. Health care professionals working with people of diverse cultural backgrounds have long recognized the challenges of providing culturally congruent care and have developed care approaches tailored to the specific needs of their clients.

This chapter provides a brief description of Arab Americans in the United States—their culture, history, religion, and values and beliefs related to health care. The focus is on the Muslim Arab community of Metropolitan Detroit. The information is derived from the author's experience as a researcher in the areas of health care values and beliefs among Yemeni Arab Americans (Kulwicki, 1987); a survey of Arab teen health needs (Kulwicki, 1989a); knowledge, attitudes, beliefs, and behaviors of Arab Americans related to AIDS (Kulwicki, 1990a); and an assessment of cardiovascular risk factors and diabetes among Arab Americans in one of the largest Arab-American communities in the United States (1990b). The author's experience as a consultant to major Detroit area hospitals serving Arab-American clients; her active involvement in community services; her expertise in development of culturally competent programs in the areas of teen health, AIDS prevention, prenatal advocacy programs, and a cardiovascular risk reduction project; and her fluency in the Arabic language have contributed to the interpretation of cultural factors that are unique to the Arab-American immigrant population.

HISTORY AND OVERVIEW OF THE CULTURE

It is estimated that around three million Arabs currently live in the United States and that in the year 2000 the number will be twelve million. Arab-American immigrants come from twenty-two Arab countries: Algeria, Bahrain, Djibouti, Iraq, Egypt, Jordan, Kuwait, Lebanon, Libya, Mauritania, Morocco, Oman, Palestine, Syria, Qatar, Saudi Arabia, Somalia, Sudan, Syria, Tunisia, United Arab Emirates, and the Yemens. The majority of the Arab immigrants in the United States are Lebanese, Syrian, Palestinian/ Jordanian, Chaldean/Iraqui, Egyptian, and Yemeni (White, 1982). Although all Arabs world wide speak one language, which is Arabic, and most are Muslims and believe in the prophet Muhammed, there are implicit and explicit differences among the Arab immigrants in the United States. For instance, there are more Christians than Muslims in the United States. Lebanese in the United States are early settlers and are more assimilated and acculturated. There are differences in occupation among Arab groups: Lebanese and Syrians usually own small businesses, Chaldeans run small grocery stores, and Yemeni work in the auto industry and as seamen.

The first wave of Arab immigrants came to the United States before World War I. Between 1889 and 1910, approximately 60,000 Arabs settled in the United States; most were males and illiterate. The majority came from Greater Syria, many of them Christians escaping the Muslim Ottoman Empire. The second wave of Arab immigrants, who came after World War II, were Palestinians, Muslims from Lebanon, and Yemeni. The Palestinian refugees immigrated after the creation of the state of Israel in 1948 and after the Arab-Israeli war of 1967. The Yemeni came after the 1950s in the wake of political conflict in Yemen. A great number of Lebanese immigrated after the civil war in Lebanon and the Israeli invasion of south Lebanon. Arab immigrants are widely dispersed throughout the United States; however, the majority are concentrated in California and in Michigan's Detroit metropolitan area (Abraham & Abraham, 1983).

The metropolitan Detroit Arabs constitute the largest concentration of Middle Eastern peoples in the country. High estimates for the number of Arab Americans living in the Greater Detroit area surpass more than 200,000. The Arab community in this area is comprised of people from a number of national and religious affiliations, including Lebanese/Syrians, Iraqui/Chaldeans, Yemenis, and Palestinian/Jordanians (Abraham & Abraham, 1983).

The first immigration from the Middle East to Detroit began in the 1890s. The "southend" community of Dearborn at that time was—and it still is—the major point of entry into the state of Michigan (Abraham & Abraham, 1983). Two thirds of the Arabic respondents to a 1979 survey (Bowker, 1979) were born overseas, emigrating to the United States after 1974.

According to the 1980 Census, the Middle Eastern population differs from the general population in that Arab Americans tend to be younger (median age = 23.2 years). Some 54 percent of the population is male. The large number of males is due to the high levels of immigration into the United States by single men as well as married men, who reside here on their own for a short period of time before sending for their families. Arab Americans rank lower than the general population in educational attainment; the mean number of years of school they have completed is 9.2. Only 23 percent report that they have completed high school (Paine, 1986; U.S. Bureau of the Census, 1980).

The mean level of income is also low. Compared to roughly 5 percent of the general population in the Greater Detroit area who fall below the poverty level, the estimate of the Arab population who earn less than poverty-level wages ranges from 20 percent to 27 percent. A recent survey by the Wayne County Health Department found that 45 percent of the respondents had an annual income of less than $10,000 (Gold, 1987). More than 70 percent of those interviewed for Kulwicki's (1990b) cardiovascular and diabetes risk assessment survey reported income under $10,000.

LANGUAGE

Although Arabic is universally written and understood by Arabs, there are distinct differences in Arabic dialects. The Arabic language belongs to the Semitic languages, and its alphabet contains twenty-eight letters. The written language is used extensively by numerous countries such as Afghanistan, Indonesia, Malaysia, some parts of China, the Philippines, and Russia. The Arabic script reads from right to left. European languages, such as Spanish, Portuguese, French, Italian, and English contain many words borrowed from Arabic (e.g., *algebra, alchemy, soda, sherbet, genius*).

COMMUNICATION STYLES

Arab Americans are highly contextual in nature; they prefer to develop feelings before developing a work relationship with strangers (Meleis,

1981). Hence, Arab Americans would engage health care providers in lengthy personal conversations prior to agreeing to any type of treatment. This kind of relationship may be annoying to health care professionals, who may find that Arab clients need more time and personal attention than their other patients.

Although most educated Arabs speak English, a large number of new immigrants may not speak or write English. Arabs who come from rural backgrounds or who are undereducated or illiterate have difficulty reading or understanding medical information and tend to avoid lengthy explanations. Abraham, Abraham, and Aswad (1983) reported that approximately one third of the Arab Americans in Dearborn speak no English, two thirds speak a limited amount of English, and one fifth read and write a limited amount of Arabic. Many have limited proficiency in spoken English. Many first-generation immigrant Arab Americans, particularly women, are illiterate in their native language. Availability of bilingual interpreters may alleviate communication difficulties. If bilingual interpreters or translators are unavailable, the use of a family member as an interpreter may be advisable. However, health care professionals must be aware that a family member may delete or misrepresent information if the information is considered to bring shame or disrespect to the individual.

RELIGION

The majority of the Arabs immigrating to the United States are Christians; in contrast, the majority of Arabs in the Middle East are Muslims. Although the predominant religion of the Arab world is Islam, there are other religious groups in the Middle East such as Copts, Greek Orthodox, Greek Catholics (Melchites), Maronites, Druze, Syrian Orthodox, Nestorians, Chaldeans, Coptic Catholics, Armenian Orthodox, and Jews.

Islam, unlike some other religions, is not only a spiritual practice but a way of life—it is the world in which a Muslim lives (Nasr, 1964). Islam is much broader than Christianity in that the *Quran* prescribes politics, economics, law and justice, and social behavior as well as theology (Roberts, 1982). Therefore, to be a true believer is to exercise the lifeways the prophet Muhammed has emphasized.

Muslims believe in the prophet Muhammed, who is recognized by all Muslims as the messenger of Allah (God). Muslims believe that God is almighty and unique; therefore, no one can have a direct relationship with God, not even Muhammed himself. Allah is the Supreme Being for all Muslims. All acts that are necessary to human life are given religious meaning and direction by the *Shari'ah*, or the Islamic religious law. The *Shari'ah* sets rules of religious observance and practice, marriage and family law, rules of social conduct and interaction, dietary regulations, and general rules of cleanliness (Nasr, 1964).

The *Quran* is the sacred book of Islam. All Muslims are expected to observe five basic duties of Islam: Profession of Faith, Prayer, Pilgrimage, Fasting, and Charity. The Profession of Faith, or *Shahada* in Arabic, requires the believer to profess the unity of God and the mission of Muhammad. Prayer, *salat*, is required five times a day—at dawn, noon, midafternoon, sunset, and dusk. Friday is designated as a day of rest. Ritual ablution must be performed before *salat*, including washing of hands, face, and feet. If water is unavailable, sand is used. Almsgiving, *Zaka* or *Zakat*, involves sharing one's wealth with the public. Fasting, or *Saum*, is complete abstinence from food and drink from dawn to sunset every day during Ramadan. All Muslims are expected to do pilgrimage at least once in their lives to *al hajj the kaaba*, the holy shrine of Mecca. The poor, persons with disabilities, and minors are exempted.

One common perception among Westerners is that Muslims have a fatalistic view of life. While Islam teaches that humans must follow their faith when making decisions and bear responsibility for their actions, it stresses that freedom in its absolute sense belongs to God. Therefore, in matters of health, illness, and death, Muslims are more limited in their sphere of influence by human action than are non-Muslims. Arabs are greatly offended by diagnoses that make predictions in terms of time. Since they believe that God makes the final determination of life and death, they cannot accept such diagnoses. When such a prediction is made, a Muslim may withdraw from medical care altogether. Therefore, in situations in which grave outcomes are expected, health care professionals should provide some hope or acknowledge God's role in the prognosis. The expression *In Sha' Allah* (if God wills) used commonly by Arabs is an indication of the Arab's belief in God's role in life and death.

Islamic law is precise regarding the ritual of ablution required after urination, defecation, and sexual relations. Muslims believe that the religion of Islam is based on cleanliness. The *Shar'iah* describes things that are by nature unclean and therefore to be avoided by Muslims, especially in prayer and eating. They include the following: urine and stool, blood and semen, corpses, unclean animals (pigs and dogs), intoxicating liquids, and non-Muslims (Roberts, 1982). Islamic dietary restrictions include the avoidance of blood and blood products, pork, and alcohol. Meats must be prepared in the Hallal way to meet Islamic law. If this is not available, kosher meats can be substituted.

THE ARAB-AMERICAN FAMILY

The family is the strongest social unit in Arab culture. The Arab family is patrilineal, and it usually consists of the father's brothers' families, grandparents on the father's side, and children (Aswad, 1988). The extended family unit, incorporating the three generations, is a close unit wherein each member is obligated to provide emotional and financial support to the other members. At times of crisis, family members are expected to show support by their presence and by offering financial assistance. The strong kinship ties among members of Arab families are also demonstrated by their active involvement in family matters such as mate selection, marriage, birth, death, and hospitalization. Within the extended family there is a sense of openness and shared experience. Family members express pride in the family and are protective of their members. If a family member does well, the whole family shares the honor (*sharaf*). On the other hand, if someone disgraces the family (*Ayb*), the whole family shares the burden of disgrace. The concept of honor and shame in Arab society has a strong influence in guiding individual behavior, especially the behavior of women. Mothers are held responsible for the upbringing of their children. They are extremely aware of their role to raise their daughters, who are expected to bring honor to the family. A woman must be a virgin before marriage; premarital sex by a girl is considered shameful to the family and, therefore, at times is severely punished by the family. Although in modern Arab countries females are allowed to date, female chastity is still highly valued.

In the United States, where premarital sex is considered to be more acceptable, Arab mothers are under extreme pressure to control their daughters' sexual activity for fear that they may bring shame to the family by losing their virginity (Aswad, 1988). In some instances, mothers encourage their daughters to marry early to avoid the possibility of premarital sexual activity. In health care settings, the concept of honor and shame is also apparent when family members conceal medical conditions that are perceived to bring shame to the family. For instance, members of a family may conceal a genetic disorder that may be considered detrimental to the family's honor and thus limit the daughters' and sons' opportunity to marry. Examples of such illnesses are mental retardation, seizures, and mental disorders.

The Islamic philosophy of procreation and the prophet's famous statement, "Marry and reproduce so that I may be proud of you before God" (Beck & Keddie, 1980, p. 87), have made marriage and procreation one of the most important aspects of the Muslim tradition. Children are much desired by the family and a source of pride for the married couple. Through children a female gains respect, power, and recognition. Pregnancy within the first year of marriage is anxiously awaited, and a missed menstrual period is greatly rejoiced.

Segregation of the sexes in Arab society is found primarily in the public arena, but it also may extend to private life. The male is considered to be the head of the household, the breadwinner, and the major decision maker, caring for the economic needs of the family. He is also considered the disciplinarian and the protector of the family honor. The role of the female is that of childbearer and childrearer, who attends to the physical and emotional needs of the family. She is the educator, responsible for the behavior of the children. Mothers are often blamed for their children's misbehavior. The oldest daughter and the oldest son are considered closest to the parents.

In the Arab culture, children are raised to obey and conform to societal expectations, not to question authority, and to respect elders. If a child does harm, the family is held responsible for the child's behavior. The reputation of the individual reflects on the family. Children are usually spoiled within the first few years of life by constant fondling, caressing, and carrying around. Western culture views Arab children as undisciplined, immature, and lacking self-control. Arab families usually view children as children until they approach puberty. After puberty, the girls are expected to behave as adults and help their mothers in household tasks. The boys, although expected to help their fathers, are allowed more freedom. Although there is little information on child abuse among Arab Americans, physical punishment is exercised by some Arabs. Corporal punishment is used as a disciplinary measure when a child misbehaves or is thought to bring shame to the family.

Sexual matters are considered exclusively male or female topics of conversation. Males and females do not discuss sexual matters between them—even between spouses. However, sexual concerns are openly discussed between individuals of the same sex. Contraception, infertility, or matters concerning family planning often are not discussed between partners and, in some instances, females may make decisions about family planning without the knowledge and consent of their spouses.

Childbirth in the Arab society is considered a female experience. In some countries, especially in rural areas of the Middle East, pregnancy is considered a healthy condition, and prenatal care is often provided by family members such as the mother-in-law or the mother. In countries where health care is available, prenatal care is provided by midwives or medical professionals. Once a woman is pregnant, her mother-in-law or her mother will be the chief advisor for prenatal practices. Frequently a pregnant woman will seek the advice of an older kin before contacting a physician. Medical care is often sought when a condition is considered complicated and difficult to treat by home remedies. For women who have limited experience with health care professionals, doctors are usually sought during the last stages of pregnancy and often when close to delivery.

Prenatal visits are considered uncomfortable and often feared by some rural immigrant women who have not experienced physical examinations by male physicians. For this reason, most women would choose a female obstetrician over a male one, preferring to avoid body exposure to male physicians. During delivery, most women prefer to have their mother, mother-in-law, or next of kin present in the delivery room. The majority of husbands prefer to wait outside the delivery room. Male children are often preferred, and the birth of the first son is often more celebrated than the birth of a daughter. After delivery, a woman is expected to rest for forty days, and her mother or mother-in-law is put in charge of performing household duties. Babies are often breastfed, although Arab-American women prefer to bottle feed.

It has come to the attention of some researchers that Arab Americans experience a high rate of infant mortality. There have been no direct studies of annual infant mortality rates among Arab Americans in the United States; however, a study conducted on infant mortality in Dearborn (Mesa, 1987), Detroit suburb, suggested that infant mortality among first-generation Arab-American women may be as high as 38.5/1,000. Kulwicki (1987) documented 79.6 deaths per 1,000 experienced by Yemeni Arab women of Dearborn over their childbearing ages, including births in Yemen. Macki's (1985) study reported that 34 out of 101 Arab women surveyed experienced infant deaths either in the United States or in their country of origin. Although the rates reported in these studies were cumulative rates of infant deaths, and not direct annual rates usually reported by health officials, they suggest a high rate of infant mortality.

Some contributing factors for such a high rate of infant mortality among Arab Americans include poverty, low levels of education, lack of knowledge of reproductive organs and functions, pregnancy at an early age, family stresses due to immigration, and smoking (Kulwicki, 1989b).

HEALTH BELIEFS

The most important determining factor in understanding Arab health care values is an understanding of Arab religious values. Inherent in these values is the belief that God is omnipotent and cause for all health and illness and that man has a limited sphere of influence when it comes to matters of illness and death. A person is healthy if she or he is in harmony with God (Kulwicki, 1987). Illness occurs when human beings have lost their relationship with God and allow supernatural forces such as evil to take over. Although germ theory is widely accepted by Arab Americans, especially in physical conditions, the fact that God has the ultimate power to cure and cause illness is pervasive among members of this culture. A disease may be a punishment from God. Preventive beliefs and rituals are exercised to promote harmony with God. Praying, the use of amulets or religious relics, herbs, and fumigation are all believed to ward off disease. Eating a balanced meal is also considered to prevent disease and promote health.

Folk health beliefs are expressed in illnesses such as infliction with the evil eye. The source of the evil eye is believed to be jealousy. Some Arab Americans believe that jealousy is often expressed by casting the evil eye. Victims of the evil eye are generally children or adults who possess good health, beauty, or good fortune. Women who possess the evil eye are considered to be envious of children or people enjoying good fortune. It is believed that when a woman with the evil eye stares at or admires beautiful children and does not mention the name of God or the prophet Muhammed when praising them, illness will befall them. One way of expelling the evil eye is the use of amulets such as Quranic verses sewn in the children's clothing or the ritual act of fumigation (Kulwicki, 1987).

The concept of the evil eye in the Arab world has persisted in the Middle East among both Muslims and non-Muslims after the conversion to Islam. The *Quran* does not mention the evil eye, but certain passages are believed to support the belief. Muslim theologians do not endorse this concept. The evil eye is believed to cause illness and death to its victims. A person possessing the evil eye could be one who is in full envy. Possible examples are a beggar, a barren woman, a loner, or someone with a physical disability. In the Muslim world, women are especially suspect because they start out with a physical and social disadvantage and are expected to show envious traits. Even something such as having a blue eye (a rarity in Arab countries) can evoke suspicion.

Arab Muslims believe that if a person loses faith in God then illness may befall that person, Madness (*Jinaan*) is an illness attributed to a loss of faith. The only cure for such illness is a person's reaffirmation of faith in God. This may require the advice and counseling of a religious intermediary who is an expert in exorcism. Muslims believe that knowledge of illnesses caused by possession is outside the realm of the American medical or mental health practitioner; therefore, they seek treatment from a religious or folk healer.

HEALTH PRACTICES

Few studies have explored Arab Americans in the U.S. health care setting. Meleis (1981) differentiated Arabs according to the social, political, and economic background of the country from which they emigrated. Meleis reported that Arabs differed in their approach to and expectations of the health care system based on the kinds of health care they experienced in their own countries. Arabs who came from oil-rich countries expected free medical care. Arabs from poorer countries expected to pay for services. Many Arab Americans who are used to paying for medical services and who come from a lower socioeconomic background may resort to home remedies until their medical condition is worsened. Thus, Arab Americans who have paid for services in their country of origin and who have limited financial resources in this country would use emergency rooms more frequently than the average North American population.

Arabs have made many historical contributions to science and medicine, and most Arabs are aware of this fact and take great pride in it. A healer who possesses knowledge is thought to possess power and authority. Doctors and other medical experts are judged as having power and authority radiating from their knowledge of science and medicine. An Arab without any education may demonstrate an exaggerated respect for the powers of the physician. But since the sequence of events of western medicine is not well understood, Arabs may revert to their traditional practices.

Arab Americans sometimes have difficulty questioning medical authorities and being actively involved in medical decision making. An Arab-American client may expect a physician to make medical decisions without the benefit of a health history or consultation with the client. In fact, if an Arab American is asked to participate in making the decision, he or she may lose trust in the medical person and stop all treatment.

Arab Americans value Western medicine highly and consider themselves privileged to be able to use such facilities. However, they consider highly technical invasive therapies superior to noninvasive treatments. Oral medication is not seen as effective as surgery. Any invasive therapy is considered superior to therapies aimed at preventing or promoting health. Arab Americans usually expect cure from medical treatments, regardless of the severity or chronicity of the condition. This expectation may cause problems when the treatment is aimed not at a cure but at symptom control, as is the case for diabetes, heart disease, or hypertension. Many times Arab Americans stop treatments once they have begun to feel better. When the condition or disease recurs, they may reject any further Western treatment and resort to folk remedies.

HEALTH STATUS OF ARAB AMERICANS

There are no available studies on disease prevalence among members of the Arab community living in the United States, and no data to describe the epidemiological patterns of disease occurrence among this population. In an effort to overcome this deficiency, a medical outreach team survey conducted in the summer of 1992 collected information from households in the Detroit metropolitan area (Arab Community Center for Economic and Social Services, 1992). Based on the data collected from 259 responding households, the five most common health problems comprised nearly two thirds of the total number of problems reported (71 percent): high blood pressure, arthritis, allergies, diabetes, and heart disease. Among the few children and adolescents for whom data were provided by adult members of the household, asthma was reported to be the most common problem, similar to its frequency of occurrence among the general population (Taylor & Newacheck, 1992).

Despite the fact that there is no solid epidemiological information on the health status of the Arab population living in the United States, several studies conducted in Michigan have provided a series of findings specific to the health status of Arab Americans. Data are available from a study on the knowledge, attitudes, and behaviors of Arab Americans related to HIV/AIDS (Kulwicki, 1990a), a cardiovascular and diabetes risk assessment among Arab Americans (Kulwicki, 1990b), and a study that assessed the health needs of Arab-American adolescents (Kulwicki, 1989a).

A study by Kulwicki (1990a) surveying the knowledge, attitudes, beliefs, and behaviors of Arab Americans identified a low level of self-assessed knowledge about AIDS and HIV transmission as compared to that of the general U.S. population. Among those surveyed, 46 percent had little or no knowledge of AIDS, 36 percent believed AIDS could be contacted from sitting on a toilet, and 47 women were identified as having absolutely no knowledge of HIV/AIDS. Of the 411 people surveyed, a large proportion were young males, and 12.3 percent of those surveyed had no formal education.

In another recent study, Kulwicki (1990b) randomly sampled a population of Arab-American adults (mean age = 40) who resided in Dearborn and assessed their cardiovascular and diabetes status. Findings showed that of the 237 surveyed for 15 cardiovascular risk factors, 15 percent had elevated blood pressures (greater than 140/90); 38 percent of these individuals smoked one or more packs of cigarettes per day; 26 percent were overweight; 23 percent had blood sugars greater than 120 mg; 70 percent did not engage in purposeful exercise; and 3 percent had experienced a cardiac event. Sixty-three percent of the sample had three or more of the risk factors assessed.

Another study by Kulwicki (1989a) of 362 Arab-American adolescents found that they were underutilizing the health care system, were using preventive services less than the general population, were experiencing concern for and conflict over growing up as minority Arab Americans, expressed a need for general medical services, participated in risky behaviors at rates similar to the general population, and desired greater access to health services for persons their own age. The underutilization reported for Arab teens follows a similar pattern reported among Arab women who were studied earlier.

Arab women generally marry between the ages of 15 and 19 (Macki, 1985). Some may have parenting skills, but others may be separated from female kin who might provide them with instruction on prenatal child care (Lazarus, 1990; Macki, 1985). A demonstration project of the Michigan Public Health Department found that 30 percent of the pregnant women received prenatal care after the first trimester (Gold, 1987). This may confirm the observation that poor women are "more tolerant of labor pain" (Lazarus, 1990), or it may indicate a lack of access to prenatal care. Unpublished data from 52 Arab women who called the Infant Health Promotion Coalition in 1990 indicate that most of them use hospital emergency rooms almost as much as they use private physicians, but very few are inclined to use clinics where only English is spoken (Arab Community Center for Economic and Social Services, 1990).

Kulwicki (1987) found that the Arabic population in the urban metropolitan Detroit area had a need for outreach programs that would promote health through education about healthier life-styles. This same study also found that Arab men preferred discussing their problems with other men or their brothers, and they preferred private physicians as caregivers. They used emergency room services as often as they used physician services, and they used public facilities much less frequently. The Arab community was found lacking in awareness of the community resources available to them, demonstrated limited knowledge about health issues that should have been taught through the school systems, and, overall, showed a need for health care services that are bilingual as well as culturally relevant.

BARRIERS TO HEALTH CARE ACCESS BY ARAB AMERICANS

The inability of Arab Americans to access the health care system is dependent on a number of factors, owing to the barriers created by language, transportation, education, and culture. The inability of Arab Americans in the metropolitan area of Detroit to speak English and poor comprehension skills in understanding and reading English, for example, serve as primary barriers to their accessing the existing health care system.

Recent data gathered by Kulwicki through an assessment of teen health (1989a) and a study of cardiovascular-diabetes risk factors (1990b) found low levels of English language skills. The persons with whom young people communicate at home are an important aspect of the process of internalizing the norms and values (Schlegel & Barry, 1991) they will take with them in later years. Among the norms and values they may learn and share with family members are those concerning the health care system.

Lack of transportation is a significant barrier inhibiting members of the Arab community from accessing the health care system. Few new Arab immigrant families have automobiles, and for those that do, the single car the family may own is used to transport the wage earner to and from work. This means that the family members remaining at home have no available means of transportation except for weekends and evenings.

The level of education of new immigrants ranks lower than that of the general U.S. population. Based on a stratified sample ($N = 237$), more than one half of the respondents who were interviewed for the study of the cardiovascular-diabetes risk factors conducted by Kulwicki (1990b) reported that they had not attended school or had not completed high school. Level of education is important in considering the ability to read information concerning the scheduling of health services and medical instructions for prescribed and over-the-counter medications.

Members of first-generation Arab-American communities for the most part are an unskilled workforce, according to field research conducted among this population (Abraham, & Aswad, 1983; Aswad, 1974; Kulwicki, 1987, 1989a, 1990b). One of the major obstacles to employment already identified is low level of education, to which can be added little training in marketable job skills. Most of the Arab community is male, and most are young, having found jobs in the automobile industry and its subsidiaries in Michigan. When the economy experiences a downswing, which is reflected in the automobile industry, many of those who find themselves unemployed are workers of Arab descent. Estimates of Arab-American unemployment from the 1970s and 1980s for example, range from the teens to highs of more than 30 percent, rates that are higher than those for other minority populations.

Cultural values play an important role in the health-care-seeking behaviors of the Arab population. The Arab family provides cohesiveness to the structuring of the Arab community, and interpersonal skills are crucial in facilitating communication within the community. At the same time, aspects of the Arab culture may serve as barriers to accessing the health care system. One of the primary issues is modesty regarding the human body, especially as it expressed, experienced, and viewed by, for, and among females.

Notions of modesty are cultural values that are learned and shared among members of the Arab community as norms of expected acceptable behavior. The rules for modesty are codified in religious texts, most notably the *Quran*, and concern expectations for covering the extremities (arms, legs, face) of the female body when in the presence of men who are not kin (Fernea, 1977, 1985; Fernea & Fernea, 1979; Kulwicki, 1987; Lipson & Meleis, 1983). This sense of modesty is held in high regard, and it occurs among women who may not practice veiling or covering the head, as it is commonly practiced among traditional Muslim women. Therefore, the issue of modesty is especially significant when considering the number of physicians who are male and to whom a family may be reluctant to send a kinswoman.

Cultural attitudes toward time and punctuality among the Arab population can lead to missed appointments or, more seriously, failures to make any kind of health arrangements, such as regular preventive care. Bilingual, culturally relevant health care programs that are currently available have been shown to be lacking in the full range of both preventive and therapeutic services needed.

CONCLUSION

The information presented in this chapter is based on data collected primarily about Arab Americans residing in the metropolitan Detroit area, the largest and most cohesive Arab community in United States. The chapter is intended to provide health care professionals with a better understanding to Arab-American clients and their backgrounds. An understanding of Arab-American customs, beliefs, and practices can assist the health care professional in providing culturally competent care and avoiding conflict with clients of Arab heritage.

Health care providers need to be sensitive and attentive to cultural differences between Arab Americans and the general Anglo-American population when providing care to Arab clients. They should realize that individual beliefs and practices exist within this cultural context. Knowledge of the values of any group or individual assists a health care provider in fitting a care plan to meet the individual client's expectations. Some folk treatments or cultural beliefs may be incorporated into health care procedures to encourage client acceptance and cooperation.

GLOSSARY

Abuka'ab   Mumps.
'adaa   Infectious.
aHmar   Red.
Aidin   Both hands.
'Ain   Eye.
Allah   God.
'Aql   Brain.
Al   The definite article *the.*
'Amaa   Blind.
Amraad zahriya   Venereal disease.
Anfaas   Spirits.
Arjul   Legs.
Asaab   Nerves.
Azmaa   Asthma.
Bard   Cold.
BaTn   Abdomen.
Baul   Urine.
Bawasiir   Hemorrhoids.
Da'f   Weakness.
Daght   Pressure.
Damn   Blood.
Dars   Tooth.
Faza'a   Fear.
Haml   Pregnancy.
Hammaam   Bath.
Humma   Fever.
Hasad   Envy, jealousy.
Hasiba   Measles.
Hassasiya   Allergy.
IHmiraar   Redness.
Iltihaab   Inflammation.
Iltihaab al-ma'ada   Gastritis.
Iltihaab al-masariin   Enteritis.
Iltihaab al-ri'a   Pneumonia.

Iltihaab fi-dmaagh   Meningitis.
Jaraatiim   Germs.
Jinaan, majnuun   Madness, being mad.
Jinn   Demon.
JiraaHa   Operation.
Jism   Body.
Judari   Smallpox.
Khalal   Disorder.
Kalaawi   Kidneys.
Kasr   To break, fracture.
Kazaaz   Tetanus.
Khurafaat   Superstititions.
Kiis maay   Cyst.
Kitaab   Book.
Kolera   Cholera.
Liifa   Fibrosis.
Ma'ada   Stomach.
Mal aarya   Malaria.
Man'   Prevent.
MaraD ol-kibd   Hepatitis.
Marad pl.amraD   Illness, Illnesses.
Mashaakil   Difficulties.
MuTahhar   Pure.
Mush   Not.
Nafsiya   Psychological.
Naqs   Deficiency.
Narf   Nerve.
Naas   People.
Naziif   Bleeding.
Nazilf daakhly   Internal bleeding.
Nazla siD'riya   Bronchitis.
QaHHa   Cough.
Qalb   Heart.
QarHa   Stomach ulcer.

REFERENCES

Abraham, S., & Abraham, N. (Eds.). (1983). *Arabs in the New World.* Detroit: Wayne State University Press.

Abraham, S., Abraham, N., & Aswad, B. (1983). The southend: An Arab Muslim working-class community. In S. Abraham & N. Abraham (Eds.), *Arabs in the New World.* Detroit: Wayne State University Press.

Arab Community Center for Economic and Social Services. (1990). *961-baby.* Unpublished manuscript.

Arab Community Center for Economic and Social Services. (1992). *Summer outreach activities: Summary report* (Tech. Rep.). Dearborn: Michigan Department of Public Health.

Aswad, B. (1988). Strengths of the Arab family for mental health considerations and therapy. In I. Ahmed and N. Gray (Eds.), *The Arab American family: A resource guide for human service providers.* Ypsilanti: Eastern Michigan University, Department of Social Services.

Aswad, B. (1974). *Arabic speaking communities in American cities.* New York: Center for Migration Studies.

Beck, L., & Keddie, N. (Eds.). (1980). *Women in the Muslim world.* London: Harvard University Press.

Bowker, J. P. (1979). *Health and social service needs assessment survey.* Unpublished manuscript.

Fernea, E. W. (1977). *Muslim women speak.* Austin: University of Texas Press.

Fernea, E. W. (1985). *Women and the family in the Middle East: New Voices of change.* Austin: University of Texas Press.

Fernea, E. W., & Fernea, R. A. (1979). A look behind the veil. *Human Nature, 2*(1), 68–77.

Gold, S. (1987). *Wayne County Health Department infant mortality outreach demonstration project: Dearborn Arab community survey* Preliminary report. Detroit: Special Projects Section, Wayne County Health Department.

Kulwicki, A. (1990a). *Arab AIDS knowledge, attitudes, beliefs and behaviors (KABB)* (Executive report). Lansing: Special Office on AIDS Prevention, Michigan Department of Public Health.

Kulwicki, A. (1990b). *Executive summary: SAHHA project cardiovascular diseases and diabetes survey* (Technical report). Lansing: Office of Minority Health, Michigan Department of Public Health.

Kulwicki, A. (1987). *An ethnographic study of illness perception and practices of Yemeni-Americans.* Unpublished doctoral dissertation, Indiana University, Indianapolis.

Kulwicki, A. (1989a). *Executive summary: Arab teen health survey* (Report). Lansing: Bureau of Community Services, Michigan Departemnt of Public Health.

Kulwicki, A. (1989b). Infant mortality among Arab Americans in Michigan is cause for concern. *Michigan Nurse, 62*(9), 12–13.

Lazarus, E. S. (1990). Falling through the cracks: Contradictions and barriers to care in a prenatal clinic. *Medical Anthropology, 139,* 854–861.

Lipson, J. G., & Meleis, A. I. (1983). Issues in health care of Middle Eastern patients. *Western Journal of Medicine, 139,* 854–861.

Macki, N. (1985). *The Arab American parenting study.* Unpublished manuscript.

Meleis, A. (1981). The Arab American in the health care system. *American Journal of Nursing, 81,* 1180–1183.

Mesa, V. (1987). *Arab American maternal risk survey, southeast Dearborn community* (Technical report). Detroit: Infant Mortality Outreach Demonstration Project, Wayne County Health Department.

Nasr, S. (1964). *Ideals and realities of Islam.* London: George, Allen, & Unwin.

Paine, P. (1986). *A study of the Middle Eastern community in the Detroit metropolitan area.* Detroit: Research Department, United Community Services.

Roberts, D. (1982). *Islam.* New York: Harper & Row.

Schlegel, A., & Barry, H. (1991). *Adolescence: An anthropological inquiry.* New York: The Free Press.

Taylor, W. R., & Newacheck, P. W. (1992). Impact of childhood asthma on health. *Pediatrics, 90,* 657–662.

U.S. Bureau of the Census. (1983, April). *1980 census of population, ancestry of the population by state: 1980* (Supplementary report No. PC 80-S1-10). Washington, DC: U.S. Government Printing Office.

White, G. (1982, January 5). Detroit's Arab-American community: Thriving and active, *Christian Science Monitor.*

SUGGESTED READINGS

Abraham, S., & Abraham, N. (Eds.). (1983). *Arabs in the New World.* Detroit: Wayne State University Center for Urban Study.

Aswad, B. (1974). *Arabic speaking communities in American cities.* New York: Center for Migration Studies.

Bowker, J. (1979). *Health and social services needs assessment survey.* Unpublished manuscript.

Kulwicki, A. (1987). *An ethnographic study of illness perceptions and practices of Yemeni Arab-Americans.* Unpublished dissertation. Indiana University, Indianapolis.

Kulwicki, A. (1988). Hot iron treatment among Yemeni Arab Americans. *The Journal of Nursing Science and Practice, 1*(3), 20–21.

Meleis, A. (1981, June). The Arab American in the health care system. *American Journal of Nursing,* 1180–1183.

Meleis, A., & Sorrel, L. (1981). Arab American women and their birth experience. *Maternal Child Nursing, 6,* 171–176.

Michigan Department of Public Health. (1988). *Minority health in Michigan: Closing the gap.* Lansing: Michigan Department of Public Health.

Paine, P. (1985). *A study of the Middle East community in the Detroit metropolitan area.* Detroit: United Community Services.

Penchansky, R. (1972). *Study of southeast Dearborn.* Unpublished manuscript.

Quran. Egypt: Dar Al-kitab Al-Masir.

► 6

Asian Americans

ELIZABETH L. CHUNG

Numerous factors have caused the migration of Asians to the United States, including political unrest, economic opportunity, family reunification, higher standards of living, and higher education. Asian Americans come from a broad geographic region with multiple ethnic identities. The continent of Asia stretches from the southwest, which includes India and Pakistan, as far east as China and Japan, encompassing countries such as Thailand, Cambodia, Laos, and Vietnam. Also included are the Philippines, Singapore, Malaysia, and Indonesia, located in the southern part of the continent.

This chapter focuses primarily on Southeast Asian Americans. Included in this category are Vietnamese, ethnic Chinese, Laotians, Hmong, and Cambodians. Although they are geographically adjoined and they have some similarities in tradition and custom, these countries are different from each other in terms of their ways of life, languages, and belief systems. Therefore, it is important to remember that not all Southeast Asians are alike. They are an extremely heterogeneous population. The chapter provides a broad overview of the cultural backgrounds of these ethnic groups in order to illustrate the similarities and differences among them. Aspects of their medical beliefs and practices are identified, with an emphasis on maternal and child health, for health care professionals to consider. Finally, recommendations are made as to how western practitioners can best cooperate with Asian Americans in promoting their well-being within the context of both eastern and western cultures.

OVERVIEW

The Southeast Asians who came to the United States are mostly represented by five ethnic groups: Vietnamese, ethnic Chinese, Cambodians (Khmer), Laotians, and Hmong. All except the Hmong are lowland delta people who have a long tradition of state-level political organization. The Hmong are primarily highland swidden people and accustomed to village-level politics (Kingston, 1978).

Southeast Asians became Americans mostly because of their refugee status. Refugees are not to be viewed as immigrants. Immigrants leave their countries by conscious choice; they spend years in planning to be prepared both financially and psychologically to emigrate. In contrast, refugees have no choice but to leave their homeland for survival. They become displaced and suffer loss, guilt, deprivation, and nightmares of the turmoil of their exodus. Between 1975 and the late 1980s, more than 1.5 million Southeast Asians fled their homelands to escape war, revolution, genocide, political turmoil, and famine. According to the U.S. Committee for Refugees (1988), Vietnamese (including ethnic Chinese) account for 60 percent of this population, Laotian (including Hmong) for 20 percent, and Cambodians for 20 percent. Most of these refugees were men (56 percent), and 44 percent were women. Age distribution seemed skewed to the younger segment, with the median age being 23.9 years. An estimated two hundred thousand children were born in the United States to the refugee population (Rhumbaut & Weeks, 1986).

Since their arrival, Southeast Asians have resettled throughout the United States, with the greatest concentration (about 40 percent) in California. There also has been a trend toward a second migration from state to state for better jobs, family reunification, familiar climate, and well-established Southeast Asian communities. California, New York, Washington, and Minnesota are among the states with large Southeast Asian populations (S. Nguyen, 1982). According to the Asian and Pacific Islander Center for Census Information and Services (1992), there was a 108 percent growth in Asian and Pacific Islander population between 1980 and 1990. The increase in some other refugee populations is even more striking: Hmong—1,371.0 percent; Cambodian—600 percent; Laotian—312 percent; Vietnamese—150 percent; and Chinese—102 percent. According to the Center, the growth is not by natural increases, but as the result of constant immigration and refugee exodus (Shinagawa, 1992).

Major Cultural Groups

Vietnamese

Vietnam is about one and one-half times the size of Minnesota, with a population of about 53 million in 1985. The majority of its population is Vietnamese, and the rest are urban ethnic Chinese, rural montagnard dwellers, and Cambodians who live in the delta of the Mekong River. Vietnamese comprise the majority of the Southeast Asians who migrated to the United States. The Vietnamese were dominated by the Chinese for over one thousand years, resulting in significant Chinese influence on their culture. After the Chinese domination, Vietnam passed through an era of national dynasties before it was united by the French. French was established as the second language, and there was great French influence on education, architecture, and medicine (Stringfellow, Nguyen, & Linda, 1981). During World War II France withdrew, and Vietnam was occupied by Japan until Ho Chi Min established the Democratic Republic and a million people were allowed to go south. Even though the country was divided into North and South Vietnam, the Vietnamese culture maintained its homogeneity throughout the society. In 1954, with the withdrawal of the French, some Vietnamese began to flee from Vietnam as refugees. That was also the time when the United States became involved in helping to settle refugees.

The first and formal wave of refugees lasted from April 1975 to December 1977, following the fall of Saigon. These refugees were hastily evacuated by helicopter or by sealift with the help of the U.S. government. Among them were many refugees who were affiliated with either the Americans or the South Vietnamese forces. The second wave occurred between 1978 and 1980, when political repression intensified. These refugees' attempts to flee were mostly in small boats. Their mass exodus was filled with horrors including brutal attack by pirates, rape, torture, and even cannibalism because of lack of food. It is important to realize that those who came during the 1970s were mostly professionals from the elite class who had some command of English and who had western or urban exposure. Those who came in the early 1980s were the working class and peasants who were mostly from rural areas and had virtually no experience with Western culture. Many of these immigrants were believed to be illiterate.

Ethnic Chinese

The history of Chinese migration extends over two thousand years. Many Chinese came by sea, primarily from three provinces of southeast China, Kwantung, Fukien, and Kwangsi. The Chinese in Southeast Asia comprised five sixths of the total overseas Chinese population. They were successful traders, money lenders, and rice producers. Chinese ownership of junks (big fishing boats) and sampans (smaller vessels) meant control of ports for goods, particularly rice. The Chinese gained a competitive edge over French traders because of their familiarity with local culture and an extensive network of contacts and associations.

The long history of contact between Vietnam and China would suggest positive relations between them, but this was not the case. Although they contributed materials and spiritual benefits that were highly valued by the Vietnamese, the Chinese were not welcome. Use of phrases such as the "Chinese cyst," the "Chinese stranglehold," or the "Jew of Asia" illustrated that they were never completely accepted in Southeast Asia. Their economic domination had been a source of resentment and a justification for attempts to integrate the Chinese by both the French and Vietnamese governments. By 1978, the ethnic Chinese began to flee. By 1980, four hundred thousand ethnic Chinese had fled, only half making it into China. Many others were resettled in the United State and other countries. It is important to note that while there were already Chinese in the United States, the Chinese from Southeast Asia brought with them experiences far different from those who emigrated from Hong Kong, Tai Wan, China, and the Pacific Islands.

Laotians

Laos is surrounded by Thailand, Burma, China, Vietnam, and Kampuchea (formerly Cambodia). Laotians first migrated from China and created the Kingdom of Lan Xang, the Land of a Million Elephants, in 1353. Lang Xang was colonized by the French until 1953, and it then enjoyed twenty years of independence until a civil war erupted, leading to the formation of the Lao People's Democratic Republic (Cerquone, 1986). Prior to the disruption caused by the wars in Southeast Asia, approximately half of its four million citizens lived in the lowlands. Laos is a landlocked country, a little smaller than Oregon. Its primary economic activity is wet rice agriculture. The majority of its people live in small rural villages. In the village, daily life depends on the family and is based in the WAT, which is the Buddhist temple that also serves as the village school. The Lao people view their families and the community as a stable and integrated unit.

There are basically three different ethnic groups among the Laotian refugees. The largest population are the lowland Lao (Lao-Loum), who are usually farmers from along the Mekong River. They speak Laos (related to Thai). The second group is the midland Lao (Lao Theung). The rest are highland Lao known as Hmong. The lowland Lao are known as gentle and easygoing people. The most often heard phrase in their language is "baw bpen nhyung" ("never mind; it doesn't matter"). Two values are very important to Laotian people. The first is *piap*, which means pride, self-esteem, honor, and disgrace. One's *piap* is a reflection of the family background. The second is *kengchay*, which makes up the personality of the Lao. *Kengchay* helps the Laotian people to be nonassertive and nonaggressive.

At the fall of the Laos, shadowed by the turmoil in Vietnam and Cambodia, many Laotians fled their country, crossed the Mekong River, and entered Thailand. As their numbers increased, the level of enthusiasm of the Thai government decreased. They were often forced into "humane deterrence camps," where they lived in substandard conditions for years. In 1986, the Thai government decided to open its humane deterrence camps and allow the refugees to be resettled in the west (Cerquone, 1986).

Hmong

The Hmong's origin can be traced to Siberia before they migrated to northern China. Early missionaries reported that European traits such as blonde hair and blue eyes found among the Hmong suggested a non-Asian origin (Quincy, 1988). There are more than six million Hmong, and the majority of them live in China. The rest are found in the mountain ranges of Southeast Asia. They had been at war with the Chinese because of their constant refusal to embrace Chinese culture. They took pride in their own rich culture and their shamanistic religion, both of which they had preserved for thousand of years.

The Hmong migrated south beyond the reach of the Chinese and enjoyed a relatively peaceful and independent state until the eighteenth century, when the emperors of the Manchu dynasty waged a war of extermination against them (Quincy, 1988). After that, persistent persecution has forced the Hmong to become perpetual migrants. From the middle of the nineteenth century onward, thousands of them found new homes in Southeast Asia (Quincy, 1988).

The Hmong in Southeast Asia preferred to settle in high-altitude, mountainous areas where there was less competition for land and fewer chances to be infected with the tropical diseases that often devastated the lowland dwellers. There, in the isolated mountain regions, they settled down and enjoyed generations of relative peace and prosperity in which their culture flourished. They have a high degree of ethnic identity and social solidarity.

The political unrest in Southeast Asia forced the Hmong to fend for themselves. It was the Laotian Hmong who fought America's "secret war" in Laos, and they sacrificed almost one third of their population to prevent the Vietnamese Communists from turning Laos into a puppet state. They paid a high price for their involvement with the U.S. government. By the end of the civil war in 1975, they had suffered casualty rates that were pro-portionately ten times higher than those of the Americans (office of Refugee Resettlement, 1985). In recent years, thousands of them have abandoned their homeland for the west because of the continued political unrest in Southeast Asia.

Cambodians

No one knows for sure the origin of Cambodia. Prehistoric evidence suggests that there were inhabitants there as early as 4200 B.C. (Chandler, 1983). There has been much debate about whether these people migrated from China, India, or the Southeast Asian islands. With land of about seventy thousand square miles, Cambodia is about the size of Minnesota. The Cambodian language is believed to have existed at the beginning of the Christian era. What is so striking to researchers is that Cambodia went through a period of several thousand years of changelessness. As a Cambodian proverb states, "Don't choose a straight path, and don't reject a winding one. Choose the path your ancestors have trod." This conservatism, perhaps, is the most notable characteristic of this subsistence-oriented society. The notion of changelessness came to an end when Cambodia was "Indianized" around the Christian era. Indianization lasted for about one thousand years. Buddhism, ancestor worship, folk religion, and village customs were well established in the lives of the Cambodians, but they gradually recognized Hinduism, the court, and Sanskrit. During this period, there was adoption, adaptation, exchange, and revision, as well as rejection by both societies. Since Indianization, Cambodia has gone through many periods of transformation, including the formation of the Angkorean era (eighth–ninth centuries A.D.) and the invasion of Cham in 1177 (Chandler, 1983).

Cambodia went through its darkest era during the seventeenth and eighteenth centuries. After a brief period of independence under King Duang (1848–1860), Cambodia became a French colony. Then, in 1922, during the period of Jayavarman VII, there was a conversion of Shaivistic Hinduism to Theravada Buddhism. Cambodia remained colonized until it gained its independence from France in 1953. Unlike the other countries of mainland Southeast Asia, Cambodia has no mountain ranges running north to south as protective barriers. Its vulnerability to attack is a recurrent feature of its history as well as its cultural transformation. During the 1970s, particularly after 1975, the entire Cambodian historical perspective was attacked vociferously by the regime of the Democratic Kampuchea.

The Cambodians fled their homeland in three irregular waves between 1975 and 1985. The first phase was in 1975, when the United States-backed Lon Nol regime was overthrown by the Khmer Rouge forces of Pol Pot.

These refugees were mostly high-ranking government officials, professionals, and the educated, along with their families. The second phase was after
the Vietnamese invasion of Cambodia in 1978. This heterogeneous group of
refugees included Khmer Rouge political and military personnel fleeing
from the Vietnamese occupation forces; starving peasants; and urban, educated people. The third phase was in 1979, when conditions in Cambodia
had reached a crisis because of famine, internal instability, and political
turmoil. During the three waves, more than one hundred fifty thousand
refugees entered the holding center in Thailand awaiting to be resettled.
The Cambodians suffered the worst ordeal of all refugees even years before
their exodus. Almost all of their educated were killed. Those who were able
to come to the United States were mostly illiterate even in their own language, making it more difficult to adjust to their new life.

Despite their differing political statuses, the Laotians, Hmong, and
Cambodians shared very similar exodus journeys, facing minefields,
ambushes, starvation, exhaustion, disease, and even death. Their ordeal
was no less traumatic and tragic than that of the Vietnamese and Chinese
by boat. However, unlike the Vietnamese, Laotians, and Hmong, the Cambodians could not claim political asylum for admission to the United
States, because few had ties to the U.S. presence. Nonetheless, the United
States agreed to resettle thirty thousand Cambodian refugees in 1979 (U. S.
Committee for Refugees, 1982). The resettlement efforts are still in
progress.

The Family

Although many members of Asian ethnic communities may have gone
through stages of cultural change depending upon their own experiences
prior to entering the United States, the family is regarded as an important
aspect of every ethnic identity. Based upon Chinese philosophy, there are
three fundamental institutions shared among these Asian Americans: family, village, and state. Of these, family is the most basic. It is believed that a
strong and prosperous village must depend on healthy families, and a uni-
fied state could not survive without strong villages. A child grows up
learning to respect the line of authority within certain relationships: son to
father, wife to husband, and subject to emperor. The family is the command post of each household. Depending on the extension of the family
tree, the dynamics of the family operate in terms of the rank and position
each person has within the family structure. It is not uncommon to see a
male pay respect to an uncle who might be much younger than himself.
Nonetheless, the father is the autocratic head of the family. He is responsible for all domestic affairs and the behavior of family members. This

responsibility exerts a great deal of pressure upon him. In order to maintain good face for the family, he makes sure his family is protected, well fed, and strictly disciplined. On the other hand, the mother is responsible for the family's finances. She also takes control over relationships with relatives and connections with in-laws.

In many of these communities, the birth of a son is a significant event because it assures the extension of the family and the continuation of the family name. Often the firstborn son is viewed as the inheritor and caretaker of the family, particularly when both parents become older (Sung, 1972). All valuable possessions of the family—jewelry, arts and crafts, special skills, and businesses—are passed on from one generation to the next through the male line (Mann & Waldron, 1977). If there is no son, families might adopt a nephew or other young male of the husband's bloodline. The Hmong believe that birth signifies the reincarnation of a soul into a new body (Quincy, 1988). Marriage signifies adulthood and the responsibilities one must assume thereafter. In death the individual's soul will leave this world in order to join the world of his ancestors and to wait for the time to be reborn.

A step beyond the immediate family, the extended family is the cornerstone of the social structure in many Asian communities. It is still common to see six to eight members residing within family. It is not unusual to see four generations living together. Elderly parents, uncles, and aunts hold honored positions within the family. They are the main support system through which advice and counsel can be found. Asian people are not accustomed to the idea of professional counseling, because of their need to save face for the sake of the family's name. Traditionally, filial piety has assured that the aging parents would be cared for by their children in their own home. An old Chinese proverb asserts, "To store up the wheat is to protect themselves from famine; to raise a son is to protect themselves from old age." Such an expectation has also dictated patrilocal residence for all sons with the exception of Cambodians, who do not have a preference for matrilinear or patrilinear obligation. Today, this poses a dilemma for modern-day working couples who need to place their aging parents in a nursing home when the extended family is no longer available. Some younger-generation immigrants find this dilemma difficult as they assimilate the values of independence and freedom from their extended family. Couples may move away from their parents and other kin to the suburbs and yet maintain a close relationship by frequent visits. For the Chinese, living close to Chinatown provides a sense of security as well as a resistance to acculturation of the aging parents. On both the east and west coasts, the difficult situation is somewhat lessened because of the availability of Asian senior citizen housing.

Asian families value education highly, even among those who might not have had the opportunity for education in their home countries. Asians view education as a means to higher economic, political, and social status. Children's higher education has priority over a nice house, vacation, or dining out for pleasure. Children usually begin their moral and cultural education at a very young age. As soon as they are able, whether boys or girls, they join in the work of the house and the field (Char, 1975). They are taught early about the importance of collective responsibility, courteous behavior, and the need for cooperation, self-control, and self-sacrifice in order to gain face, or respect, and preserve the family's name (Queen, Habenstein, & Adams, 1961).

Asian children in the United States are usually bilingual and become acculturated at a more rapid pace than their parents. The father may learn some English at work, but the mother remains at home to care for the young. The language barriers may be more severe within some Laotian or Hmong families in which the parents are illiterate in their own language. Whenever possible, Asian children may attend language school either after the daily English school or on weekends. Asian families insist that the Asian heritage, values, and language be taught to the next generation. They usually have more success with the children when they are younger. As children grow older, their interest diminishes, and the parents' pressure subsides. Overall, raising a family in the new cultural environment prevents many difficulties and, at times, fosters feelings of inadequacy among first-generation parents who must confront language and cultural barriers between themselves and their children. When adult immigrants or refugees are asked what concerns them most about living in the United States, one of the most common responses is how to raise their children so that they are obedient, responsible, and successful in school and work and refrain from drugs, violence, and premarital sex.

Clan and Kinship

The clan is another form of family structure that is highly developed in Southeast Asia. A clan is a recognized grouping of families with the same last name and line of ancestors. They include direct descendants or those related by marriage. Within the Hmong society, the estimated number of clans varies from eighteen to twenty five. Each clan is distinguished by its last name—Yang, Vang, Xiong, Hang, Moua, and so forth. Clans function as a large group of extended family. Among them, a few elderly persons are chosen to head the family. They influence the behavior, decisions, rules, and duties of family members. As clans increase in size in the United States, it is common to see members form an association patterned after those of their native land. During the early days of Chinese immigration, benevolent associations were formed as focal points for the communities. These associations might be made up of families who have the same last name, who are from the same village, or who speak the same dialect. Some of these associations are formally chartered, recognized, and support their own language schools, entertainment, and newspapers.

The highland Laotians, or Hmong, form the closest family structure. Hmong clans recruit new members principally through marriages. Hmong are not allowed to marry someone with the same last name in the same clan organization. However, if a woman is widowed, she may marry a brother of her late husband (Quincy, 1988). Hmong subsistence productive properties are held in common under the control of the leaders. This practice is found among new settlers in the United States as they pool their resources to purchase an item such as a car for the whole clan.

These Asian community social structures exert a great deal of power and influence upon their members. They provide cohesiveness to maintain the economic base of life and to provide the social organization needed to maintain their roots. For those who work with these communities in the assimilation process, it is important to keep in mind that efforts must be made to reach out to the clan leader(s) before approaching individual Asian Americans.

Marriage and Family

Arranged marriage was common two to three decades ago, although this practice is no longer popular today. However, some Asian-American mothers might return to their own country and consult with matchmakers to find girls for their grown-up sons. Within the Hmong society, arranged marriage is still practiced so that the man can marry outside his clan. A generation ago, the age for marriage was seventeen to twenty one for the male and fourteen to seventeen for the female. Once married, with the exception of the Laotians, the newlywed couple was usually expected to reside with the groom's family. The bride was expected to perform household chores without complaint. The groom was considered ready and began to play his role as "head of household." In most Asian communities, the woman does not change her name when she marries but is formally addressed with her husband's surname. Laotian women usually take their husbands' family names. Both Chinese and Vietnamese offspring carry the paternal family name, but other Southeast Asians carry the maternal last name. In the United States, naming practices can be confusing because some individuals may use the same or different names as their official names on various documents.

Role of Women

In most Asian societies there is a distinct role delineation between genders. Mothers and daughters are secondary within the family structure of most Asian families. However, Laotians tend to view daughters and sons as being equal. As a wife, the woman gains formal recognition from parents-in-law with the birth of the first son. As a daughter, she was taught early on in her life the importance of obedience to her future family and her obligation and responsibilities as a daughter-in-law (Kingston, 1977). Traditionally, most Asian women go through the following phases once they marry: (1) the adjustment of being accepted as a daughter-in-law, (2) assumption of household responsibilities, (3) official status as part of the family after the birth of a child, and (4) existence as a respected mother and mother-in-law. Throughout they maintain a role subordinate to that of the husband. Today, the roles of these women are changing. Out of economic necessity, many Asian women have joined the workforce. Sometimes they become the breadwinners of the household either because they are widowed or because their husbands remain in the homeland. Depending on the family dynamic, the new roles may cause marital problems. Nevertheless, such role reversal may equalize the relationships between these Asian women and their families.

Religion

Buddhism, Taoism, and Confucianism are the three main schools of philosophy that exerted a significant impact on the lives of all of the Southeast Asians discussed here except the Hmong. In the seventeenth century, Roman Catholicism also reached Vietnam, resulting in an Asian Catholic population second only to that of the Philippines. Lowland Lao and Cambodian religious belief derived from Theravada Buddhism, which originated in India. This religion plays a key role in all aspects of life, and spiritual fulfillment takes precedence over material comfort. The main principle of Buddhism focuses on gaining merit. Each person can count on his or her own merit as insurance for a better life in the next incarnation. The Hmong practice shamanism. Laotians strongly believe in animism as well as Buddhism. In the last year of the Laotian war, a Hmong revitalization movement called *Cha Fa*, meaning "Lord of the Sky," was formed and continued to be practiced in the refugee camps (Tapp, 1989). But most political and military leaders were always careful to observe Buddhism as the state religion and looked at religion as an integral part of their lives, not as a set of beliefs and practices separate from everyday life. The involvement of Christian churches in bringing Southeast Asian refugees to the United

States has resulted in a significant number of conversions to Christianity among refugees. Rather than forcing the Asians to assimilate, Christian affiliation has helped them to maintain their cultural and social distinctiveness because the assemblies usually use the native Asian language and church members are often under the direction of their own Asian ministers and deacons.

Ancestor Worship

Ancestor worship is commonly practiced by Asians. It is believed that there is a linkage between the remotest ancestor and the most recently born. At the Lunar New Year celebration for the Chinese or Tet for the Vietnamese, families pay special tribute to elder members both living and dead. Many of the activities remind the family of the cycle of life and fertility. As an Asian proverb says, "When you eat the fruits, remember who planted the tree." Asians also believe that the spirit of the ancestor always hovers about to look after the welfare of the family. A family enjoying good health is expected to make special offerings or perform special rituals to their ancestors. Family members are also expected to please various important spirits such as the god of the door or the god of the four seasons. In one particular Chinese festival (Ching Ming) or at a funeral, families burn paper images of clothing, houses, servants, tobacco, animals, paper money, and other articles the ancestors might need in the spirit world. The extent of these offerings indicates the wealth of the deceased. The family tries to provide the best for the deceased. There is usually a banquet at the end of the worship service at which family or clan affairs are discussed. In most instances, a clan or association acquires a collective plot of gravesites for all of the families. The location of the gravesites is carefully chosen in terms of geomancy (Tapp, 1989).

Hmong religious belief gives a clear definition of the relationship between the living and the ancestors. Hmong religion cannot be separated from the Hmong kinship network and the commonality of the Hmong ancestral sites. Two dominant features have an impact on the Hmong way of life: the relationship between ancestors and their descendants and the relationship between religion and social structure (Lee, 1986). Hmong religious ceremonies reveal renewed social groupings, strengthened lineage solidarity, and inspiration for new members to fulfill their obligation to the living, the dead, and the unborn (Quincy, 1988). Hmong also give thanks for their own existence while they care for their offspring, to whom they will one day become ancestors (Char, 1981).

Health Practices

In general, Asian health practices originated from various belief systems, collectively making up the Eastern system, which is different from that of Western origin. While the Western system looks at disease as a function of cause and effect, the Eastern system looks at the entire person and his or her relationship with the inner and outer world. The Eastern system focuses on "why" and "who"; it tries to explain why illness happened. In the West, the focus is on "how," the solution to the illness. The best way to understand the Eastern system is to study its etiological concepts of health and illness.

There are multiple etiological concepts among Asians, and compounding the situation is that what constitutes a "cure" among Asians may be as varied as the etiological beliefs. Furthermore, the definition of illness (i.e., suffering), may vary between Eastern and Western perspectives. Thus, *sickness* and *wellness* are relative terms between the two hemispheres. A physical manifestation may be a sign of fate to some Asians and not necessarily an illness. Moreover, there are even diversities in perceptions of health and illness among various Asian ethnic subgroups.

Traditional concepts of health and illness among the Chinese, Vietnamese, and Cambodians are similar, partly because their world view is rooted in Buddhist philosophy and partly because their culture originated in China. Chinese healers use terms that are strange to Western ears. Certain illnesses are generated by "dampness," "heat," "wind," or "fire." Healers make diagnoses by interrogating, observing color and the tongue, listening to the sounds of the body, and taking a pulse rate (Kaptchuck, 1983). Physical examinations and extensive laboratory tests are not well accepted by Asians (Tung, 1980).

Chinese medicine evolved from the philosophy of *Yin* and *Yang*, which keep the universe in balance. Every aspect of the universe contains Yin and Yang. Yin represents femininity, negative force, emptiness, body, soul, earth, moon, night, water, cold, darkness, contraction, and downward movement. Yang, on the other hand, represents day, fire, heat, daylight, expansion, and upward movement. The dialectic of Yin and Yang is also expressed in terms of body parts. For example, the viscera are Yin while the bowel system is Yang. The Chinese medical system views Yin and Yang as two opposite forces in constant cyclical motion for the sake of balance. As Kaptchuck (1983) noted, Yin and Yang created each other, control each other, and transform each other in the course of this balancing act. Another schematic understanding of the Yin/Yang theory is the traditional Chinese Taoist symbol. The two half circles of Yin and Yang justify the whole. The diameter of the two signifies its dialectical logic.

Another aspect of the Chinese medical system that plays an important role in Eastern healing is the *Five Phases* (Kaptchuck, 1983). The Five Phases are a part of a system of categorization by which all things and events in the universe are organized according to the five elements: wood, fire, earth, water, and metal. The health of a person depends upon the balance of body parts and these elements. A newborn who comes into this world in a state of abundance of water will be given a name bearing a source of fire as a counterbalance. Therefore, the goals of Chinese medicine are to restore balance and bring bodily parts into what the West would call homeostasis (Frye, 1991).

For the other Southeast Asians, there is little literature discussing concepts of health and illness. Some attention is now being given to the Laotians and Hmong. Westermeyer (1988) provides a rather detailed description about the Laotians and Hmong, suggesting that there seems to be a lack of schematic presentation to describe health and illness among these two ethnic groups.

Although they are neither exhaustive nor consistent, according to Westermeyer, the Laotians and Hmong share some concepts of health and illness. One of these shared concepts concerns the presence of thirty-two souls (*khuan*) that reside in each human body and the absence of which will cause illness and even death. String tying is one way to ensure the continued presence of these souls in one's body. There is also a belief in spirits (*phii*) for everything in this universe. These spirits can scare a soul away, thereby causing illness, or they can return a lost soul and restore health. The spirits, including deceased ancestors, exert great influence on one's destiny. Like the Chinese and Vietnamese, Laotian and Hmong people pay respect to these spirits or gods through a number of benevolent behaviors. Included among these behaviors are special periodic rituals such as incense burning, and making offerings. Respect for the spirit, god, goddess, or *phii*, is viewed as a law passed on from generation to generation.

Other shared concepts have to do with the effect of bad blood, air, wind, and bile. Blood is considered the life force for healthy people. If a person is sick, it is believed that he or she has some bad blood (*Luot baw dee*) which can usually be treated with herbs or medicine. There are also environmental, climatic, or temperature conditions that exert great influence on each person. A person may become ill due to bad wind. It is believed that heavy dust may cause tuberculosis.

A few other beliefs are unique to the Laotians. They believed that magic and sorcery play a significant part in one's health and illness. Connected with magic are certain omens related to astrology and dreams. Laotians also view "too much thinking" or too many worries as causing illness. These problems go against the Buddhist belief that emphasizes moderation and is consistent with the value placed on balance, harmony, and calm composure. Illness can also be inflicted by the undesirable behavior of another person toward these spirits. Overindulgence in tobacco, alcohol, or opium may predispose one to illness. Violent death and sudden death are viewed as unnatural and are not usually publicly revealed. In these cases, it is believed that the person may have had a sinful life and is being captured by a dangerous spirit, *phii pawb*. There are also diseases such as cholera or venereal disease believed to be spread from one person to another by touch.

Folk Medicine and Therapies

Medicines come in various forms and are derived from various plants, animals, and minerals. Most Asian healers prescribe herbs in one single dose for several days. Patients are instructed to return if they do not feel better. Should the condition not improve within a few days, another regimen is attempted. Patients consider herbal medicine both an art form and a medical wonder. When choosing herbal medicines, Eastern healers must take into account the season, universal balance, availability, and the well-being of the patient, as well as how they may interact with foods, tonic drinks, or herbal teas, for they all play interrelated roles and should not be viewed separately (Van Esterik, 1988).

Ancient Chinese people placed a great deal of emphasis on diet. Appropriate diet is important not only for treating illness, but also for the purpose of health maintenance and disease prevention. Foods are categorized as "Yin" and "Yang" or "hot" and "cold." Specific foods are prescribed for pregnancy, morning sickness, childbirth, infancy, and the postpartum period, as well as the postmenstrual period. Certain foods such as shellfish may be considered the cause of certain skin problems, as the poisons within these foods (e.g., shrimp, oysters, crabs) manifest into the surface of the skin. In general, it is common to see boiled rice (*khow piek*) in warm water taken during acute illnesses. Cold water is not recommended at all for any illness within these groups.

The most common form of *physical therapy* practiced by Southeast Asians in the United States is *moxibustion*, or suction in which a heated cup is placed on the skin to draw out the "bad blood" from the body. This technique produces ecchymosis (subcutaneous hemorrhage), which is later punctured to allow the escape of bad blood. Cambodians also use this therapy to treat or prevent diarrhea or malaria. Another therapy is the use of acupuncture to cure illness and relieve pain.

Massage includes acupressure practiced by the Chinese, stroking, rubbing, kneading or pounding depending on the severity of the illness. But the most common treatment is "wind eliminating," a universal practice among all these groups. There is wind rubbing, through which a coin coated with Tiger Balm or camphor is used to scratch on the body where the physical ailment surfaces. There is also wind pinching with the index and middle finger to rid the bad wind from the body. Sometimes the process is vigorous enough that it produces bruises. Wind eliminating, as well as moxibustion and cupping, have caused great concern among Western practitioners, who have considered these therapies as abusive to the patient's body.

Southeast Asians seek various types of *medical experts* for treatment. For the Chinese and Vietnamese, there are the Eastern medical doctors who were formally trained by accredited schools of Eastern (Chinese) medicine. Another common expert is the herbalist in Chinese herbal medicine stores. For the other groups, healers are divided by area of specialty, such as spirit experts, medicine experts, and magic experts (in Lao called *maw mon*). In Thailand where many Southeast Asian refugees have spent years of waiting, there are traditional healers called *Kru Khmer* for Cambodians, and *Maw Dyaa* for Laotians and Hmong. People go to them or are referred to them when they are under a great deal of psychological distress and unable to say where their physical ailment is (Kemp, 1985). Hmong people prefer to see the shaman, who is believed to acquire this healing technique as a gift from God (Quincy, 1988). Shamanistic healing usually involves a trance ceremony to cure the patient. The shaman uses divination to diagnose the patient's problem.

Charms made out of medicinal substances, animal bones, stones, or metal, are worn around the neck, wrist, or waist to keep evil spirits from harming the body. Parents place them under the beds of their children for protection, and pregnant women use them to ensure an easy delivery and a healthy infant. It is still common to see first-generation Southeast Asians, especially infants, wearing amulets or talismans (in Khmer called *katha*) or strings with special knots. Among Cambodians, Laotians, and Hmong, string tying is considered essential for protection, and the strings should not be removed unless it is absolutely necessary to do so. It is believed that these string knots are prayers written in Pali, a Buddhist language (Kemp, 1985). Strings are perceived as the linkage between the person and his or her ancestral support system (Muecke, 1983). (One Laotian mother almost became hysterical when a nurse was about to cut the strings tied around her daughter's wrist to replace them with a hospital identification tag.) Some men also wear *Sak*, which are tattoos around the neck, shoulders, chest, and sometimes on the back and arms. Tattooing is done by a *Kru* or monk. These sacred prayers are very personal to the individuals, and Westerners must respect them.

Offerings are generally made to spirits along with Buddhist ceremonies. Offerings consists of animals, rice, flowers, or money presented to the temple's monk. The extent of an offering reflects the wealth of the family.

Prayers are said mostly by Buddhist and Christian believers. If available, Buddhist monks are hired to offer special prayers for the sick. In Laos, a shaman or a magic expert may be called upon to say a secret phrase (*mon*) upon certain charms given to the sick to hasten their recovery. Sometimes a special ceremony (*baci*) is held in the home of the sick person to reconcile with the offending spirits. During the *baci* ceremony for a sick person, there are offerings of food, chanting of Buddhist verses, and tying of strings on the affected person. Hmong people do not practice prayers, but trance or *ua neeb* ceremony is still common. However, while most others perform prayers or meditation outside their home, the Hmong often hold the *ua neeb* ceremony within the family.

MATERNAL AND CHILD HEALTH PRACTICES AMONG SOUTHEAST ASIANS

Pregnancy

Pregnancy is usually an accepted and welcomed event in Asian families. Within Buddhism, birth, aging, illness, and death are four main paths of one's life cycle on earth. The state of being pregnant is viewed as part of the life cycle and not an illness. Whatever the sex, the birth of a child means a new extension to the family, and for most Asian families the family lineage is everything. Therefore, children are cherished and enjoyed. Awaiting the birth of a child is full of anticipation and an exciting time for families, and thus the clan.

However, some taboos and restrictions should be observed during pregnancy. Physical activities are not limited, but a pregnant woman is cautioned not to carry heavy loads or work in tense situations. The Chinese believed that a pregnant women should remain in the house and avoid events such as funerals and weddings. Her attendance at a funeral may invite the spirit of the deceased to enter her womb; her presence at weddings might bring bad luck to the newlyweds and the family (Char, 1981).

Close attention is paid to the diet during pregnancy, especially if the mother or mother-in-law is present. During this time, the pregnant woman's diet consists of high-protein foods such as eggs, meat, and bean curd. Too many fruits and vegetables are believed to weaken the mother. Shellfish brings indigestion and causes bad blood in the baby, resulting in boils. Alcohol is not recommended, but *areca* (a tall palm tree in Southeast Asia with red or orange egg-shaped nuts similar to chewing tobacco) and cigarettes are considered acceptable. During the second trimester, herb tea with special roots becomes part of the daily meal as a nutritional supplement.

Adolescent pregnancy is not considered a social problem as long as it is the result of a legal marriage. In the Cambodian, Lao, and Hmong communities, it is not uncommon for married girl to become pregnant at fourteen or fifteen years of age. Hmong boys begin their courtship as young as fourteen, and Hmong girls begin when they are thirteen or fourteen. Hmong society dictates that courting occur only between different clans with different family names.

Childbirth

Traditionally in Southeast Asia, delivery occurred at home with the assistance of a midwife. Around the time of delivery, a woman received the most attention in her life from all members of the family. In the past, rituals were performed around the clock to ensure the safe passage of the unborn to this world. The mother was most vulnerable to evil spirits and needed all means of protection. Also, this was the time when the woman was most pampered. There were others to rub her back and wipe her face during her entire labor. While she was in labor, the husband was not allowed to be in the birth room. No matter how difficult the labor was, the woman was not to cry out, for this might embarrass her family. Childbirth was viewed as a painful event, and women were to endure this pain quietly and willingly, as any other suffering is endured according to the Buddhist way of life.

Today it is still possible to find women wishing to deliver at home and only call upon the ambulance at the last moment. This help-seeking behavior varies within ethnic groups. The more educated or English-proficient groups seek prenatal care earlier than those who are not as well educated. Many Laotian and Cambodian women do not seek prenatal care. In addition to cultural and language barriers, these women delay their prenatal care because of transportation and babysitting problems, the fear of having blood drawn, the "cold" food that they are given, and the entire hospital environment, which contradicts their belief in balance. These women also feel embarrassed or insulted by examinations involving more than one male practitioner. Nevertheless, most women deliver their babies in the hospital. By and large, vaginal delivery is still the preferred method. Cesarean deliveries are acceptable to most Southeast Asians, with the exception of the Hmong. If a Cesarean delivery is necessary, it is important to identify the decision maker within the family. In many situations, this is not the woman herself, but the husband, grandfather, or female clan leader of that particular community.

If a birth were to occur at home in Southeast Asia, the umbilical cord might be kept for good luck and used to brew medicinal tea if the child became ill. The placenta would usually be discarded right away so that no harm would befall the infant. If there were infertile women, or women with certain female problems within the family, the placenta might be cooked as a medicinal supplement. In the Hmong tradition, the placenta of a male infant would be placed beneath the pole of the front door to emphasize the significance of family lineage. If it were a girl, the placenta of the baby would be buried underneath the house.

Circumcision is not considered an acceptable practice. Asian mothers who deliver in U.S. hospitals may not be aware that they are giving consent to such a procedure for their newborn sons.

Traditionally, the baby was returned to the mother as soon as possible after he or she was wrapped with cloth. Only then was the father allowed to see the newborn. It is extremely important for family members of the Lao, Hmong, and Cambodians, young and old, to greet the infant because it is considered proper to welcome the spirit of the new family member.

Birth defects are viewed as a shameful mishap in most cases. There is very little understanding about such pregnancy outcomes. Buddhists may view birth defects as fate. Animists may think defects result from an act of a spirit and will call for the performance of a *baci* ceremony. As with mental illness, birth defects are believed to result from wrongdoing of one's family or ancestor; thus, no one in the family may want to discuss it. A Chinese infant with a cleft palate may be viewed as the result of too much usage of scissors by the mother, or in some cases, too great a consumption of rabbit meat.

The Postpartum Period

The postpartum period is a special time for the mother and the child in Southeast Asia. The mother is pampered and spared household responsibilities. The mother-in-law and other relatives prepare foods that are considered precious and nourishing. During this period, Chinese women eat simmered chicken with special herbs and soup from pickled pigs feet and fresh vegetables. Cambodian women receive special meals of salty eggs and rice soup with pork. They also believe that wine keeps the body warm, chases bad blood away, helps them to sweat, gives them good circulation, and regulates their menstrual flow following this period. During the "cold" state of postpartum, the heat the mother lost during the birth process must be replaced. In Southeast Asia, a brazier of wood or charcoal is placed under her bed until the mother gets up about one month postpartum. Even in the United States, Asian women are expected to stay indoors for one month. They are told not to shampoo their hair or take a bath or shower. A sponge bath, however, is allowed. For her first bath, the mother is advised to use special herbs in the bathing water. Chinese women use a large amount of ginger peels and orange rinds to prevent the wind from getting into their bodies. New mothers are expected not to have sexual intercourse for 30 to 100 days.

Breastfeeding

Traditionally, breastfeeding was the norm for Asian women, but recently there has been a decrease in breastfeeding among these women. Infant mortality has been extremely high in Southeast Asia, particularly in the refugee camps. Many of these women experienced the death of their own infants or became malnourished despite the fact that they breastfed their babies. As they became acculturated, they were impressed by the fact that formula-fed American babies appeared to be stronger and bigger. They wanted to be Americanized, so they switched to formula to be like other American mothers. In addition, they believed that using formula would enhance their independence to work outside the home.

Infancy

Southeast Asian babies are considered one year old at birth, and they become another year older at the next new year. This relates to the Chinese way of reckoning and the twelve-year cycle. At about the age of one month, the infant is honored with a party combining prayers and thanksgiving to the ancestors; this is also the time the baby's name is made official. Naming the baby is an important undertaking. Elders, temple monks, and other learned persons are consulted for the baby's name, especially if it is a boy. The precise moment when the child is born in accordance with the lunar calendar, the season, the wind, and the elements, is all taken into account for this occasion. The name must reflect the personality and characteristic of the child and must not duplicate names of relatives. For the Hmong, the newborn has to wait for three days before the shaman can come to invite the soul to be reincarnated into the baby's body; only then is the baby officially recognized into the human race.

There is a strong bond between the mother and the infant. She carries the infant around and does her housework with the infant nearby. The first year of life is secure, with a great deal of attention given to the baby by all family members. Crying is usually not well tolerated. The infant is picked up, carried in a sling on the back, or rocked in a cradle. If the grandmother lives with the family, she might have the infant sleep with her. Among

Asian families, it is usually the grandmother who assumes the major responsibility for the child as soon as the mother returns to work. Thus, it is important for health professionals to determine who is the primary caretaker of the infant.

Childrearing

Childrearing is a very important function of families. The values of the traditional family are passed on to the next generation. It is believed that as long as the child lives with the parents and other family members, he or she needs to learn the proper ways of behaving and preparing to enter into adult society. With more educated Asian families, enduring values such as the importance of the family, higher education, professional occupation, a high work ethnic, and economic accomplishment are emphasized. To achieve these goals, parents provide a nurturing environment, administer firm discipline early in life, provide good role models, and define acceptable and unacceptable behavior. Both parents usually assume the responsibility for the care of small children.

Whether in Asia or in the United States, Asian families show more permissiveness toward very young children with regard to bodily functions. Children's eating habits and schedules are not highly structured. The caretaker is accustomed to chasing after the young child with the rice bowl bite after bite. Sometimes the caretaker can be embarrassed by a health professionals who seeks information on the three meals that are eaten by the child. In rural Southeast Asia, families may eat only one large meal a day. In the United States, they may only have two main meals. Mother initiates toilet training only when the child demonstrates his or her readiness. Usually, the child is not punished for accidents. Brothers and sisters are permitted to sleep in the same bed when they are younger, and father and son may share the same bed as they grow up. The very young nursing infant frequently sleeps with the mother while the father sleeps with other offspring.

Family Planning

Family planning is not taken seriously by Southeast Asians even before coming to the United States. Southeast Asians have large families, partly because of familial obligation and partly because of a high infant mortality rate. When they come to the United States, family planning is practiced more commonly among Vietnamese and ethnic Chinese, but it is the least successful program among the Laotians, Hmong, and Cambodians. A pelvic examination to many of them is a very invasive procedure, particularly if it is done by a male practitioner. In the refugee camp, women are usually given depo provera injections for birth control; however, this is not available in the United States. Also, because of the language barrier, many of these women do not understand oral contraception, nor do they know why the twenty-eight-day schedule is so important. It is not uncommon to see older Southeast Asian women with six children or more. To them, as well as some others, tubal ligation may be an option, but it must be approached with their acknowledgment that this is an irreversible procedure. Another important step for the provider to take is to make sure that the husband is part of the decision-making process. To ensure cooperation, a male practitioner may provide counseling for the husband. Gender plays an important part in this type of health practice among Southeast Asians.

ETHNOCULTURAL BARRIERS TO AND IMPLICATIONS OF HEALTH CARE SERVICES

Asian Americans, regardless of their status prior to coming to the United States, are confronted with barriers that impose hardships in all aspects of their lives, including health, employment, education, and language. At present, there are many linguistic, structural, cultural, socioeconomic, and financial barriers that impede adequate and proper access to medical services, including preventive education, for these Asian subgroups.

Language

Language is one of the factors that most hinder appropriate health care services among Asian Americans. There are more than one hundred Asian languages representing different Asian countries. Within each country there are further subdivisions. Consequently, an ethnic Chinese from North Vietnam might express himself or herself differently from an ethnic Chinese who came from South Vietnam.

Only 4.9 percent of the newly arrived Southeast Asian refugees speak English fluently (Asian American Health Forum [AAHF], 1990). In the United States, there are too few primary health care facilities providing linguistically appropriate services that are also culturally relevant (AAHF, 1990). In most health care situations, translators and interpreters are used. However, these individuals may not be trained to meet the demands of their roles, and they may be unfamiliar with both Eastern and Western beliefs and practices or unable to translate medical terms and concepts from one language to the other. Furthermore, the gender and age of the interpreter in relation to those of the client may affect the language used by the client. Children who have some command of English may accompany their parents or older relatives to seek health care services, but they are not appropriate interpreters. Also, an Asian woman may not want to communicate her illness through a male interpreter because of modesty. Information passed along from patient to provider through an interpreter may not be interpreted correctly when terminology about the body and signs and symptoms vary significantly (Muecke, 1983). Chinese people tend to describe illnesses in terms of "wind" and certain conditions of their heart as manifestation of their illness. Hmong people describe different liver conditions to illustrate physical discomfort. Thus, the language barrier is not only a matter of linguistics or speech, it is also a matter of vocabulary, usage, and, most important, the expression of thoughts and feelings.

Cultural Perception

There are marked differences in cultural perception between the West and the East regarding disease etiologies, illness behaviors, treatment modalities, and patterns of decision making and accessing care (Frye, 1991). Despite acculturation and assimilation, the margin of difference has not changed much because ethnic identity continues to be the one element determining these cultural perceptions.

The notion of gender continues to be an important factor in decision making and accessing health care. Many Asian women dislike, and some refuse, vaginal examination by a male doctor, especially if the doctor is of a different ethnic background. Some may not seek family planning services because of their fear of pelvic examinations. It is important to identify who is the key decision maker in the household when it comes to medical treatment or procedures, including family planning services. In Laotian and Cambodian families, the husband influences family planning substantially. In Hmong culture, the family may wish to consult their clan leader, who in turn may seek advice from a shaman.

Providers of services to Asian groups also need to understand the body image within a cultural perspective. According to Confucian teaching, all flesh, including hair and skin, is given by the parents, and any surgical procedure would be viewed as a disrespectful act. On the other hand, the Hmong would be afraid that the soul might be upset and leave one's body in the course of any surgical procedure, and the person may become "ill" without the soul. The head, as described by Muecke (1983), is the seat of life, and, therefore, having head treated, touched, or looked at is a threatening experience to Southeast Asians.

Folk practices also vary among Southeast Asians with regard to herbal medicines and folk therapies. Southeast Asian Americans appear to have a higher tolerance for illness than their counterparts of European descent. They are not accustomed to bed rest unless it is absolutely necessary or is approved by the head of the household. If a person is sick, the initial treatment would include folk medicines that are usually available at home, prayers to god(s) and the ancestors, and consultation with fortune tellers or astrology books. However, there may be simultaneous treatment using both folk practices and Western medicine (Kulig, 1988). Most refugees and immigrants have high regard for Western practices. However, they view the health care system as the dispensing of medicines. In Vietnam, Hong Kong, and Thailand, a trip to the Western medical practices is undertaken with the expectation of an injection and some medication. When no injection or drugs are given, the result is disappointment and a feeling of being denied.

Financial Implications

In addition to the barriers posed by language, culture, and belief systems, there are financial and socioeconomic factors that impede access to adequate and appropriate medical services for Southeast Asians resettled in the United States. Analysis of the income level of specific Southeast Asian ethnic groups found that Cambodians, Hmong, Laotians, and Vietnamese had significantly lower family incomes than the U.S. average or the average of all Asian populations. Among them the Hmong differ the most from the U.S. population as a whole. The Hmong are, by and large, younger and less educated and have lower incomes than the U.S. average and that of the other Southeast Asian groups.

Like many other lower income Americans, these Asian Americans live in poverty, and they have just as many unmet health needs. In spite of efforts made by individuals or social service agencies to secure employment for them, many Southeast Asians cannot keep their jobs. Language and cultural barriers and lack of understanding between them and their employers might contribute to their employment termination. They might also prefer to rely on the welfare system because it provides other benefits such as food stamps, housing, and medical coverage. The complexities of applying for public health benefits may also deter the medically indigent refugee or immigrant from accessing these resources.

Public Policy Factors

While much attention has been focused upon the problems these newcomers have, the government is not without its share of responsibilities. There are public policy factors that contribute to the disparity in health status for Southeast Asians. Sufficient support for programs and services targeting these ethnic subgroups is lacking. This situation is exacerbated by the scarcity of reliable data on these special-needs groups. Because of lack of sufficient data, Asian Americans are often excluded as a targeted population for federal grant competitions, as in the case of the recently established Centers of Excellence authorized as part of the Minority Health Improvement Act of 1990. Funding is also an issue at the local level because the number of Asian Americans may be small, and program development for them may not be considered cost effective. Also, the reluctance of the Southeast Asians to seek medical care may give the impression that they do not have significant unmet health needs. Although Asians are widely considered to be overrepresented in the medical profession, as viewed by the Public Health Service and the Association of American Medical colleges, these ethnic groups are still not well represented in the allied health professions. In the past twenty years, the gains for these professionals have been made mostly by second- and third-generation Chinese and Japanese Americans (AAHF, 1990). According to the Asian American Health Forum,

> *The mere existence of A/PI health professionals does not in itself assure adequate service provision. . . . While this methodology suggests that a generic A/PI physician can serve a diverse group, in reality, a third generation Japanese neural surgeon in New York cannot be expected to communicate with or provide appropriate care to a newly arrived Hmong seeking prenatal care in California. (p. 5)*

There is a need to further train or develop indigenous community workers or advocates in order to overcome the language and cultural barriers.

Finally, there is an inadequate number of health centers or organizations that provide comprehensive services to Asians. The few that exist are located mostly along the two coasts or in metropolitan areas where there are large Asian populations. Even if health and social services exist for the other Southeast Asians, they are fragmented and dispersed physically, which poses another problem, transportation. Most Southeast Asians do not drive cars, and they find using public transportation to be difficult and frightening.

SUMMARY

The Southeast Asian population is one of the fastest growing minority groups in the United States. To provide effective, appropriate, and adequate health and human services to meet their needs, one must be aware of not only who they were prior coming to the United States but also their acculturation processes. This chapter has attempted to provide some historical and political perspectives as well as cultural and religious background in order to further an understanding of their health beliefs and practices. It has also discussed the barriers they have to face daily. It is important that health and human services providers keep the following points in mind in their delivery of services to Southeast Asian Americans:

The Culture of the Homeland

1. Asians look at health and illness as resulting from the relationship between the person and elements in the universe. Religious beliefs and health practices often cannot be distinguished from one another.
2. Chinese and Vietnamese view illness as an imbalance between Yin and Yang. Laotians, Cambodians, and the Hmong may view illness as due to soul loss, witchcraft, and evil spirit possession.
3. Folk remedies are widely practiced, including the use of herbs, acupressure, acupuncture, and dermabrasive practices of cupping, pinching, rubbing, and burning.
4. Traditional healers are popular among the Chinese, Vietnamese, and Cambodians. These healers include fortune tellers, herbalists, and martial arts practitioners. The Hmong prefer to use a shaman, who is believed to have healing power from the gods.
5. Gender is an important consideration. The roles of males and females are tacitly defined in all aspects of the Asian's life. To a lesser degree, a person's rank and age or position in the family also play an important role in daily life.
6. Religious beliefs and health practices cannot be easily distinguished from each other. The Chinese and Vietnamese practice Buddhism, Taoism, and Confucianism. Cambodians and Laotians believe in Thervada Buddhism. Laotians and the Hmong believe in animism focusing on the supernatural, demons, and loss of souls.
7. Respect for the head of the household and the clan leader is a strong tradition in most Asian families. These individuals play significant roles in decision making for many aspects of life.

The Culture of the War

1. Whether by boat or by land, many Southeast Asians experienced or witnessed trauma during their exodus to the West. They or their family members were raped, beaten, and killed. Death, hunger, starvation, and exhaustion were common.
2. Fragmentation of families shattered the entire support system.
3. There are mixed emotions about the war and its causes and effects.

The Culture of the U.S. Health and Human Services System

1. Neither the U.S. nor the Asian cultures were well prepared to accept each other as Southeast Asians began their resettlement in the United States some twenty years ago. Many Americans still feel overwhelmed. As the memories of the war begin to fade, so does the enthusiasm of the host to accept newcomers and deal with their problems.
2. Much effort on the part of U.S. institutions is focused upon one-way assimilation, rather than a mutual give and take process.
3. Despite open public policies and the availability of federal financial aid, the establishment of resettlement services has not had the impact on self-sufficiency desired for these populations.
4. The rate of acculturation is greater in children, adolescents, and working mothers or wives. This discrepancy results in inter-generational gaps and role conflicts. Such family tensions often lead to an increase of domestic violence, substance abuse, mental illness, and dysfunctionalism within the family.
5. Language is by far the most critical problem in regard to barriers to the accessibility of health and human services.
6. There is a lack of strategic planning within the general public health arena to promote the training of bilingual health care workers such as nurses, social workers, outreach workers, and health educators. There is also inadequate training of effective translators and interpreters for health and human services providers.

CONCLUSION

Today the health care system is challenged by the rapid growth of a multicultural society. Service providers need to be sensitive to the possible differences and subsequent incongruence of perceptions of those they serve. They also need to be cognizant that there are differences among Southeast Asians and among individuals within these groups. The Southeast Asian refugees and immigrants are making inroads to adjust to their new way of life in the United States. Among the various groups studied in this chapter, the ethnic Chinese and Vietnamese are more ready to adapt and adopt the American way of life, including Western medical practices such as regular check-ups, early prenatal care, and routine child care and immunization. Their educational experience was relatively higher than that of the Laotians and Hmong prior to coming to the United States. They had more previous experiences to observe, learn, and form opinions about the Western world.

Successful intervention for Southeast Asians requires a holistic approach that looks at the relevant cultural, religious, and health beliefs in an interrelated manner. Improving the overall well-being of this population requires a commitment from a partnership of public policy makers, local agencies, and refugee communities.

Finally, although service providers are challenged by those from other cultures, they need not shy away from these challenges. As Confucius (551–479 BC) stated: "By nature men are alike; through practices, they have become far apart."

GLOSSARY

Amulet Small articles such as miniatures of Buddha, saints, special nuts, medallions, or pendants are worn to ward off evil spirits. These are usually worn around the neck or waist or are sometimes sewn into clothing. Amulets are highly regarded by those who wear them. Should it be necessary to remove them for a medical procedure, the patient or a relative must be asked to remove them. The amulets must be easily retrieved later on.

Cold As described in terms of Chinese medicine, one of the six pathogenic factors in the environment, or simply the result of not enough fire (*Yang*) in the body. It is benefited by application of warmth (e.g., a heating pad) or warming foods and herbs.

Dampness As described in Chinese medicine, one of the external causes of disease that disturbs the normal flow of energy and particularly the digestive functioning of the spleen and stomach, characterized by heaviness, stagnation, and turbidity; fluid accumulation due to impaired water metabolism.

Dryness As described in Chinese medicine, one of the six pathogenic factors in the environment. A disorder with dryness is associated with thirst, dry mouth and throat, fever, constipation, scanty concentrated urine, dry cough, emaciation, and similar symptoms.

Fire As described in Chinese medicines, one of the six pathogenic factors in the environment. It manifests in high fever, feverish sensation around the eyes and nose, redness in the face or tongue, and the like.

Heat/hot As described in Chinese medicine, a condition usually cased by heat, one of the six pathogenic factors in the environment, or a lack of water (*Yin*) to counterbalance in the fire (*Yang*) in the body. It is benefited by cooling foods and treatment and is aggravated by heat. This is usually an acute, excess condition such as infection, fever, and the like.

Khow piek (boiled rice) Gruel, congee, or porridge. Usually, rice or grain that has been cooked with extra water and cooking time to the point of being soupy. The "rice soup" is used for infants with diarrhea. In times of sickness, this is very common among the Chinese and Southeast Asians.

Moxibustion (Och) A traditional healing technique that is common in Asia and Southeast Asia to remove a cold condition in the body. A herbal substance (*moxa*) is heated on or near the affected area (typically the periumbilical area), introducing heat while dissipating the cold condition. In the Chinese practice of moxibustion, a slice of ginger or a pinch of salt is placed on the skin over an identified acupuncture point before the moxa is applied.

Sanskrit Prayers or spiritual phrases. Cambodians, Laotians, and Thai males tatoo these as protection from evil spirits, knives, spears, or other weapons.

Talisman, katha Strings or cords tied around the wrists, ankles, or neck of Southeast Asians to keep their protective souls within the body or to prevent the entry of evil spirits into the body. These strings can be tied by special religious specialists or elders in the family. There are also special occasions such as marriage, pregnancy, or leaving upon or returning home from a journey when special rituals are held to invite protective spirits to come in and be bound with the person's body for good luck.

Wind One of the external causes of disease; a syndrome characterized by fever, chills, headache, and body aches. Internally, wind can also disrupt the balance, manifesting such symptoms as dizziness, fainting, convulsions, tremor, numbness, or pain that moves around (like the wind).

Yang Relating to the male, active, positive, energetic side of life or nature of a person.

Yin Relating to the female, passive, negative, watery, cool, substance side of life or nature of a person.

REFERENCES

Asian American Health Forum. (1990). *Dispelling the myth of a healthy minority.* San Francisco: Author.

Asian and Pacific Islander Center for Census Information and Services. (1992). *Our ten years of growth: A demographic analysis of Asian and Pacific Islander Americans.* San Francisco: Asian/Pacific Islander Data Consortium.

Cantanzaro, A., & Moser, R. (1982). Health status of refugees from Vietnam, Laos, and Cambodia. *Journal of the American Medical Association, 247,* 1303–1307.

Cerquone, J. (1986). Refugee from Laos in harm's way. In V. Hamilton (Ed.), *American Council for Nationalities Services.* Washington, DC: U.S. Committee for Refugees.

Chandler, D. P. (1983). *A history of Cambodia.* Boulder, CO: Westview.

Char, T. Y. (1975). *The sandlewood mountain.* Honolulu: The University Press of Hawaii.

Char, T. Y. (1981). The Chinese family. In A. L. Clark (Ed.), *Culture and childrearing* (pp. 140–164). Philadelphia: F. A. Davis.

Frye, B. A. (1991). Cultural themes in health care decision making among Cambodian refugee women. *Journal of Community Health Nursing, 8*(1), 33–44.

Kaptchuck, T. J. (1983). *The web that has no weaver: Understanding Chinese medicine.* New York: Congdon & Weed.

Kemp, C. (1985). Cambodian refugee health care beliefs and practices. *Journal of Community Health Nursing, 2*(1), 41–52.

Kingston, M. (1977). *The woman warrior.* New York: Random House.

Kingston, M. (1978). *San Franciscan Chinatown. American Heritage, 1*(30), 47.

Kulig, J. (1988). Childbearing among Cambodian refugee women. *Canadian Nurse, 84*, 46–47.

Kuykendall, K. (1972). *Acculturative change in family structure among Chinese Americans.* Unpublished doctoral dissertation, University of Colorado, Boulder.

Lee, G. Y. (1966). Culture and adaptation Hmong refugees in Australia. In G. Hendrick, B. Downing, & A. S. Deinard. (Eds.). *The Hmong in transition* (pp. 56–72). New York: Center for Migration Studies.

Mann, E., & Waldron, J. (1977). Intercultural marriage and childrearing. In T. Wenshing, J. McDermott, & T. Maretzki (Eds.), *Adjustment in intercultural marriage* (pp. 62–80). Honolulu: The University Press of Hawaii.

Muecke, M. A. (1983). Caring for Southeast Asian Refugees in the USA. *American Journal of Public Health, 73*(4), 431–438.

Nguyen, S. (1982). The psycho-social adjustment and the mental health of southeast Asian refugees. *Psychiatric Journal of the University of Ottawa, 7*(1), 26–35.

Office of Refugee Resettlement. (1985). *The Hmong resettlement study.* Washington, DC: U.S. Department of Health and Human Services.

Queen, S. A., Habenstein, R. W., & Adams, J. B. (1961). *The family in various cultures.* New York: Lippencott.

Quincy, K. (1988). *Hmong: History of a people.* Chaney: Eastern Washington University Press.

Rhumbaut, R. G., & Weeks, J. R. (1986). Fertility and adaptation: Indochinese refugees in the U.S. *International Migration Review, 20*(2), 428–466.

Shinagawa, L. (1992, September). Growth and diversity among the Asian Pacific American populations in the United States. *Partners in human service: Shaping health care and civil rights policy for Asian and Pacific Islander Americans.* (Final Report. Publication No. 93-50218). Washington D.C. Office of Minority Health, U.S. Department of Health and Human Services.

Stringfellow, L., Nguyen, D. L., & Linda, D. L. (1981). In A. L. Clark (Ed.), *Culture and childbearing* (pp. 228–241). Philadelphia: F. A. Davis.

Sung, B. (1972). *The Chinese in America.* New York: Macmillan.

Tapp, N. (1989). *Sovereignty and rebellion: The White Hmong of northern Thailand.* Singapore & New York: Oxford University Press.

Tung, T. M. (1980). *Indochinese patients.* Falls Church, VA: Walter Brothers.

U.S. Committee for Refugees. Cambodian refugees in Thailand: The limits of asylum. (1982). *Refugee Reports, 8*(1), 1–16.

U.S. Committee for Refugees. New life and frustrations. (1988). *Refugee Reports, 9*(3), 1–15.

Van Esterik, P. (1988). To strengthen and refresh: Herbal therapy in South East Asia. *Social Science Medicine, 27*(8), 751–759.

Westermeyer, J. (1988). Folk medicine in Laos: A comparison between two ethnic groups. *Social Science Medicine, 27*(8), 769–778.

SUGGESTED READINGS

Baldwin, L. M., & Sutherland, S., (1988). Growth patterns of first-generation Southeast Asian infants. *American Journal of Diseases of Children, 142,* 526–531.

Barker, J. C. (1992). Cross-cultural medicine, a decade later. Cultural-diversity: changing the context of medical practice. *West Journal of Medicine, 157,* 248–254.

Barry, M., Craft, J., Coleman, D., Coulter, H. O., & Horowitz, R. (1983). Clinical findings in Southeast Asian refugees, child development and public health concerns. *Journal of the American Medical Association, 249*(23), 3200–3203.

Boehnlein, J. (1987). Clinical revelance of grief and mourning among Cambodian refugees. *Social Science Medicine, 25*(7), 765–772.

Brown, M. S. (1977). Child rearing in cross-cultural perspective. *Health Values: Achieving High-Level Wellness, 1*(2), 77–81.

Chen, M. S., Jr. (1993). A 1993 status report on the health status of Asian Americans and Pacific Islanders: Comparison with *Healthy People 2000* Objectives. *Asian American and Pacific Islander Journal of Health, 1,* 37–55.

Chen, M. S., Jr. (1993). Cardiovascular health among Asian Americans/Pacific Islanders: An examination of health status and intervention approaches. *American Journal of Health Promotion, 7*(3), 199–207.

Chen, M. S., Jr, Zaharlick, A., Kunn, P. et al. (1992). Implementation of the indigenous model for health education programming among Asian minorities: Beyond theory and into practice. *Journal of Health Education, 23,* 400–403.

Cheng, L. R. L. (1990). Asian-American cultural perspectives on birth defects: Focus on cleft palate. *Cleft Palate Journal, 27*(3), 294–300.

Chung, R. C., & Okazaki, S. (1991). *Counseling Americans of Southeast Asian descent: The impact of the refugee experience.* Washington, DC: National Research Center on Asian American Mental Health, National Institute of Mental Health.

Colomb, L. (1988). The interplay of traditional therapies in south Thailand. *Social Science Medicine, 27*(8), 761–768.

Feldman, K. W. (1984). Pseudoabusive burns in Asian refugees. *American Journal of Diseases of Children, 138,* 768–769.

Fingerhut, L. A., & Kleinman, C. (1990). International and interstate comparison of homicide among young males. *Journal of the American Medical Association, 263*(24), 3292–3295.

Fishman, C., Evans, R., & Jenks, E. (1988). Warm bodies, cool milk: Conflicts in postpartum food choice for Indochinese women in California. *Social Science Medicine, 26*(11), 1125–1132.

Fox, P. (1991). Stress related to family change among Vietnamese refugees. *Journal of Community Health Nursing, 8*(1), 45–56.

Fung, L-C. (1992). *Breast health days: A breast cancer education and screening program for Chinese American women.* Proceedings from the Sixth International Conference on Health Promotion Related to the Chinese in North America, 48.

Gann, P., Ngheim, L., & Warner, S. (1989). Pregnancy characteristics and outcomes of Cambodian refugees. *American Journal of Public Health, 79*(9), 1251–1257.

Golomb, L. (1988). The interplay of traditional therapies in South Thailand. *Social Science Medicine, 27*(8), 761–768.

Hardwood, A. (1981). *Ethnicity and medical care.* Cambridge, MA: Harvard University Press.

Hurie, M., Mast, E., & Davis, J. (1992). Horizontal transmission of hepatitis B virus infection to United States-born children of Hmong refugees. *Pediatrics, 89*(2), 269–273.

Jackson, L. E. (1993). Understanding, eliciting and negotiating clients' multicultural health beliefs. *Nurse Practitioner, 18*(4), 30–43.

Jenkins, C. (1986). Vietnamese needs assessment. In C.P. Quock & J. Louie (Eds.), *Proceedings of the First Asian American Health Forum* (pp. 185–191). Washington, DC: U.S. Public Health Service.

Koschman, N. L., & Tobin, J. J. *Working with Indochinese refugees: A handbook for mental health workers and human service providers.* Chicago: Department of Public Aid.

Kumabe, K. T., Nishida C., & Hepworth, D. H. (1985). *Bridging ethnocultural diversity in social work and health.* Honolulu: University of Hawaii School of Social Work.

Labun, E. (1988). The Vietnamese woman in Canada. *The Canadian Nurse, 84*(8), 49–50.

Laderman, C., & Van Esterik, P. (1988). Techniques of healing in Southeast Asia. *Social Science Medicine, 27*(8), 747–750.

Lee, J., & Kiyak, H. A. (1992). Oral disease beliefs, behaviors, and health status of Korean-Americans. *Public Health Dentistry, 52*(3), 131–6.

Levin, B., Nachampassack, S., & Xiong, R. (1988). Cigarette smoking and the Laotian refugee. *Migration World, 16*(4/5), 32–38.

Lin, K. M., Tazuma, L., & Masuda, M. (1979). Adaptational problems of Vietnamese refugees: Health and mental health status. *Archive of General Psychiatry 36*, 955–961.

Lin-Fu, J. S. (1987, March). Meeting the needs of Southeast Asian refugees in maternal and child health and primary care programs. In *Maternal-Child Health Technical Information Series*, (pp. 2–9). Rockville, MD: Health Resources and Services Administration.

Lin-Fu, J. S. (1988). Population characteristics and health care needs of Asian Pacific Americans. *Public Health Reports, 103*(1), 18–27.

McKenzie, J. L., & Christman, N. J. (1977). Healing herbs, gods, and magic: Folk health beliefs among Filipino-Americans. *Nursing Outlook, 25*(5), 326–329.

Manderson, L., & Mathews, M. (1981). Vietnamese attitudes towards maternal and infant health. *The Medical Journal of Australia, 1*, 69–72.

Mollica, R., Wyshak, G., Lavelle, J. et al. (1990). Assessing symptom change in Southeast Asian refugee survivors of mass violence and torture. *American Journal of Psychiatry, 147*(1), 83–88.

Murphy, G., & Frey, L. (1988). *A mutual challenge: Training and learning with the Indochinese in social work.* Boston: Boston University School of Social Work.

Nolan, C. M., & Elarth, A. M. (1988). Tuberculosis in a cohort of Southeast Asian refugees: A 5-year surveillance study. *American Review of Respiratory Disorders, 137*, 805–809.

Pandit, R. D. (1989). Ethics in infertility management: Asian aspects. *Asia-Oceanic Journal of Obstetric Gynecology, 15*(1), 79–85.

Pham, C., & McPhee, S. (1992). Knowledge, attitudes and practices of breast and cervical cancer screening among Vietnamese women. *Journal of Cancer Education, 7*(4), 305–310.

Putsch, R. (1985). Cross-cultural communications. *Journal of the American Medical Association, 254*, 3344–3348.

Quock, C. P. (1992). Health problems in the Chinese in North America. *Western Journal of Medicine, 156*(5), 577–588.

Richman, D., & Dixon, S. (1985). Comparative study of Cambodian, Hmong, and Caucasian infant and maternal perinatal profiles. *Journal of Nurse-Midwifery, 30*(6), 313–319.

Roberson, M. H. (1987). Folk health beliefs of health professionals. *Western Journal of Nursing Research, 9*(2), 257–263.

Rosenberg, J. A. (1986). Health care for Cambodian children: Integrating treatment plans. *Pediatric Nursing, 12*(2), 118–125.

Rosenberg, J. A., & Givens, S. S. (1986). Teaching child health-care concepts to Khmer mothers. *Journal of Community Health Nursing 3*(3), 157–168.

Santopietro, M., & Lynch, B. A. (1980). Indochinese moves to Main Street: What's behind the "inscrutable" mask? *RN Magazine, 43*(10), 55–62.

Santopeitro, M., & Smith, C. (1981). How to get through to a refugee patient, *RN Magazine, 44*(1), 43–48.

Scheper-Hughes, N. (1990). Three propositions for a critical applied medical anthropology. *Social Science Medicine, 30*(2), 189–197.

Schumacher, L., Pawson, G., & Kretchmer, N. (1987). Growth of immigrant children in the newcomer schools of San Francisco. *Pediatrics, 80*, 861–868.

Scott, C. (1974). Health and healing practices among five ethnic groups in Miami, Florida. *Public Health Reports, 89*(6), 524–532.

Shelton, D., Merritt, R., Giovino, G. et al. (1992). *Cigarette smoking among Asian/Pacific Islanders: National estimates, 1987–1990.* Presentation at the 1992 American Public Health Association Annual Meeting.

Sich, D. (1988). Childbearing in Korea. *Social Science Medicine, 27*(5), 497–504.

Stein, J., Berg, C., Jones, J. A., & Detter, J. C. (1984). A screening protocol for a prenatal population at risk for inherited hemoglobin disorders: Results of its application to a group of Southeast Asians and Blacks. *American Journal of Obstetrics and Gynecology, 150*(4), 333–341.

Toole, M., & Waldman, R. J. (1990). Prevention of excess mortality in refugee and displaced populations in developing countries. *Journal of the American Medical Association, 263*(24), 3296–3302.

Tracy, T. J., Glidden, C., & Leong, F. T. (1986). Help seeking and problem perception among Asian Americans. *Journal of Counseling Psychology, 33*(3), 331–336.

Tripp-Reimer, T. et al. (1984). Cultural assessment: Content and process. *Nursing Outlook, 32*(2), 78–82.

Uba, L. (1992). Cultural barriers to health care for Southeast Asian refugees. *Public Health Reports, 107,* 544–548.

Watkins, E. G., & Johnson, A. E. (Eds.). (1985). *Removing cultural and ethnic barriers to health care.* Chapel Hill: University of North Carolina.

Westermeyer, J. (1989). An epidemic of opium dependence among Asian refugees in Minnesota: Characteristics and causes. *British Journal of Addiction, 84,* 785–789.

Yu, E. S. H. (1991). The health risks of Asian Americans. *American Journal of Public Health, 81,* 1391–1393.

Yu, E. S. H., & Liu, W. T. (1992). U.S. national health data on Asian Americans and Pacific Islanders: A research agenda for the 1990s. *American Journal of Public Health, 82*(12), 1645–1652.

Zaharlick, A., & Brainard, J. (1987). Demographic characteristics, ethnicity and the resettlement of Southeast Asian refugees in the United States. *Urban Anthropology, 16*(3–4), 326–373.

Zaharlick, A., & Brainard, J. (1989). Changing health beliefs and behaviors of resettled Laotian refugees: Ethnic variation in adaptation. *Social Science Medicine, 29*(7), 845–852.

Understanding the
Hispanic Community

HILDA BURGOS-OCASIO

> *. . . increasing communication across . . . [cultural*
> *and ethnic] lines to destroy stereotypes, to halt*
> *polarization, to end distrust and hostility, and*
> *to create common ground for efforts toward*
> *common goals for public order and justice.*
> —DILLARD, 1985, P. 1

By the year 2000 it is estimated that Hispanics will be the largest minority group in the United States. According to the United States Bureau of the Census, (U.S. Bureau of the Census 1991), in 1990 there were about 22.4 million Hispanics in the United States, representing 10 percent of the total population. The Hispanic population increased by about 53 percent between 1980 and 1990. However, because of problems with data-collection procedures and the high number of temporary workers, the exact number of Hispanics living in the United States is difficult to establish. A long-range projection is that 140 million Hispanics may live in the United States by the year 2080.

Hispanics in the United States present different realities. This chapter provides general information about the Hispanic culture, similarities and differences among Hispanic subgroups, and issues to be considered by health care professionals. It also discusses health and illness beliefs and practices of Hispanic people. Issues of assimilation and acculturation are identified. The goal of the chapter is to provide concrete information to help health care professionals gain sensitivity, knowledge, understanding, and competency in dealing with the Hispanics in the United States. As Torres (1992b) indicated, the diversity of this group makes it imperative that health care providers be sensitive to and knowledgeable about their patients' cultural background and beliefs. More and more literature points out that the use of treatment models that include the psychological, social, and cultural aspects of the individual will improve treatment.

THE CONCEPTS "HISPANIC" AND "LATINO"

To understand Hispanics as a cultural group, it is imperative to define and clarify who they are based on where they come from. Hispanics, in general, identify themselves as members of the same ethnic group not by demographic characteristics but by their cultural values and language (Marín & Marín, 1991). In the spectrum of ethnicity and language, the term *Hispanic* emerges as a common bond that unifies those who claim Spanish as their heritage. As Pérez-Stable (1987) indicated, Hispanic is basically the name that has been officially used by the federal government to classify individuals who claim ties to Spain in their heritage. It also implies that the Spanish language is a unifying element (Cortes, 1991). The use of the term *Hispanic* has been controversial because many definitions do not include people from the South of the United States who did not immigrate to this country, but whose land was invaded and then occupied (Falicov, 1982). People of Spanish ancestry who consider themselves Hispanics can be classified as Hispanics regardless of the number of generations who have been living in the United States. The word *Latino*, which is commonly used to refer to this same group of individuals, clusters those Spanish-speaking countries where the integration of Spanish, indigenous people, and Africans has occurred. This term includes all Latin American individuals (including Brazilians).

Whether an individual prefers to be called Hispanic or Latino is a matter of choice. Some Hispanic/Latinos feel comfortable with either term, while others feel strongly about their preference. Because of the differences, it is recommended that when referring to individuals or to a specific ethnic group the name of the country of origin be utilized (e.g., Mexicans, Puerto Ricans, Cubans, etc.) (Cortes, 1991). This chapter uses the term Hispanics to refer to those subgroups in the United States that identify themselves with the Spanish culture and the Spanish language. It will be taken into consideration that according to the U.S. Census Mexicans, Puerto Ricans, and Cubans are the predominant subgroups in the United States.

HISTORY

Before the English, French, or Dutch arrived on North American shores, the blood of Spanish ancestors was mixed with that of the indigenous people of Mexico's lands, reaching farther north than today's Mexican boundaries. The Spanish had reached Florida, Texas, California, the Caribbean Islands, and the shores of South America.

Hispanics can be viewed as people who come from countries that have undergone colonization, first by the Spaniards, and later on by the Anglo-Americans, Dutch, French and British, and with it classical colonialism. In contrast to the English colonization patterns, the Spanish colonization process relied on strong initiatives led by the royal Spanish crown and the Roman Catholic Church. The Spanish royalty wanted to acquire more lands and precious metals; the Church wanted to save the souls of the natives. The Spanish were more successful in converting the natives to the ideas of Christianity—or at least to its religious practices. The Spanish policy of including the Indians, although in low ranks as laborers, established a sense of conformity to the effects of colonization. This led to an ideology of "La Raza" (the race) rather than an exclusionary view of people who were considered "different." The general philosophy of the Hispanic culture has evolved from a collection of influences from many cultures, leading to personalized beliefs about the family, the community, religious practices, and rules governing interpersonal contacts.

With the arrival of Christopher Columbus to the "New World" shores, language became one of the important elements of identification among Latin Americans. As Cortes (1991) indicated, most Hispanics in the United States are linked by Spanish as the single language of heritage. It is important to note that although not all Hispanics in the United States speak Spanish, most of them recognize its symbolic importance.

RELIGION

As a result of the Spanish colonization, the primary religious influence on Hispanics is Catholicism. Many Hispanics do not actively practice religious rites, but they do recognize Catholicism as their religion, while others are devout and practice Catholicism faithfully. Many traditional families, particularly the family elders, have altars where statues and pictures of saints are openly displayed. Some Hispanics practice fundamentalist faiths such as Jehovah's Witnesses, Pentecostal, and Baptist religions. Other variations of religious practices by Hispanics include a combination of African rituals intertwined with sanctioned saints of the Catholic Church (known as

Santería and a respect for supernatural beliefs and spiritism (known as *Espiritismo*).

MIGRATION

Hispanics are unlike many other immigrants because many of them have not migrated from any other country. Their identity as a group has changed over the years because of political needs and decisions made by governmental decrees (Blasini-Perk, 1990). For example, since 1898 all Puerto Ricans have been considered to be born in the United States because that was the year Puerto Rico became an incorporated territory of the United States as a result of the Spanish-American War. The same treaty changed the geographic boundaries of the Mexican-American borders. Since the early 1800s, Cubans have developed roots in areas of Miami and New York through their import and export trades. Other Latin Americans also have been linked to the United States through economic ties since the eighteenth century.

By the 1960s and 1970s, Hispanic immigration into the United States expanded to include other peoples from the Caribbean and Central and South America. Salvadorans began to migrate to the United States in 1976, and Nicaraguans and Guatemalans arrived in the late 1970s. Panamanians, Dominicans, and Ecuadorans escaped the pressures of poverty, government upheavals, and political conflicts by emigrating to the United States in the 1980s.

As the 1980s gave way to the 1990s, the cluster-residence patterns of Hispanics in the United States changed greatly. From California to the Midwest to New York to Southern Florida, Hispanics began to settle and cluster in distinct communities.

The Hispanic population is a heterogeneous group that reflects distinctive economic classes, ethnic subgroups, and races. The Hispanic heritage can be traced back to the many centuries of conquest of Spain by the Moors, the Spanish enslavement of the Aztecs and Caribbean indigenous people, and the Africans brought in to replace the natives. Intermarriage of the Spanish with the subordinate people resulted in new groups of *mestizos* (a mixture of Indian and White) and *mulattos* (a mixture of African and White). Also, the cultural heritage of the Dutch, French, and other Europeans who explored and colonized other areas of South and Central America and the Caribbean was mixed with that of the indigenous population. Therefore, there is a widespread racial mixture in Latin American countries. Mestizo and mulatto are very much part of the Hispanic reality.

While the United States operates within a rigid system of ethnic and racial categorization, this seldom occurs in Latin American countries.

The racial and physical makeup that Hispanics represent has resulted in identity problems and discrimination against Hispanics in the United States.

Just as the heritage patterns of Hispanics vary, so do the migration patterns of the various Latin nationalities and ethnic groups. *Campesinos* or *jíbaros* from rural areas, displaced migrant farm workers, urban dwellers from *pueblos* (towns) experiencing their own urban-blight struggles, middle-class or rich families who have lost their wealth to new governments or military coups—all are seeking to improve their lives in the United States.

Hispanic migration in the United States has been greatly influenced by political and economic patterns. During the period around 1917 many Mexicans came to the United States to serve as farmhands and railroad workers because of the labor shortages during World War I. By 1924 the U.S. government imposed refugee quotas regulating the numbers of incoming Europeans. Again, Mexicans were brought in by the government through *bracero* programs, which established employment contracts through 1964 (Blasini-Perk, 1990).

Puerto Ricans, on the other hand, have been establishing themselves in New York City since the nineteenth century looking for a better way of life, particularly since the Depression. Between 1900 and 1945, industrial and agricultural labor was the primary reason for Puerto Rican settlement in New York, but this migration has spread widely to other states. Since the 1940s, Puerto Ricans have settled in Hawaii, California, Arizona, Illinois, Indiana, Wisconsin, Ohio, and other states (Blasini-Perk, 1990). This interesting migratory factor is referred to as the "revolving door migration." According to the U.S. Census, many Puerto Ricans are returning to the island to retire or to raise their families in traditional settings. On the other hand, more and more professionals are coming to the United States looking for better economical conditions and professional growth.

Economic and political changes in Latin America have led to migration trends. Many Hispanics come to the United States with transferable job skills, some settle for any job in order to escape political persecution, and still others face the label of "no marketable job skills" while dealing with the loss of trade work or agriculture-related employment. Language barriers and competition with other marginal populations for low-skill, entry-level positions also affect the lives of Hispanic migrants. Health care professionals interacting with Hispanic populations need to consider the various factors impacting Hispanics in cultural transitions, such as who migrated and why, class and racial factors, political ideology, and religious and philosophical values.

Although Hispanics have entered the United States in different ways and have different backgrounds, they experience similar problems of discrimination, segregation, and exploitation in language, culture, education, politics, society, and economics (Cortes, 1991).

ACCULTURATION AND ASSIMILATION

According to Bash (1981), *acculturation* is the adoption of cultural traits and factors on a piecemeal and/or formalistic basis. The degree of acculturation and identification with the host culture as a reference group varies with the individual. *Assimilation* occurs when an old set of traits is relinquished through interaction, participation, and communication in the new society (Bash, 1981). Assimilation involves processes of psychological adjustments, cultural adaptation, and social structural integration.

Hispanic assimilation is complicated by issues of race and color. Unlike European immigrants, Hispanics comprise many races. Hispanics are identified in the United States as an "other" racial group by virtue of physical appearances. Given the differing ethnic and racial composition, education and economic backgrounds, and political and religious views, the acculturation and assimilation rates of the Hispanic population are hard to gauge.

Acculturation and assimilation are also influenced by residential segregation or concentrations (Blasini-Perk, 1990). The proximity of the United States mainland to Mexico, Central America, and the Caribbean allows Hispanics to commute between cultures, which makes culture-specific foods, toiletries, and newspapers available for purchase. Cable television programming allows Hispanics to view international news, *novelas* (soap operas), and other entertainment programs. Spanish-language radio programs are produced in many large cities, and bilingual education programs and public information laws have enhanced Hispanic access to community institutions.

Biculturalism refers to the process of integrating values and behaviors from two cultures—the ethnic and the dominant culture—into an individual's identity. *Bilingualism*, on the other hand, refers to an individual's ability to communicate in two languages (e.g., English and Spanish). Most Hispanics do not wish to abandon their culture, language, and identity. Many become bicultural and/or bilingual rather than assimilated. Moreover, different Hispanic groups manifest different degrees of acculturation and assimilation. Assimilation patterns include identification with the dominant culture; intermarriage; and employment in skilled labor positions, white-collar industries, and service jobs. Large urban settings attract mostly higher education instructors and medical professionals. Most Mexicans living in the Midwest are active in all aspects of social and economic strata in their communities.

The first migration of Cubans, unlike the Mexicans and Puerto Ricans, assimilated quickly. During the 1950s and 1960s, a great number of Cubans migrated to the Miami area and later to other coastal cities. Most of them were fleeing Fidel Castro's political persecution and were well-educated, middle-class or higher citizens. Many were professionals or skilled workers who were easily employed. Others settled for service jobs until they were able to establish their own enterprises. Many of the Cuban immigrants assimilated into the dominant culture but maintained their own cultural values and beliefs. A second wave of Cubans (*Marielitos*) came to the United States in the late 1970s. Unlike the first group, this second group lacked professional or job skills, which resulted in the emergence of refugee camps across the country. Many of these immigrants have become recipients of public assistance and have not developed the skills necessary for adapting to the Anglo-American culture.

Puerto Ricans, unlike any other Hispanic immigrant group, enter the United States mainland as citizens who can vote, serve in the armed forces, and, due to an open border, travel easily to the land of their birth. Puerto Ricans on the mainland represent a vast cross-section of economic and social class groups. Many are the second generation of children of some of the first Puerto Rican migrants. Migrants of the late 1800s and early 1900s were well-educated islanders seeking better employment opportunities. Later, waves of Puerto Rican migration brought to the United States mainland displaced agricultural workers who had been affected by industrialization that increased unemployment on the island. Others came as "family helpers" for those who were already working on the mainland.

During the 1970s, the change from industrial to technological employment resulted in greater numbers of Puerto Rican migrants at the unemployment and public assistance lines in many northeastern and midwestern cities. Today's Puerto Ricans represent several groups—those who were born on the island who have been living on the mainland for many years, those who were born on the mainland, and those who are second- and third-generation children educated in mainland schools and universities or who still remain in urban ghettos.

South Americans who come to the United States tend to bring higher labor skills along with their migration needs. They tend to assimilate more quickly because of access to employment and the smaller number of population concentrations for this group. Many migrate as a results of political or economic changes that impact the powerful old families and their enterprises.

Central Americans, on the other hand, have migrated to the United States with limited work skills. Most of them are *campesinos* (farmers) escaping the military forces that are vying for power. Central Americans along with border-city Mexicans comprise a large part of the illegal aliens in the United States. Central Americans (i.e., Salvadorans, Nicaraguans, Guatemalans, Hondurans, and Panamanians) who migrate tend to be employed as domestic workers, child care providers, office cleaners, or in other low-skill positions. Their acculturation is limited by their limited access to opportunities outside of their employment and social circles. Assimilation of this group will not be fully measurable for years to come.

Generally, most Hispanics accept the Anglo-American culture as the general pattern of their new country for entry into economic, employment, educational, or political structures. However, as they continue to live in the United States, they keep many of their traditions and cultural beliefs alive. However, for a large number of Hispanics, acceptance of their new cultural environment is a slow and painful process. This pattern of slow adaptation to the general U.S. culture causes them to remain separated from the Anglo-American culture. Many Hispanics learn to speak English, but many do not. Some rarely venture out of their own neighborhoods and never have to speak English to meet their basic needs. In some families the children speak English only outside of the home. In others, the parents speak only in Spanish, and their children respond only in English. Others are functionally illiterate in both languages. And still others have their own "Spanglish" (mixture of Spanish and English) dialects.

As expressed by Blasini-Perk (1990), stress and acculturation pressures can contribute to family violence, strict childrearing practices and spanking, wife battering, socialized acceptance of male drinking and smoking, and increased at-risk behaviors by teens or Hispanic men. *Verguenza* (shame) and *pena* (guilt) pressures imposed by the family discourage open discussion about unacceptable behaviors. Acculturation pressures also affect Hispanic teens in the United States, especially in the areas of multiple unwed teen pregnancies, dating, and sexual contacts.

SOCIAL VALUES

All Hispanics share a clearly identifiable bond to Spanish traditions and heritage. To a certain extent, that heritage provides common social values including a characteristic sense of openness toward others (*confianza*), a gregarious and amiable regard for social interaction, and a preference for *personalism*—simple, personal relationships and contacts rather than extreme formality, although awareness of social class status remains.

Hispanics also focus on interpersonal (*simpático*) contacts rather than on the need for isolation or extremely imposed rules of privacy. They reflect an intense awareness of the dignity (*dignidad*) of each human being, regardless of social status, and a strong sense of shared responsibility for the well-being of others. The personal for Hispanics comes before the institutional. People and relationship needs are more important than time, work, and money. Greater importance is placed on the heart and emotions than on the head and intellect; passionate displays of emotion in public are acceptable. Hispanics also possess a strong sense of justice regarding all human, personal, and social needs.

The values of *individualismo* (individualism), *personalismo* (personalism), and *familismo* ("familism") are clearly common among Hispanic cultures. *Individualismo* and *personalism* stress the inner qualities that constitute the individual's uniqueness and personal identity. *Familismo*, on the other hand, places great emphasis on the family's identity as a unit. Simply defined, it is the strong sense of family that Hispanics share, and that, according to the literature (Zayas & Palleja, 1988), pervades all Latin American countries. *Familismo* includes the "extended family's cohesion and willingness to accommodate those in need" (Zayas & Palleja, 1988, p. 261). Adherence to this value demands the active involvement of nuclear and extended family members. *Familismo* serves as an adaptive function, mainly to hold the family together in times of stress. For this reason, the family intervenes first with the individual, leaving professionals as the last resource.

According to Cortes (1991), Hispanics tend to have perceptions of gender and intergenerational relationships that sometimes differ from those of the U. S. mainstream. In traditional settings, men have emphasized the domain of work outside of the home, and women have taken primary responsibility for *la familia* as well as for the preservation and transmission of culture (Cortes, 1991). Largely because of economic demands, however, women have entered every aspect of U. S. working life and have long been at the forefront of Hispanic political and labor struggles.

THE FAMILY

Hispanics hold a strong kinship view of family, often including non-blood-related family members, which is extended beyond family ties to include community members.

Hispanics highly respect the extended family system. The Spanish concept of *respeto* (respect) is so strong that it is more akin to deference to the needs or wishes of others above one's own (Blasini-Perk, 1990). This value has an impact on all levels of relationships and is especially recognized within the family hierarchy. Elders are valued for their knowledge, children for their potential. All family members are recognized for their contribution to the well-being of the entire family. As García-Preto (1982, p. 164) indicated, "In times of stress Puerto Ricans turn to their families for help. Their cultural expectation is that when a family member is experiencing a crisis or has a problem, others in the family are obligated to help, especially those who are in stable positions."

However, a double standard does exist for males, who may be afforded certain privileges or liberties related to independence, social interactions, and rites for reaching manhood. The role of "man of the house" is an important part of the family governing structure; it is assumed by a son or other male relative in the absence of the father figure (head of the family). Many Hispanic families are still intact, with a husband, wife, and children. Consensual marriage is widely accepted, but legal marriages are the norm. Hispanics tend to marry early, and marriages of teenagers (fourteen–eighteen years old) are not uncommon. In some cases, extramarital affairs by the husband are tolerated. In some instances, the offspring from extramarital affairs are recognized by the family and may be acknowledged openly during social interactions (Blasini-Perk, 1990).

Hispanic families are not limited by blood relationships and they can include *hijos de crianza*, sons or daughters by rearing, not by birth. Children and adolescents in need of parenting or economic support frequently are taken in by families. This can be initiated by the *compadres/padrinos*, by aunts or uncles, or by others in the community. This relationship is not often formalized through legal procedures unless it is enforced by outside forces as required for guardianship.

The Hispanic family in the United States is changing, leaving some Hispanics facing what they consider the crumbling of the *familia*. Single-mother households are becoming more prevalent, whether they result from death, separation, abandonment, or personal choice. In these cases, women become the primary breadwinners, sometimes discovering that their roles in the traditional culture conflict with Anglo-American ways.

CHILDREN

Most of the time, children are a welcome part of the Hispanic family and are considered a blessing from God. Older children are taught to be responsible for younger siblings or to help in the caretaking of grandparents or older relatives. Although they are vested with adult responsibilities, children are also exposed to daily interactions with their peers. Children are included in almost every family interaction. The Anglo-American concept of babysitting is not common among Hispanics, since it is expected that all family members participate in the caring of the children.

Rituals of baptism include the *compadrazgo* (coparenting) system. Special friends or other family members are identified as godparents for the child. Each child may have a *madrina* (godmother) and *padrino* (godfather) *de agua o casa* (of holy water or home, prior to the formal church baptism) and/or *de iglesia* (traditional godparents). These ties are very strong, and the child grows up with high regard for both sets of parents.

The unbaptized infant is carefully guarded against evil forces. Amulets may be worn by the child, special blessings may be bestowed on the child by adults who come in contact with him or her, and *Dios te bendiga* (God bless you) is often repeated in an effort to protect the child from *mal de ojo* (the evil eye) associated with jealousies or evil wishes directed at the child. Pierced ears (in girls) and gold jewelry are common for very young infants.

Children and preadolescents are "protected" from sexual information, but are exposed to adult conversations and are therefore aware of human sexuality and sensual messages early in their development. The gender roles are defined to include a belief in *marianismo* (the sanctification of women, much like the Virgin Mary) and the acceptance of *machismo* (the high regard for masculine ability), which includes elements of courage, honor, respect for others, and providing fully for one's family.

Once a young girl reaches puberty and begins her menses, she is no longer considered to be a child; she is a *señorita*. This is a special time because the girl is now viewed as possessing the potential for marriage and childbearing. Her virginity is highly valued and protected by the family, and sexual experimentation is not tolerated.

When a young boy reaches puberty, he is considered *un hombrecito* (a little man) and will experience freedom not allowed for his sisters. Sexual experimentation is tolerated, and many male behaviors such as smoking tobacco and drinking alcohol usually begin at this time.

Grandmothers in a Hispanic family tend to have much input in the rearing of grandchildren, and they often provide the primary parenting support for the mother. Disciplining by adults can range from severe scolding and veiled threats of withholding privileges to spanking. The mother in the Hispanic family is responsible for providing the disciplinary and parenting role. Men are seen as breadwinners and heads of the family, consulted about major decisions and major disciplinary issues.

HEALTH ISSUES

According to De La Rosa (1989), a study conducted by the U.S. Department of Health and Human Services found that Hispanics in the United States were at higher risk than the general population of heart disease, stroke, cirrhosis, and diabetes. It also found that this population has a high infant mortality rate. Torres (1992a) indicated that "illness related to poverty and socioeconomic status such as substance abuse, diabetes mellitus, cancer, infant mortality, and AIDS, are extremely prevalent in Hispanics" (p. 2b). The Hispanic Health and Nutrition Examination Survey, conducted between 1982 and 1984 by the National Center for Health Statistics, found that Hispanics are at higher risk for diabetes mellitus, have a high consumption rate of tobacco usage, and display a high level of cholesterol (Torres, 1992b).

Another study, performed by Andersen et al. (1981), suggests that Hispanics residing in the southern United States have limited access to medical care, are less likely to see a doctor, rarely practice preventive medicine, are generally more dissatisfied with the medical services that they receive, and are more inclined to use informal systems (home medicines) than seek medical assistance.

According former United States Surgeon General Novello (1992), cancer-related deaths are twice as high for Hispanics as for non-Hispanic Whites. For example, cases of cervical cancer are reported to be double for Hispanic women than for non-Hispanic Whites.

Hispanics also present a higher incidence of other diseases such as tuberculosis and measles. According to Novello (1992), the incidence of tuberculosis among Hispanics is four times higher than for non-Hispanic Whites. An increase in the cases of measles among Hispanic youths is becoming a matter of concern. Hispanics are at three times higher risk for diabetes, and it is of greater metabolic severity than in non-Hispanics.

Currently AIDS is one of the areas of major concern among Hispanics. Among men, Hispanics represent approximately 15.7 percent of all AIDS cases, with a full 39 percent of these cases due to drug use by injection (Novello, 1992). Hispanic women, on the other hand, represent 20.5 percent of all AIDS cases among women. Novello (1992) reported that 50 percent of these cases are due to drug use by injection and 39 percent are due to heterosexual contact with an infected partner.

According to Novello (1992), Hispanic children represent approximately 24.5 percent of all AIDS cases in children under the age of thirteen. Of these, 80 percent acquired HIV from their mothers. Novello (1992) also reported that 48.2 percent of these children had a mother who was infected by drug injection, and for 32 percent the mother had a sexual partner who was injected drug user.

Health care decisions in the Hispanic family usually become the responsibility of the "wisest" family member (usually an elder) who is knowledgeable about folk remedies (Blasini-Perk, 1990). Traditional home remedies are used before any medical care is sought. Herbal teas, special foods, periods of resting, and isolation or special massages are all methods used by folk healers or family members. Medical attention is sought, usually by word of mouth, from trusted providers or sanctioned hospitals.

Religious influences, passed on from generation to generation, also play a part in the response to health and illness. Life and death are considered matters controlled by God, and conscious interference with fate is considered to be disrespect of God's will. In fact, disease and epidemics are thought by some to be punishment from God. According to Guendelman (1983), this acceptance or surrender to God's will might be interpreted by health professionals as fatalistic, clashing with the medical model.

Preventative medicine is not a norm for most Hispanics. This behavior may be related to the Hispanic "here and now" orientation, as opposed to a future-planning orientation. Economic limitations or reliance on folk medicine could be explanations as well. According to the Hispanic Health and Nutrition Examination Survey (as cited by Novello, 1992), Hispanics were almost twice as likely as non-Hispanic Whites to indicate that they did not have a regular source of care. Novello also indicated:

> *Twice as many Hispanics as non-Hispanic Whites report using hospital emergency rooms as their primary source of health care.*
> *Data from the 1990 Current Population Survey indicate that as many as 32% of Hispanics lack health insurance. (Novello, 1992, p. 33)*

An Hispanic's active seeking out of health care will greatly depend on the individual's prior experiences with health care delivery systems, level of acculturation, and urban or rural upbringing. The inability of many migrants to speak English is problematic enough, but the complexity of the U.S. health care system is another main source of confusion. Many Hispanics rely on interpreters, who may be friends, family members, or employees of the health care system. Since Hispanics have a strong sense of modesty and privacy about physical exposure and emotional self-disclosure, the interpreting situation can be a cause of stress and anxiety. Also, interpretation is not the same as translation. Translation is a literal word-for-word repetition of the language, which leaves out personal understanding and feelings. Interpretation is a repetition of what has been said, often colored by the interpreter's personal understanding of what is heard (sometimes stated with personal nuances, emphasis, or explanations).

When a family member becomes ill and is hospitalized, it is a concern of the nuclear and extended family and friends. Assistance in child care, housework, emotional support, translating, and moral support are tasks taken on by all significant individuals around the person who has become ill. It is not uncommon to have several family members accompany the patient, often bringing in food and other goods. This is most evident at times of birth and terminal illness or in deathbed situations. Since death is in the hands of God, group and family support is extended to protect the survivors as well. Guendelman (1983) described the role family can play when Mexican-American children are in the hospital:

> *The interdependence among family members is strong and acts as a natural support system in times of stress. It extends to embrace compadres, relatives and godparents who may be closely involved in providing emotional, practical and financial assistance. The network plays a significant role in maintaining family stability. (p. 5)*

In other words, in instances of illness the Hispanic family will band together to provide supports at all levels. In cases of chronic illness, the expectation is that the individual will be permitted to die with dignity. Traditional mourning rituals may last up to one year, with varying degrees of public emotional displays and symbolic dressing (shades of gray, white, and black).

Most Hispanics from rural backgrounds have mixed feelings about hospitals. There is an unspoken fear, which might stem from personal experiences or from stories told by others, that hospitals are places of death. However, most Hispanics have great respect for the health professions. Whether doctor, nurse, social worker, *curandero* (ritual healer), *santiguador* (one who lays hands/massages), or *espiritista* (spiritual guide/healer), each is viewed as an authority based on training or education, or as gifted by God with a special talent. According to Guendelman (1983), some of these health beliefs conflict with Western medicine and tend to create a view of Hispanic clients as naive or unsophisticated. This lack of appreciation of cultural differences creates a barrier built of fear and lack of trust between health provider and client.

One innovative way of meeting individual and community needs is through folk medicine. Folk medicine emerges from the native, African, and European cultures and values that define Latin America. It involves "those health care practices which have been developed mostly out of beliefs and usage over time, and handed down from earlier generations and/or borrowed from other cultures as being in the folk medical system" (Dennis, 1985, p. 14). This practice, which is characterized by the belief that the mind and body have to work together, is based on the Christian belief that God can and does heal and that people with a special gift can heal in His name (Ripley, 1986; Hentges, Shields, & Cantu, 1986). For Hispanics, spirituality is an important component in the utilization of folk medical practices. Because of the diversity of cultures in Latin America, several terms have emerged to classify and define folk healing. As discussed before, the most common ones are *espiritismo* (spiritism) and *curanderismo* (healing). Folk healing serves as an important community support system for many Latin American individuals suffering from mental health problems or life stressors.

Folk psychiatry is practiced in many Latin American countries. Folk psychiatry is defined as "the diagnosis and treatment of behavioral disorders by techniques that are appropriate to a cultural or ethnic group. The techniques might be effective even though they are not based on scientific procedures" (Goldenson, 1984, p. 329). In Rio-Sao Paulo, Brazil, for example; there are more than seventy-five folk psychiatric hospitals that integrate medical and folk techniques (Hohmann et al., 1990). The practitioners of folk medicine usually have their practice in the same community in which they live. Folk medicine practitioners are usually older people who traditionally inspire respect. They speak the common-day language and do not charge exorbitant fees. Hohmann and colleagues (1990) have concluded that the establishment of these institutions came as a result of trying to complement a deficient psychiatric system that is not meeting the needs of the community.

WOMEN AND HEALTH CARE ISSUES

Hispanic women's health care has been negatively affected by lack of knowledge about reproduction, human sexuality, and body image. Open discussion of sex-related concerns is generally taboo. Infertility is most commonly perceived as a woman's problem, and fertility methods are relatively unknown for Hispanics. Most childless couples adopt or continue to be providers for other family members' children or younger siblings.

Pregnancy is welcomed in the Hispanic culture. Once pregnant, an Hispanic woman is well cared for by all around her (Blasini-Perk, 1990). The woman is viewed as a vessel carrying life. If the family has its way, the woman is not permitted to smoke, drink alcohol, or become overly tired or hungry. In a large number of cases prenatal care registration and compliance are absent during pregnancy, mostly because the other women in the family share their expertise and care for the pregnant women.

Childbirth is often approached with fear and misinformation, given the taboos associated with sexuality. Once the infant arrives, much care and special treatment are bestowed on the woman and the immediate family. Hispanic men, unless acculturated to do so, rarely participate in the labor and birth experience. Breastfeeding is common, and circumcision is practiced by choice based on family preference. Circumcision is not openly discussed or celebrated. Much attention is given to caring for the infant's umbilical cord. Sometimes a clean coin is belted on the healing cord to flatten it or to prevent an umbilical hernia. The caretaker also worries about and provides protection for the infant's anterior fontanelle. Symptoms such as diarrhea, vomiting, restlessness, and irritability are all associated with *caida de mollera* (sunken fontanelle) (Blasini-Perk, 1990). Feeding and child care are carefully monitored. Providing food and being good parents are highly valued by Hispanics.

Maternal postpartum care is affected by economics, time constraints, economic resources, and other competing life forces. The return to sexual activities is important and quick for most couples. Closely spaced pregnancies are not uncommon. Birth control arrangements are usually left up to the woman's choice. Oral contraceptives and the rhythm method are the most common methods of birth control. Condoms are often associated with clandestine sex and are not generally associated with marital sexual contacts. Choices of partial or total hysterectomy and tubal ligation also depend on exposure to medical care providers and economic access to services.

GLOSSARY

Aztecas   Aztecs. Civilization of the native Indians from Mexico, who had a very advanced civilization prior to the Spaniard conquest.

Bautismo de agua o casa   Baptism of holy water. An informal ceremony usually celebrated in the parents' home. Parents, godparents, and in some instances family members gather to Christianize the child by pouring holy water on the child's head and praying. The belief is that in case of sudden death the child will die a Christian.

Bautismo de iglesia   Traditional church baptism. An official church ceremony, it is considered an important event in the child's life and is celebrated by family members and community at large.

Caida de mollera   Sunken fontanelle. An important milestone in the child's life. Determines the healthy and fast growth of the child.

Campesino   Farmer; peasant; countryman. Sometimes used as a target for jokes because of naiveté, but very well regarded and respected because of dedication to and love of the country.

Compadrazgo   Inherited or adopted kinship; coparenting. A spiritual affinity between the godfather and the parents of the child. This relationship extends to the point of inclusion of godparents in the child's family.

Compadre   Coparent. It refers to the relationship between the parents of the child and the godparent.

Confianza   Confidence; trust. A social value that is characterized by the sense of openness and friendliness toward others.

Curandero Healer; ritual healer; medicine man. An individual who heals the body, the mind, and the spirit through herbs and natural remedies.

Dios te bendiga God bless you. A special blessing usually used to denote good wishes. It is commonly used when an adult greets a child, in an effort to protect the child from the "evil eye."

Dignidad Dignity. Awareness of the dignity of each human being, regardless of social status.

Espiritismo Spiritualism; spiritism. Practiced among certain groups, it is the result of a combination of African rituals intertwined with saints of the Catholic Church. It is used for the healing of the body, the mind, and the spirit.

Espiritista Spiritual guide; spiritual healer. An individual who practices healing through spiritualism.

Familismo "Familism." A value that places great emphasis on the family's personal identity as a unit. This value implies an active involvement of the nuclear and extended family, and it is usually expanded to include non-blood-related family members.

Familia Family. A social structure that is extended beyond family ties. Family is not limited to nuclear and extended relationships. It usually expands to include non-blood-related family members.

Hijo/hija de crianza Son/daughter by rearing, not by birth. A child usually taken in by the family for parenting or economic support. The relationship is usually not formalized by legal procedures, but more by social support.

Hombrecito Little man. A term used to refer to a young boy once he reaches puberty or exhibits characteristics associated with male roles.

Individualismo Individualism. A value that stresses the individual's inner qualities that make him or her unique.

Jíbaro Farmer; peasant; countryman. A concept used in Puerto Rico to define individuals who live in rural areas.

Madrina Godmother. A female who participates in the child's formal and/or informal baptism and/or confirmation ceremony and makes a commitment to help raise the child (financially and spiritually).

Mal de ojo Evil eye. A curse associated with jealousy. It can be targeted toward any person or material possession.

Machismo High regard for masculine ability. Important in the definition of roles, especially among family. Implies that men have to take charge, be strong, angry, rough, et cetera.

Marianismo Marianism. The sanctification of women. Women are viewed and expected to act with the same sanctity that the Virgin Mary is viewed with by the Catholic Church. Based on this, woman are attributed characteristics such as purity, devotion, gentleness, etc.

Marielito The second wave of Cuban immigrants, who came through the Port of Mariel in the late 1970s.

Mestizo Children born of native Indians and the Spaniards who came to conquer.

Mulato Mulatto. The children born of African slaves and the Spaniards who came to conquer or those of native Indians and African slaves.

Orgullo Pride. A value cherished by Hispanics; puts a lot of pride in the sense of being.

Padrino Godfather. A male who participates in the child's formal and/or informal baptism and/or confirmation ceremony and makes a commitment to help raise the child (financially and spiritually).

Padrinos Godparents. Those who participate in the child's formal and/or informal baptism and/or confirmation ceremony and make a commitment to help raise the child (financially and spiritually).

Pena Guilt. Pressures by the family that discourage the discussion of certain topics such as sex, drugs, teen pregnancy, et cetera.

Personalismo Personalism. A value cherished by Hispanics. A gregarious and amiable regard for social interaction, personal relationship, and contacts rather than extreme formality, although there is a conscious awareness of social class status.

Pueblo Town. Each town has unique characteristics and customs. The term can be used also to define a common cultural sentiment that embraces a whole country.

Raza Race, ethnicity. A concept that establishes that a mixing of races and ideologies occurred, producing what today are known as Hispanics/Latinos. Basically, it refers to the fact that a collection of influences from many cultures led to the personalized beliefs and values that constitute what the Hispanic/Latino is today.

Respeto Respect. A value highly regarded by Hispanics. It is akin to the deference to the needs or wishes of others rather than those of oneself.

Santería Healing through the saints. A religious practice among certain groups resulting from a combination of African rituals intertwined with the saints of the Catholic Church. It is used for the healing of the body, the mind, and the spirit.

Santiguador Healer. An individual who uses massages, herbs, and prayer to heal.

Señorita Young woman. This term is used to refer to girls when they reach puberty. Specifically, it is used to indicate that the young woman has already menstruated and should no longer be considered a child.

Simpático Congenial, pleasant, nice, agreeable. Interpersonal contacts are valued more than the need for isolation and extreme imposed rules of privacy.

Spanglish Mixture of Spanish and English languages used by a large number of Hispanics/Latinos in day-to-day speech.

Verguenza Shame, disgrace. Pressures that, together with guilt, the family imposes to discourage the discussion of certain topics such as sex, drugs, teen pregnancy, et cetera.

REFERENCES

Andersen, R. et al. (1981). Access to medical care among Hispanic population of the southern United States. *Journal of Health and Social Behavior, 22*, 78–79.

Bash, H. (1981). *Sociology, race, and ethnicity.* New York: Gordon and Breach.

Blasini-Perk, Z. (1990). *Hispanics.* Unpublished manuscript.

Cortes, C. E. (1991). Latinos/Hispanics. In *A teacher's guide to multicultural perspectives in social studies.* Boston: Houghton-Mifflin.

De La Rosa, M. (1989, May). Health care needs of Hispanic Americans and the responsiveness of the health care system. *Health Care and Social Work, 14*(2), 104–113.

Dennis, R. (1985). Health beliefs and practices of ethnic and religious groups. In *Removing cultural and ethnic barriers to health care* (pp. 12–28). Based on proceedings of a national conference, Chapel Hill, NC.

Dillard, J. M. (1985). *Multicultural counseling: Toward ethnic and cultural relevance in human encounters.* Chicago: Nelson-Hall.

Falicov, C. (1982). Mexican families. In M. McGoldrick & J. Giordano (Eds.), *Ethnicity and family therapy* (pp. 135–155). New York: Guildford.

García-Preto, N. (1982). Puerto Rican families. In M. McGoldrick & J. Giordano (Eds.), *Ethnicity and family therapy* (pp. 164–186). New York: Guildford.

Goldenson, R. (Ed.). (1984). *Longman dictionary of psychology and psychiatry.* New York: Longman.

Guendelman, S. (1983). Developing responsiveness to the health needs of Hispanic children and families. *Social Work in Health Care, 8*(4), 1–13.

Hentges, K., Shields, C., & Cantu, C. (1986). Folk medicine and medical practice. *Texas Medicine, 82*(10), 27–29.

Hohmann, A. et al. (1990). Spiritism in Puerto Rico: Results of an island-wide community study. *British Journal of Psychiatry, 156,* 328–335.

Marín, G., & Marín, B. (1991). *Research with Hispanic populations.* Newbury, CA: Sage.

Novello, A. C. (1992). *Hispanics.* Unpublished manuscript. The Ohio State University, College of Medicine.

Pérez-Stable, E. J. (1987). *Issues in Latin American care.* Newbury, CA: Sage.

Ripley, G. (1986). Mexican-American folk remedies: Their place in health care. *Texas Medicine, 82*(11), 41–44.

Torres. R. (1992a). Need for screening for CV risks, family history: Results of the Adolescent Cardiovascular Examination Survey Among Hispanics (ACES). *The Vanguard, 1*(2), 21–13.

Torres, R. (1992b). *Hypertension in Hispanics.* Handout.

U.S. Bureau of the Census. (1991). *The Hispanic population in the United States: March 1991.* (Current Population Reports, Series P-20, No. 455). Washington, DC: U. S. Government Printing Office.

Zayas, L., & Palleja, J. (1988). Puerto Rican familism: Considerations for family therapy. *Family Relations, 37*(3), 260–264.

SUGGESTED READINGS

Bernal, G. (1982). Cuban families. In M. McGoldrick & J. Giordano (Eds.), *Ethnicity and family therapy* (pp. 187–207). New York: Guildford.

Comas-Diaz, L., & Griffith, E. (1988). *Clinical guidelines in cross cultural mental health.* New York: Wiley.

Cooper, E. J. (1977). Group and the Hispanic prenatal patient. *American Journal of Orthopsychiatry, 47*(4), 689–700.

De Anda, D. (1984). Informal support networks of Hispanic mothers: A comparison across age groups. *Journal of Social Service Research, 7*(3), 89–105.

Delgado, M., & Humm-Delgado, D. (1982). Natural support systems: Source of strength in Hispanic communities. *Social Work, 27*(1), 83–89.

Estrada, L. F. (1985). The dynamics of Hispanic populations: A description and comparison. *Social Thought, 11*(3), 23–29.

Fabrega, H. (1990). Hispanic mental health research: A case cultural psychiatry. *Hispanic Journal of Behavioral Sciences, 12*(4), 339–365.

Falicov, C. J. (1982). Mexican families. In M. McGoldrick & J. Giordano (Eds.), *Ethnicity and family therapy* (pp. 134–163). New York: Guildford.

Gaviria, M., & Stern, G. (1980). Problems in designing and implementing culturally relevant mental health services for Latinos in the United States. *Social Science Medicine, 148*, 65–71.

Guendelman, S. (1985). At risk: Health needs of Hispanic children. *Social Work in Health Care, 10*(3), 183–190.

Le-Vince, E., & Franco, J. N. (1981). A reassessment of self-disclosure patterns among Anglo Americans and Hispanics. *Social Work, 28*(6), 522–524.

Markides, K. S. (1983). Mortality among minority populations: A review of recent patterns and trends. *Public Health Reports, 98*(3), 252–260.

Queralt, M. (1984). Understanding Cuban immigrants: A cultural perspective. *Social Work, 29*(2), 115–121.

Queiro-Tajalli, I. (1989). Hispanic women's perception and use of prenatal health care services. *Affilia: Journal of Women and Social Work, 4*(2), 60–72.

Slesinger, D. P., & Cautley, E. (1981). Medical utilization patterns of Hispanic migrant farm workers in Wisconsin. *Public Health Reports, 96*(3), 255–263.

► # 8

Culturally Relevant Care: The Orthodox Jewish Client

DARYLE SPERO

Health care providers encounter Jewish patients in almost every city throughout the United States and Canada. In most cases, Jewish patients do not differ from other patients. However, health care providers need to be aware of particular cultural considerations that can affect how they deal with Jewish clients. While sometimes it is difficult for the caregiver to differentiate between religious needs and personal needs, or even personality quirks, demanding behavior is definitely not meant to be a part of any Jewish practice. The information in this chapter, which focuses on maternity patients, should help the caregiver understand which behaviors have a religious basis and which do not.

BACKGROUND

Jewish religious practice is based on laws originating in the Old Testament. The laws were explained more fully in the Talmud (a rabbinic text dating from the second through fifth centuries) and finally codified in the *Shulchan Aruch* (Code of Jewish Law) in the fifteenth century. These laws delineate the conduct of the Jew from morning until night, from birth until death. While it can be confusing and difficult to anticipate all of the nuances of the

Jewish client's life, by showing sensitivity and awareness and asking the patient for clarification the caregiver can help the patient feel more at ease and the patient, in turn, will help the caregiver by identifying her needs. To traditional Jews, the Code of Jewish Law is very important. Violating the laws is distressing, especially in times of crisis such as hospitalization. The caregiver, by helping the patient adhere to these laws, can enhance her recovery from and her perception of delivery.

The following quote from the report of a labor and delivery nurse (Lutwak, Ney, & White, 1988) illustrates the need for understanding a client's cultural context:

> *I have some real concerns about this couple. Although they attended childbirth preparation classes, the father wasn't physically supportive of his wife. Oh, he was verbally supportive, but he wouldn't touch her at all—no hand-holding or back-rubbing! Any time we checked his wife or gave her physical care, he left the room and didn't return until we called him back. He refused to enter the delivery room, too. He stayed in the labor room, reading! In the recovery room he kept his distance. None of the hugging and kissing we usually see after the birth. They both say they're happy with the baby and yet they won't call her by name. (p. 45)*

It is easy to misinterpret culturally induced behaviors. Rather than suspecting this couple of having marital discord or, perhaps, a potential attachment problem, the caregiver needs to recognize that this Orthodox couple is observing the religious laws of *Tzniut* (modesty), *Niddah* (family purity), and Orthodox baby-naming practices.

To understand the differences among their Jewish clients, caregivers need to be familiar with the three branches of Judaism: Orthodox, Conservative, and Reform.

- The *Orthodox* Jewish patient adheres closely to the Talmudic laws and is guided by a strict interpretation of them. Caregivers are more likely to encounter the various behaviors described in this chapter in Orthodox Jewish patients. Even among Orthodox patients, however, there are differences. While the *law* tends to be fixed, the *customs* may lead to a variety of interpretations. Therefore, among Orthodox Jewish patients, there are differences in observance depending on their individual backgrounds and how they interpret the customs. For example, one sect of Orthodox Jews, known as *Hasidim*, follow the dictates of a particular rabbi, strictly obeying the laws and customs including a dress code that is much like that of the Amish.

- The *Conservative* Jewish patient takes a moderate approach to these laws and customs, and health providers are not likely to encounter many of the behaviors described in this chapter with this patient.
- The *Reform* Jewish patient tends to identify more with Jewish culture than with Jewish laws and customs. It is unlikely that caregivers will observe the behaviors described here in encounters with Reform Jewish patients.

Further differences may be encountered in dealing with Jewish immigrants from Russia, Iran, or Israel who are now in the United States. In working with Jewish immigrants, caregivers must be aware of differences in cultural backgrounds as well.

Caregivers may also find that a patient has changed during her own life; she may have once been Orthodox and is now Reform. A Reform patient might be considering a *Brit* (religious circumcision) or following traditional Jewish naming practices, and she may wish to discuss these with the caregiver. An Orthodox patient may choose not to discuss anything, but within the framework of the hospital the caregiver should be aware of the Jewish practices and work with the patient to make her comfortable.

Reform Judaism, which began in Germany in the early nineteenth century, sought to eradicate the differences between Jewish practice and the practice of the majority population. By the mid-nineteenth century, most Jews in the United States were Reform. However, the mass immigration of Orthodox Jews from Eastern Europe in the later nineteenth century changed these demographics, and the two groups—one adhering strictly to the old ways and the other rejecting the old ways completely—clashed.

One result of this clash was the Conservative movement, which included both Reform Jews who wanted more traditional practice and Orthodox Jews who wanted less. The Conservative movement, a strictly American phenomenon, even today struggles for identity. There are Conservative Jews who are committed to virtually all Orthodox practices and others who can hardly be differentiated from Reform Jews. After World War II, the large influx into the United States of European Orthodox Jews who survived the Holocaust was instrumental in establishing networks of Jewish day schools. This has led to a renaissance of Orthodox Jewish practice and the increasing numbers of "born again" Jews who follow many of the practices described in this chapter.

ORTHODOX JEWISH BEHAVIORS

Laws of Tzniut: Modesty and Dress

Tzniut refers to the laws of modesty that maintain the dignity of the human body. Orthodox women usually wear clothing that covers both elbows and knees. Some also keep their hair covered at all times, either with a wig or a scarf or beret. In labor and delivery, an Orthodox patient may be offered a surgical head covering instead. The patient will also feel more comfortable with a second hospital gown to cover her back. Whether or not she keeps her hair covered, personal modesty is an important issue to the woman and her husband.

In this context, the husband's behavior may vary depending on the couple's level of observance. Some men leave the room during examinations and procedures, while others choose to stay in the room, but not watch. The husband does not watch out of respect for the dignity of his wife. Extra draping for the wife during examinations and delivery can help make the husband feel more comfortable and therefore better able to support his wife during labor and delivery. Some husbands remain for the birth itself, while others leave the room and sit outside, saying special prayers from the book of Psalms for the safe delivery of mother and baby.

Niddah: Laws of Separation Between Husband and Wife

The *Niddah* laws require that husband and wife separate whenever there is uterine bleeding. This separation refers to physical touching and intimacy. Every month, from the start of the woman's menstrual period until seven days after the bleeding has stopped, the couple refrains from sexual relations. This causes the couple to develop and draw upon other, nonphysical aspects of their relationship. At the end of the seven-day period, the woman immerses herself in a special ritual bath called a *mikveh* and makes a special blessing. At this time the couple can resume marital relations. The result of this separation is a physical and spiritual renewal of the sexual relationship. These laws, which are also referred to as the "laws of family purity," are a profoundly spiritual and religious institution that serves to keep the marital relationship fresh and special.

These laws also apply to the bleeding that occurs during labor and delivery. Couples vary in their observance of this aspect of the laws of *Niddah*. Some rabbis interpret the laws of *Niddah* to begin with the onset of contractions, others at the appearance of bloody show, at the rupture of membranes, at full dilation, or when the woman can no longer walk during contractions. Caregivers should be sensitive to this, as the patient may need more hands-on support from the nurse. The father can still be encouraged to participate in nonphysical moral support. In many cases the father will remain in the birthing room during delivery, maintaining his position at the mother's head but observing carefully the laws of both *Tzniut* and *Niddah* by not touching his wife or by standing at her head and not watching the birth of the baby. In other cases the father will prefer to leave the room and pray instead. A caregiver may suggest that an Orthodox couple use a *doula* (female support person) during the birthing process.

The laws of *Niddah* forbid premarital sex. Therefore, when a couple decides to marry, the engagement period is kept short. These laws keep the problem of adolescent pregnancy to a minimum among Orthodox Jews. Social stigma is attached to any pregnancy out of wedlock, and such pregnancies are kept as quiet as possible.

Brit Milah (or Bris) (The Covenant of Circumcision) and Naming the Baby

A *brit*, or *bris*, is a covenant with God. The *Brit Milah*, which was a covenant between God and Abraham, is one of the most important commandments in the Torah. Historically, the *Brit Milah* is considered to have been one of the first commandments given, preceding even the Ten Commandments given at Mount Sinai. The Torah explicitly states that the *Brit Milah* must take place on the eighth day of a baby boy's life. It cannot be performed before the eighth day, but it may be postponed if the baby is ill, jaundiced, or premature. In Jewish law the "day" starts at the nightfall of the preceding day.

The *Brit Milah* must be performed by a trained, certified *mohel* (the Hebrew name for the man performing the circumcision and sometimes pronounced "moil"), and it can take place in the home, the synagogue, or any other place chosen by the family. This joyous celebration for the Jewish family can range from a small family gathering to a large reception. The *Brit Milah* itself, as performed by the *mohel*, is a valid surgical procedure, performed under conditions of sterility by a well-trained practitioner. However, the bris ceremony transforms the "cold" surgical circumcision into a meaningful religious experience, one of the most significant in the life of a Jew. There are many beautiful ceremonies associated with the *Brit Milah*. Godparents (the *kvattern*) are chosen, and they will hand the baby to the *sandek*, who holds the baby during the *Brit Milah*. This is a great honor for those chosen by the parents. There is also a chair set aside for the prophet Elijah, who is said to attend every bris. Although the mother and baby have been discharged well before the *Brit Milah*, the arrangements may cause some added stress to the newly postpartum mother in the hospital, because planning a *Brit Milah* is like planning a large party. Grandparents often take over much of the planning to relieve the new parents of this responsibility. Care must be taken by the hospital staff to ensure that a routine hospital circumcision is not performed.

A problem may occur in the case of a mixed marriage in which the mother is not Jewish and has not undergone an acceptable conversion. According to Jewish law, the religion of the child follows that of the mother; therefore, in this situation, the child is not considered Jewish even though the father is Jewish. Some *mohels* are reluctant to perform a *Brit Milah* in this situation. Others will perform the bris with some changes in the ceremony.

The *mohel* usually visits the home the day after the *Brit Milah* to check on the baby. He will also instruct the mother on the proper care of the baby after the circumcision. However, it is appropriate for the postpartum nurse to give postcircumcision instructions before the mother and baby go home, just as she would to any other mother of a male infant.

The baby boy is officially named during the bris ceremony. In fact, many Orthodox Jews will not disclose the name of the baby before the bris, which means that they may have to fill out the birth certificate later. Baby girls are officially named by the father during a reading of the Torah in the synagogue, usually within the first week after birth. Babies (male or female) are often given both Hebrew names and English secular names. The Hebrew name (and sometimes even the secular name) may be in honor of a deceased relative or have another significant meaning, such as a relationship with a particular holiday. Sephardic Jews, those who descend from Jews who lived in countries bordering the Mediterranean Sea, often name their children after a living relative. The Hebrew name is used in many religious ceremonies in the life of a Jew. Many families will dedicate a *kiddush*, a party named after the blessing said on a cup of wine at the beginning of the celebration after synagogue services on a Sabbath, in honor of the naming of the baby girl. No time limit need be observed with reference to the *kiddush*.

In addition to the *Brit Milah*, there are other birth practices observed by Orthodox Jews that result in gatherings of family and friends. These include *Sholom Zachor*, a welcoming of the baby boy, held in the family's home the first Friday night after birth, and *Pidyon Haben*, a ceremonial Redemption of the First Born, which occurs if the firstborn child is male.

There are several sects of Jews with a more mystical bent (Hasidic Jews or Sephardic Jews) who may want to put prayer cards or amulets inside the baby's crib to protect him until after the bris. This custom is meant to ward off the "evil eye." Caregivers should not question these practices, but should work with the family to keep them comfortable and to keep the baby safe.

Kashrut: Laws Pertaining to Food

Orthodox patients require "kosher" food—that is, food prepared in a kosher kitchen. Kosher practice excludes certain types of food (e.g., pork products), as well as even acceptable foods that have not been prepared in the religiously prescribed manner. It is not permitted to mix meat and dairy products, and separate cooking and eating utensils must be used for each. Once she has eaten meat, the patient must wait three to six hours (depending on her custom) before she can eat dairy foods again. Between dairy and meat she can wait a much shorter time. This must be understood in trying to meet the added milk requirements needed for breast-feeding. Some food products contain neither diary nor meat ingredients. These are called *pareve* and can be eaten with dairy or meat at the same meal. Fresh fruits and vegetables are always permitted. Before eating bread, patients may want to perform a ritual washing of the hands together with a blessing.

Some hospitals in urban centers may have a kosher kitchen, supervised by a rabbi (called a *mashgiach*), which prepares regular patient meals and snacks for patients requesting kosher food. All special diets can be obtained kosher as well. Kosher guest trays can be ordered for the patient's family members, and kosher food is available in a designated area of the cafeteria for staff and visitors who eat kosher. The kosher kitchen might be a small section of the main hospital kitchen. In hospitals without a kosher kitchen, kosher frozen dinners are kept available. These are often prepared by local kosher caterers and need only be heated or microwaved. Under normal circumstances however, food should not be prepared or heated on the Sabbath.

If no kosher meals are available, the patient will need to have food brought in. She may want to keep it wrapped and labeled in the unit refrigerator. The wrapping assures her that it was not mixed with nonkosher food in the refrigerator. She may request use of the microwave if there is one available. If the patient is providing her own food, a dietitian may help her or her family determine what would best meet her nutritional needs.

Baby formulas, like other general food products, need to be certified kosher, because some formulas may contain animal products. Most kosher products have a symbol certifying that they are kosher somewhere on their label. The most common of these symbols is the Ⓤ (a letter O with a smaller U imbedded inside it) or Ⓚ (a letter O with a smaller K imbedded inside it).

The kosher symbol is given to a product by a rabbinical authority when the manufacture of the product is under rabbinical supervision. In fact, kosher food can be prepared in any kitchen (hospital, hotel, factory) where rabbinical supervision is available.

The Sabbath (or Shabbos) and Holiday Laws

Sabbath begins at twenty minutes before sundown on Friday afternoon and continues until about forty minutes after sunset on Saturday. The Sabbath is considered a day of rest. The patient is not permitted to do many things that non-Jews take for granted. The following examples illustrate how Jewish law defines *work*, which is prohibited on a day of rest.

- A patient cannot use electricity or the telephone, which means she will be unable to use the lights, the television, and more important, the nurse's call button and the electric bed. If she is on an intravenous medication requiring a pump, she will not want to disconnect it to get up from the bed to go to the bathroom. She will also not want to operate a PCA (patient-controlled analgesia) pump after a cesarean birth, since she will not be able to push the button to dose herself. More frequent rounds by the nurse may be indicated to anticipate the patient's needs on the Sabbath and holidays. Some patients are embarrassed to explain this or ask for help with these seemingly demanding requests. In the case of an emergency, the patient is not only permitted, she is commanded by Jewish law, to do whatever is necessary to handle the emergency.
- Tearing of paper is prohibited on the Sabbath. Therefore, if sanitary pads are individually wrapped, the patient will want to tear them open before the Sabbath begins. She may also wish to tear toilet paper for the Sabbath, which she will keep in a stack on a bathroom shelf.
- The patient will not travel by car on the Sabbath. In an emergency, such as labor, travel is permitted, so Orthodox patients arrive at the hospital and deliver on the Sabbath. On the other hand, the patient cannot be discharged on the Sabbath because there is no longer an emergency.
- The patient cannot write on the Sabbath, so she cannot fill out forms or menus.
- The patient will want to light Sabbath candles on Friday night or on the eve of a holiday. Some medical centers provide an electric cande-

labrum for this purpose. This avoids the problem of an open flame in the hospital and is accepted by the rabbinical authorities.

- There are additional considerations that pertain to the spouse and other family members. If the patient delivers on the Sabbath, while her spouse was able to bring her to the hospital, he will not be able to drive home, use an elevator or telephone, sign papers, or handle money until the Sabbath ends. If the distances involved are not unreasonable, he may walk home after he has assured himself that all is well with his wife and their newborn. On the other hand, he may need to stay until the end of the Sabbath. If kosher food is available, a guest tray would be appreciated, to be paid for after the Sabbath. Some hospitals provide cots and a room for fathers to stay over until the end of the Sabbath.
- The patient will probably not have telephone calls or visitors on the Sabbath unless the hospital is within walking distance or someone has stayed over at the hospital. This lack of visitors should not be interpreted as an indication of poor family support.

Many of the Jewish holidays (Passover, Pentecost, Tabernacles, Rosh Hashana, and Yom Kippur) have the same basic set of laws and customs as the Sabbath. These holidays also begin at sundown the evening before. These holidays (except for Yom Kippur) last for two days, which can further complicate matters. Sometimes a two-day holiday may lead directly into the Sabbath, giving rise to three days of restricted behavior. With short maternity stays, this can complicate the discharge time. The patient may need to be discharged from the unit but remain as a boarder until the holiday or Sabbath is over. Yom Kippur is a day of fasting, abstaining from all food and drink. However, a laboring or newly delivered mother is exempt from fasting.

The Passover holiday, which occurs in the spring (usually April), has additional food restrictions. Any food products using flour must be made from a specially prepared flour. In addition, any eating utensils that might have come in contact with products made from regular flour are prohibited during Passover. Because of this, all food used during Passover must be certified as "kosher for Passover." Passover is the most complicated time for the person observing kosher laws. For example, during this holiday, even coffee, which is rarely a problem, cannot be used unless prepared in a "kosher for Passover" coffee maker.

Caregivers who frequently encounter Jewish patients may find a calendar helpful. A Jewish calendar can be obtained from any local Jewish or Hebrew bookstore or from the local Bureau of Jewish Education, as can reference books explaining these laws and customs.

Birth Control, Abortion, and Sterilization

According to the strict interpretation of Jewish law, birth control is not generally permitted unless the mother's physical or psychological health is at risk and a rabbi's counsel has been sought. Practice varies among young couples according to their level of observance. Conservative and Reform Jews are more likely to practice birth control, and even Orthodox Jewish couples may use natural family planning or even a diaphragm, birth control pills, or an IUD, as female methods are preferred.

The postpartum nurse should show sensitivity in her attempts to discuss contraception before discharging her patient. While breastfeeding is encouraged for its own sake, some Orthodox couples will consider breastfeeding for one to two years, hoping this will also work as a contraceptive.

To "be fruitful and multiply" is considered one of the most important commandments. Having children is considered a blessing and the primary means of promoting the continuity of the Jewish people. The Jewish family is obligated to have at least two children—a boy and a girl—educate them, help them develop good moral character, and eventually facilitate their marriages. Infertility is always a serious problem for the Jewish couple, and, among the strictly Orthodox, it can even lead to divorce. Couples will go to great lengths to correct infertility; however, not all methods (such as donor sperm) are rabbinically acceptable to the strictly Orthodox. A couple facing infertility problems will need to work closely with both a rabbi and an infertility specialist.

Adoption is an acceptable option for Jewish families, but great care is taken to ascertain the background and religion of the child. If the child is not Jewish by birth, adoption is still permitted, but a conversion will be required when the child is older.

Sterilization and abortion are not permitted in the Jewish religion unless the mother is in a life-threatening situation. In Jewish law the mother comes first until the baby is born; then both are considered equally important. Each individual case can be decided by a rabbi after consulting with medical professionals. As is the case with birth control, Reform or Conservative Jews are less likely to follow the dictates of the strictly Orthodox. It is difficult to make assumptions, however. In times of great stress, the couple may adopt a more religious response, although the opposite behavior can occur as well.

Prenatal Testing and Stillbirth

Prenatal testing is not chosen by many Orthodox patients since abortion would not be permitted unless the mother's health or safety were at risk.

Since the testing process itself is permitted, some couples still choose to have the testing as a means of preparing themselves for a suspected problem such as Tay Sachs disease, a congenital disorder that occurs mostly in Jewish families of East European descent. The disease, characterized by weakness beginning at six months of age, progressive mental and motor deterioration, blindness, paralysis, and dementia and seizures, results in death, usually by three years of age. Estimates indicate that one in thirty European Jews may be carriers of this trait. If both parents are carriers, there is a one in four chance that the couple will have a baby with this disease.

Prenatal screening (a blood test) can determine whether either parent is a carrier. Intrauterine diagnosis is done by amniocentesis. Screening for a Jewish couple is recommended before marriage, and many cities have screening programs for young adults of marriageable age. Once a woman is pregnant, the decision regarding whether to have amniocentesis is a controversial one among the Orthodox. There is disagreement among rabbinic scholars as to whether abortion would be permitted in case of a Tay Sachs baby. While abortion is usually prohibited, if the mother's physical or mental health will be seriously affected, an abortion is permitted. The decision is made for each case based on previous history and circumstances.

When a baby is born alive with serious birth defects or anomalies, the Orthodox family may wish to keep the defects a secret, seeming to distance themselves. This requires sensitivity and understanding on the part of the caregiver. The parents will often ask their rabbi to manage the situation, and he will contact various national Jewish support groups who keep rosters of the top medical specialists in every field. The rabbi will consult with one of these specialists and then work with local physicians in helping the parents make decisions (e.g., regarding resuscitation). Parents may seem aggressive in treatment. They feel that life, no matter how short, has value. In fact, euthanasia in any form is prohibited in Judaism. As was mentioned earlier, while Reform or Conservative Jews are less likely to follow the dictates of the strictly Orthodox, in times of great stress the couple may adopt a more religious response.

It is often difficult for a neonatal intensive care staff to understand how a family can allow a rabbi to make medical life-or-death decisions for their infant. It should be understood that in all likelihood the local rabbi is in contact with medical-rabbinic professionals who help with the decision making and are closely involved with the medical staff. Caregivers in this situation should try to support the family in the decisions that they finally make even if they are contrary to the caregiver's beliefs. There will be no funeral or *shiva* (formal seven-day mourning period) for an infant born with anomalies incompatible with life. A burial will take place in any case.

While Judaism teaches the immortality of the soul and the existence of an afterlife, every moment of life is considered precious and the extension of life, however brief, worthwhile. Jews seek out the best medical care available in every situation and rarely get involved in nontraditional healing such as folk remedies.

Family Practices

The Jewish family embraces a broad spectrum of values that have important implications for parenting. Many of these values are visible in all segments of the Jewish community and cross all social and economic boundaries. For example:

- In the Jewish family there is a strong emphasis on rituals that families do together. The Shabbat dinner, the Passover seder, and the lighting of Chanukah lights are examples of family-based rituals that even Reform Jewish families observe.
- The extended family is very important in Judaism. "Honor thy father and mother" is much emphasized, and it includes grandparents as well. Uncles, aunts, brothers, and sisters are all interested and involved, and the caregiver may find many people looking over his or her shoulder in the hospital.
- Education, both religious and secular, is a religious obligation and is taken very seriously by Jewish families. Both parents play an active role in this, and in particular at many of the family celebrations that are the framework for family-based rituals the father will teach something from the tradition. This is called a *D'Var Torah*. The Passover seder, in fact, emphasizes this.
- Jews are encouraged to have large families, and support is provided for such families.
- In every community of Jews, the community itself becomes an extended family. Newcomers to the Jewish community are welcomed and invited for Sabbath meals. Members of the community, especially among the Orthodox, take responsibility for meals for the family when the mother and baby first return home. Groups of visitors come to the hospital to visit any Jewish patient there. In situations where either the mother or the child is seriously ill, the community will rally around the family, even in the hospital, with prayers and well wishing as well as practical help.

Childbirth Classes

Some Orthodox couples may attend regular Lamaze classes, but they may or may not participate in the hands-on coaching that the classes encourage. Caregivers must accept and work with this fact.

Some couples may request a private Lamaze class, as they would feel more comfortable discussing intimate subjects on a one-to-one basis. The private class is very effective for this population. It enables the father to obtain needed information in a comfortable setting. Otherwise, he might choose not to participate at all. These couples would also find the group exercises unacceptable in a mixed setting.

In larger communities, ultra-Orthodox Jews may request women-only classes. Those attending can be encouraged to bring female coaches with them. This affects how the instructor teaches the coach's role, in that often the nurse has to assume some of the coach's hands-on role during labor and delivery.

The couple will not want to share the baby's name in advance. There will be no baby showers, as gifts are not given in advance, and in some cases no baby items will be brought into the house until the baby is born. This couple may not have baby clothes to bring to an infant care class, so an instructor needs to work with the couple and not make them uncomfortable or embarrass them.

CONCLUSION

The practices of Orthodox Jewish women that a caregiver is likely to encounter have been highlighted to orient caregivers to the special needs of this cultural group. For fuller understanding and background, a caregiver may wish to explore Judaism in depth to fully appreciate its observances and practices. Caregivers are encouraged to ask patients what they need. People generally take great pride in their cultural beliefs and background and will be happy and relieved to know that the caregiver is aware. Learning about the childbearing family's beliefs and incorporating them into the care plan can both enhance the patient–caregiver relationship and promote positive perceptions of the childbirth experience.

ACKNOWLEDGMENTS

I would like to acknowledge several people who were especially helpful in the development of this chapter. Rachel Chesner copresented with me on this topic at several workshops. Our discussions served to crystallize many of the ideas presented here. Marilyn Berger's suggestions on Jewish parenting were very useful in the development of that topic, as were discussions with Dr. Jeff Schwersinksi, Dr. Shia Wexler, and Rabbi Ephraim Spero. The editorial comments and suggestions of my colleague at Mount Sinai Maternity Matters, Susan Biasella, were, as always, right on the mark. The article by Lutwak, Ney, and White cited as a reference was especially helpful. Finally, special thanks to my husband, Sam Spero, for his encouragement and support.

GLOSSARY

Brit Milah (BRIS)   Ritual circumcision.

Dvar Torah   Statement of a Biblical insight.

Elijah   Jewish prophet thought to attend all Brit ceremonies.

Hasidic Jews (HASIDIM)   Particular sect of Orthodox Judaism noted for devotion to a "rebbe" (rabbinic leader).

Kashrut (KOSHER)   Laws pertaining to food and its preparation.

Kiddush   Ceremony sanctifying the Sabbath and holidays.

Kvattern   Godparents.

Mashgiach   Person supervising preparation and serving of kosher food.

Mikveh   Ritual bath.

Mohel   Person trained to perform ritual circumcision.

Niddah   Condition of menstrual impurity.

Pareve   Kosher food product having neither dairy or meat ingredients.

Passover   Jewish holiday lasting eight days, occurring in spring. During this period, no bread or leavened products are consumed.

Pentecost   Jewish holiday celebrated seven weeks after Passover, lasting two days.

Pidyon Haben   Ceremony of the redemption of the firstborn male child.

Rosh Hashana   Jewish New Year.

Sandek   Man who holds infant during circumcision ceremony.

Sephardic Jews   Jews originating in Spain, North Africa, and Asia Minor. Some of their customs may differ.

Shabbos (SABBATH)   Begins Friday, twenty minutes before sundown, and ends after dark on Saturday. Considered a day of rest.

Shalom Zachor   Ceremony celebrating birth of baby boy. Occurs on the first Friday evening after the birth.

Shiva   Seven days of mourning following funeral.

Shulchan Aruch   Book of Jewish Law.

Talmud   Oral tradition codified between second and fifth centuries.

Torah   Five Books of Moses.

Tzniut   Modesty.

Yom Kippur   Day of Atonement on which adults are required to fast (abstain from food and drink).

SUGGESTED READINGS

Abraham, A. S. (1980). *Medical Halachah for everyone: A comprehensive guide to Jewish medical law in sickness and health.* New York: Feldheim.

Abramov, T. (1990). *Straight from the heart: Torah's perspective on mothering through nursing.* New York: Feldheim.

Bell, R. (Ed.). (1989). *The Hadassah magazine Jewish parenting book.* New York: Free Press.

Bleich, J. D. (1981). *Judaism and healing.* New York: KTAV.

Chill, A. (1979). *The Minhagim: The customs and ceremonies of Judaism, their origins and rationale.* New York: Sepher-Harmon.

Cohen, S. (1992). *Yevoraich Es Hana'Orim: Anthology of Halachos and Menhagim regarding pregnancy, childbirth and children.* New York: Feldheim.

Donin, H. H. (1977). *To raise a Jewish child: A guide for parents.* New York: Basic Books.

Feldman, D. (1968). *Birth control in Jewish law.* New York: New York University Press.

Feldman, D. (1986). *Health and medicine in the Jewish tradition.* New York: Crossroad.

Finkelstein, B., & Finkelstein, M. (1993). *B'Sha'Ah Tovah: The Jewish woman's clinical and Halachic guide to pregnancy and childbirth.* New York: Feldheim.

Goldberg, C. (1991). *Mourning in Halacha.* New York: Mesora.

Goldberger, Y. (1991). *Sanctity and science: Insights into practice of Milah and Metzitza.*

Kolatch, A. J. (1981). *Jewish book of why.* Middle Village, NY: Jonathan David.

Krohn, P. (1985). *Bris Milah.* New York: Feldheim.

Lamm, N. (1966). *A hedge of roses.* New York: Feldheim.

Lutwak, R. A., Ney, A. M., & White, J. E. (1988, January/February). Maternity nursing and Jewish law. *Maternal Child Nursing, 13,* 44.

Rosner, F., & Bleich, J. D. (Eds.). (1979). *Jewish bioethics.* New York: Hebrew Publishing.

Rosner, F. (1991). *Modern medicine and Jewish ethics* (2nd ed.). New York: Yeshiva University Press.

Rosner, F. (Ed.). (1990). *Medicine and Jewish law.* Northvale, NJ: Jason Aronson.

Schlesinger, B. (1987). *Jewish family issues: A resource guide.* (Garland Reference Library of Social Science). New York: Garland.

Trepp, L. (1980). *The complete book of Jewish observances: A practical manual for the modern Jew.* New York: Behrman House.

Wagschal, S. (1994). *The practical guide to childbirth on Shabbos and Yom Tov.* New York: Feldheim.

Relevant articles in the *Encyclopedia Judaica,* which is indexed.

Health Care Provision and the Native American

MARÍA J. ROBBINS

The serving of people is a great undertaking, one that requires patience and understanding. To give service to those who are ethnically different from oneself, it is first necessary to accept that prejudice or prejudgment is based on familiar but false stories and premises presented by movies and a slanted history. Among the Native Americans, a person who gives service to others and becomes known for efforts to place the welfare of others before his or her own welfare is held in high regard (Mankiller, 1991).

HISTORY AND OVERVIEW

When discovered by the Europeans, the American Indians occupied almost the entire landscape of North and South America. The population of the United States at the time of the first European contact has been estimated at 2.5 million. It fell to about 250,000 in 1890 and rose to 1,361,869 in the 1980 census. At that time approximately one half of the North American Indians lived in five states: California, Oklahoma, Arizona, New Mexico, and North Carolina, with California having the largest number. Physically, Native American Indians resemble Mongoloids (Central and Eastern Asians) more closely than Europeans, Africans, or Australians (*Encyclopedia*

Americana, 1986). Indians are found in every state including Hawaii and Alaska, along with the native people of those areas (*Garwood,* 1987).

When the Europeans came to the New World, they recognized no culture or religion other than their own as valid. They believed that it was "God's will" that they conquer and subdue this new land and any creatures living in it (Dippie, 1982). After years of conquest, colonization and domination, the new people, now called "Americans," observed that the land was becoming reasonably free from the natives and that they seemed to be disappearing as a threat. They began to call the natives the "Vanishing Americans" (Brown, 1982). They said that it was a kindness to remove those who remained to the distant areas of the country. It was predicted that they would soon die out or be absorbed into the general population (Dippie, 1982), especially when "shorn of tribal superstitions, armed with a trade and a Christian education, Indians would be productive citizens" (Altschuler, 1982).

On the other hand, the Native American leaders, chiefs, and medicine people realized that a superior fighting force was destroying their people and the world as they knew it. They chose to surrender and retreat in the face of this wave of destruction. However, although the native peoples retreated, they did not vanish, nor did they become extinct. A news editor in San Francisco stated in an article that he is living proof of the survival of the native peoples. He is *mestizo,* the product of a native and Spanish marriage. He believes that it is a tribute to native achievement that he and others like him exist, that the race of native peoples was willing to pay any price to survive (Rodríguez, 1990).

Among the Native Americans and other minorities who have resided on reservations or in segregated neighborhoods are three groups that may be encountered by health care providers: the "old" racial minorities, the "new" racial minorities, and the "nonminority" people of color. Among the old group are the alienated and/or elderly who prefer to speak the native language of the reservation, ghetto, or inner-city barrio. The new minorities are those who have emigrated from Asia or Latin America. They are in need of all services and are just trying to survive. The nonminority people of color are the middle-class working people—including some educated Native Americans—who, if it were not for their skin coloring, would be fully assimilated (De Hoyos, De Hoyos, & Anderson, 1986). This group may have absolutely no connection with their ancestral culture or traditions. Health care workers may encounter language problems with those Native American traditionalists and/or elderly who are isolated by poverty or choice on or near the reservations, or with urban poor living in a city ghetto.

A Native American speaker at a minority mental health conference, when asked how health care should be modified for Native Americans, suggested that anyone who is living and functioning well in a dominant society should be treated just like the general population (Holappa, 1992). That may well be true if the person is not attempting to maintain both Native American and dominant cultural values or expectations at the same time. These culturally marginal people experience an inner conflict, having on one side White middle-class expectations and advantages and on the other side a need to maintain an identity and values found in tribal dress, ceremonies, and, perhaps, native language. Many European Americans do not understand or tolerate in-between positions or "middle-of-the-road" mentality and, in defense of their own culture, expect people of various colors to be "White" in everything but skin color (Nofz, 1988).

A Lakota (Sioux) woman who had been off the reservation for less than a year spoke of her need to walk, talk, and behave in a manner typical of the nonnative or dominant society. Her people on the reservation understood what she had to do in order to survive and succeed in the larger society. But they cautioned her to remember who she was and where she came from. She showed in face and tone of voice the anguish that resulted from being torn between the cultures. When she returns to the Rosebud Reservation, she has to be Lakota, not White. But while outside, she has to be someone else. One wonders whether she will lose herself in the confusion (Anonymous interview, Columbus, Ohio, May 1993).

SACRED TRADITIONS

The native peoples traditionally considered themselves children of the Earth and related to all the other creatures rather than separate and above them. The Great Mystery's essence was in each living thing upon the Earth (Steiger & Steiger, 1991). Like a person's body, it was observed that the Earth's land and waters go through cycles of cleansing. Like the ages of a person's life, the Earth experienced spring/childhood, summer/adulthood, autumn/old age, and, at last, winter and death. But through the Great Mystery/Creator, the Earth lived again and again. And living close to the Earth, her red children lived through the seasons of life and cleansing and healing. Not demanding wealth or much land, high honors, and material possessions beyond their needs, asking only for life and enough to sustain it, they survived. Common to most Native American philosophies is that everyone has a purpose or spiritual duty—everyone has a spiritual relationship and responsibility to the Earth (Ywahoo, 1987).

The Native American spirituality is lived every day as a way of life (Atwood, 1991). There are six religious concepts that most Native Americans share:

1. A belief in the Great Mystery/Spirit/Creator.
2. A belief that all things in the universe are dependent upon each other.
3. The necessity of having a personal commitment to the Source of Life (Creator).
4. A belief in teachings on morals and ethics from persons knowledgeable in the sacred traditions.
5. Expectation that the wise ones (elders, medicine people, singers) can and will pass knowledge and sacred practices down from generation to generation by memory.
6. The recognition that humans are imperfect, weak, and even foolish and should look to "clowns" to remind them not to take themselves too seriously. (Beck & Walters, 1988)

Except among the Pueblo people, there does not exist a rigid system like those in the Christian, Judaic, or Muslim religions that spells out specifically who is a spiritual leader (Swan, 1990), nor is every practice or ritual set like that of a Catholic mass. Therefore, customs and beliefs may vary from subgroups within tribes and with individuals who are free to conceptualize religion in a personal manner (Atwood, 1991).

HEALTH CONCEPTS

Because the Native American does not consider spiritual life to be separated from physical life, health depends a great deal on what sort of life one is leading, whether one is at peace with everyone else, and whether one's own life is in balance. When a Native American of the Pueblo tradition (Hopi, Dine/Navajo, Zuni) becomes ill, it relates to disharmony and imbalance. If a ceremony called a "sing" is done, then things should come back into balance and the person should return to health. The art of sand painting is a part of this tradition, and only a skilled and knowledgeable practitioner can draw all of the images in the right manner and the proper order. The patient sits or lies down on the painting and is given bitter herbs to drink. When the patient and family have all participated in the ceremony, balance is restored and everyone in the family system is expected to recover (Aaeng, 1992).

In the Woodland tradition (Cherokee, Shawnee, Wyandotte, Miami), one must make amends if the conscience is not clear. People are often stressed by breaking rules or some wrongdoing. It may be necessary to give something to the family of the person wronged in order to achieve harmony and well-being. A practice in the Ohio/Michigan/Kentucky area is a "giveaway," in which one brings food, clothing, and other items to a gathering to be given to the less fortunate. The people receiving the goods are not made known, and no recognition is given to those who gave. But great spiritual honor is gained from this sacrifice. The "giveaway" may also be practiced during special life events when the honored person gives as well as gets gifts.

The use of herbs and roots is well known among all Native Americans, and it is the basis for many modern drugs. The use of the sweat lodge to cleanse and purify oneself has long been a custom among many tribes, and it is presently being used in some alcohol treatment modalities among native and nonnative practitioners (Foster, 1992). According to Brownlee (1978), the native people are usually too polite to tell a medical or other helping professional to his or her face that they are offended by something that was done or said. But the Papago Indians of the West will gossip behind one's back all over the village or town. The health care provider, usually nonnative, would expect a person to face him or her and talk about the problem, but this is not the Papago way.

Because beliefs concerning death are so widely varied, it is best to question a respected elder. Some native people facing death, even in a hospital, may request a medicine person so that they might prepare for death—in much the same manner as Catholics receive the last rites of the Catholic Church. In contrast, it is difficult to discover much information about such matters concerning the Dine (Navajo). It is said that they fear the idea of death so much that they avoid looking at dead animals. They do not mention the name of a dead person—even that of a loved one—and are offended by outsiders who make the mistake of using the name in expressing sympathy (Aaseng, 1992).

THE FAMILY AND KINSHIP

The family, traditionally, means not only parents and grandparents, but also includes the clan and tribe as an extended family. This inclusion of all generations results from the respect and reverence given the elderly within the family and tribal structure (Block, 1978). It has been said that native people consider the effects of their actions upon all their relations, especially their children and their children's children. The major difference between native people and nonnatives is their future planning: nonnatives leave money and possessions for their children, whereas native people leave the land and forests for their children (Durning, 1991). In a study by Neumann, Mason, Chase, and Albaugh, (1991), the importance of a strong family life was a significant factor in success among Cheyenne and Arapaho students. The students who were most successful in academic pursuits had a strong sense of self-esteem, which they traced to a caring figure who talked with them and encouraged their participation in various activities. That person did not have to be an immediate parent, but perhaps an aunt, uncle, grandparent, or older cousin. Older adult relatives, even great aunts and uncles, may function as and have an influence as strong as the biological parents (Ashbey, Gilcrist, & Miramontez, 1987).

Caring for others before oneself is encouraged in the Ojibwa people. The person who considers the needs and welfare of the family and tribe— seeing that others are fed, housed, and cared for without thought for him or herself—is rewarded with respect and esteem. Those who are selfish in their dealings, thinking of self before others, are not held in high regard (Nofz, 1988). This peer pressure undoubtedly has a strong effect upon what people say and do.

In the traditional culture of Native Americans, each individual knows that he or she is expected to behave in certain ways as a member of the tribe and can gain respect by certain behaviors and lose respect by others. Love for children is unconditional, and the parents and tribe cherish them. Other people are called "aunt" and "uncle" among the Dine (Navajo) and "grandmother" in the Great Lakes and Woodlands area. It does not matter if one has ever seen the individual before, respect for elders (of age or wisdom) is expected and given, and this promotes a sense of belonging and reverence for people of age and experience.

Traditionally, Native American children are not whipped or beaten. It is told by those of great age that when there were enemies to fear and a crying child could endanger the entire village, the mother would stop the child's crying by holding its nose. Somehow it was known that breathing through the mouth kept the child too busy to cry. This was not punishment, but undoubtedly the child would learn quickly when it was acceptable to cry and when it was not.

In the words of an Iroquois woman, in the event that actual punishment for misbehavior was required, it was carried out by a family member other than the immediate parents. The aunt, uncle, or other relative would take the child for a walk and tell him or her a story about a naughty little animal who had fallen into a dangerous situation because it had disobeyed the parents. The destination of the walk was a stream where the child was expected to stand while cold water was splashed handful by handful in his or her face. In modern times and urban settings, a cup of cool tap water might be thrown in the youngster's face. This was not merely punishment, although a splash of water might have shock value, but bathing in a running stream was also a method of purification. The water splashing was done even in winter. In the case of a stubborn boy, perhaps in his early teens, the youngster might be thrown bodily into the water. The embarrassment of walking home wet through the village may have been the true punishment. Everyone knew what had happened and why.

Because the Native American peoples are not a homogenous group but encompass many tribes and clans within the tribes, it is difficult to generalize about the authority figures and how to access the authority within any group identified as Native American. It may be said, in general, that the older people traditionally have been seen as the keepers of wisdom, the survivors, and those in the tribe most worthy of respect. It is feared that a valuable resource will be lost, and the culture as well, when the elders die (Block, 1978). A person designated as chief of a tribal group is worthy of respect if he or she behaves in an appropriate manner. A true leader is not loud, boisterous, or self-important but bears the burden of leadership with the knowledge that he or she is responsible for all the people who are depending upon him or her. Often the head person will give away his or her own food or clothing because the people need those things. Wilma Mankiller, Chief of the Cherokee Nation, is quoted as stating that the family comes first, and to her that means all of her people. When she is remembered, she wants it to be not just because she is a woman, but also because of what she has accomplished and for the help that she will have given her people. (Mankiller, 1993).

Although not all of the Native Americans in a neighborhood or area apart from the reservation may belong to Native American councils, health care providers may contact such councils for information and/or advice. Native Americans in an urban setting may be contacted just as easily through a church if a significant number belong to any one denomination. Because the Catholics have been the most consistent missionaries among the native people, many of them are Catholic, and their authority figure may well be the Church in an urban setting.

FOLK MEDICINE

Just as there are many tribes or nations of Native Americans, there are many different healing practices. There are individuals within each tribe who are respected for having special knowledge. In some tribes they are called medicine men or women, and in others "singers." Most tribes use herbs, which are still finding modern adaptations in medicine. Cocaine, quinine, cascara sagrada, ipecac, and other drugs were all used by the natives before Columbus landed (Nadar, 1973). The medicine people pray and maintain an attitude of balance in themselves so that they may help restore harmony to those who are troubled. These medicine people do not give specific information away to curiosity seekers. Healing talents come from the Creator, and methods of healing are given only to those who have demonstrated that they will not misuse them (Atwood, 1991). Traditionally, a person who seems to have "a calling" for the difficult path of the medicine man or woman will seek out an established medicine person for guidance. Some individuals are born into a family where there are medicine people and certain signs seem to indicate that this is the path the young one must follow (Ortega, 1989). Problems are usually considered as being due to a "loss of harmony" of the person with his or her associates or surroundings. The task of the medicine person is to help to restore harmony with manner and process, which is just as important as the content and outcome of the solution itself (Foster, 1992).

Among the Tsalagi (Eastern band Cherokee), mental health, physical health, and social order are an expression of the proper balance of things. In order to maintain right mind and right relationships with others, the Tsalagi practice forgiveness ("friends making new"), a ritual that releases painful memories and enables enemies to become friends again (Ywahoo, 1987).

According to Richards and Oxereok (1978), among the native people in Alaska, holding traditional and modern concepts and values simultaneously does not cause a conflict. Clients have been known to consult modern counselors for some types of concerns and local healers or medicine people in their village for others. For broken bones and illnesses that are clearly more physical than emotional or mental, most Native Americans utilize modern medical practices where they are available. People living on reservations have no choice but to utilize the local Indian Health Service clinics (Brownlee, 1978).

MATERNAL AND CHILD CONSIDERATIONS

Traditionally, sacred practices accompany the birth and naming of a child. Naming ceremonies are still conducted, according to Hirschfelder and Molin (1992). They report that children often receive many names during their lifetime, some of which are to be used only with close relatives and certainly within the tribe and are never to be known by strangers. Some names are earned by deeds, or at puberty. Some children are named after distinguished tribal relatives or ancestors, much like children of nonnative peoples.

Among the Iroquois, women traditionally separated themselves from the family and gathered together during the "moon days" or menstrual periods. When they had lodges instead of modern homes, a small "moon lodge" was set aside for this purpose. Special activities attended the onset and culmination of menstruation. Girls had special puberty rites of passage, and women joyfully celebrated their menopause with a party (Anonymous interview, 1987). Among the Apaches to this day, men and women join in celebrating the "Sunrise Ceremony," a girl's puberty ceremony, which lasts for five days and can cost more than one thousand dollars (Itule, 1992).

Most Native Americans living in the larger society observe modern practices; however, some return to the reservation for special ceremonies. Those living on distant reservations cannot be reported upon, as statistics are poor regarding these particular ceremonies. At this time, studies concerning Native Americans have "samples too small to be statistically significant and the data may be further skewed by non-Indians identifying themselves as Indians" (American Association for Higher Education, 1991, p.27). In order for a health care professional to work with a local Native American group, it is best to ask an older, respected member of the tribe for advice and support. In the case of an individual client, this approach will work if the client identifies with the local Native American group.

In a study by Bulterys (1990), northern Indians and Alaskan Natives were more likely than southwestern Indians to receive prenatal care during the first and second trimester of pregnancy. Native mothers in general were less likely to start care until late in the pregnancy and more likely to receive no professional care at all than were the typical nonnative women.

A study by Hsu and Williams (1991) pointed out that Native families living off the reservation seemed to have a high incidence of injury-related deaths in children between one and four years of age. It was determined that the children died from ingesting poisonous substances and from other accidents. The families did not seem to understand how to prevent these occurrences or how to intervene to save the children. Although the incidence of deaths in this age group was three times that of the general population, the authors of the study suggested that economic conditions, rather than culturally based differences in parenting behavior, seemed to account for these findings. The Native American families had low incomes and were similar to low-income families of other races in not using smoke detectors, possessing a fire extinguisher, or regularly checking heating systems.

In a study by Fingerhut and Makuc (1992) reviewing the statistics from the National Center of Health Statistics on mortality among minority populations in the United States as a whole, it was noted that Black and Native American children ages one to fourteen had much higher death rates than did Asian, Hispanic, and White children. These were specifically deaths related to injury, and to a large degree, auto accidents. While it was not mentioned in the study, anyone who has seen poor families loaded into battered old cars in cities, near reservations, or even in coal mining areas will no doubt have noticed children sitting on laps and unrestrained by seatbelts or car seats. This is a reflection of poverty, not race or neglect. So often health care professionals or child service workers assume intent to neglect and remove children from the homes of anxious and struggling parents. These professionals need to look at the resources available to poor families of any race before assuming willful neglect. While love and support are traditionally strong among Native Americans, it is obvious that poor economic circumstances make it difficult to raise healthy children.

ELDER CARE ISSUES AND CONSIDERATIONS

Isolation and distrust of service providers in the dominant society, especially among elderly Native American Indians, seems to play a part in the conflicts and unease with which the Native American population utilizes health care. Delivery of services to the elderly depend upon their ability to access those services. According to Block (1978), the Native American elderly are often left behind on the reservation when the younger family members move away to find work. The elderly live in isolated areas and fear leaving the communities they know to go to hospitals or nursing homes, where they are marooned in a nonnative culture without family or friends. They have been known to lose spirit, fall ill easily, and die prematurely in such surroundings. The situation off the reservation is little better, as the elderly may be left alone at home with little or no money to pay for services from people who may speak a different language and who look and act differently from the people to whom they are accustomed.

Nofz (1988) has suggested that internal conflicts exist within Native American individuals who realize a commitment to the elders they have left behind on the reservation or at home in the urban community, and yet feel the need to pursue all possible work opportunities and be successful according to the American work ethic. This conflict may lead to a feeling of isolation from both value systems and result in maladaptive behavior such as drinking in those who might appear most successful.

INDIAN YOUTH ISSUES AND CONSIDERATIONS

Isolation and alienation from family play an important role in the number of suicides suffered among the Native American and Alaskan Native populations. The suicide rate in 1987 among Native American adolescents was double the national rate of all other adolescents combined. In 1988, the

Indian Health Service conducted a survey of 7,254 students in grades six through twelve on the Navajo reservation. Nearly 15 percent (N = 971) reported a previous suicide attempt. Nearly all knew a family in which a suicide had occurred (Grossman, Milligan, & Deyo, 1991).

A study among Native American college students revealed that while they valued well-educated counselors of any race for career counseling, they preferred same-race counselors who shared their value systems when faced with personal problems (Bennett & Bigfoot-Sipes, 1991). Therefore, while it might be supposed that education would be a deciding factor in overcoming Native American distrust of nonnative counselors, this is not necessarily true when matters relevant to values and life-styles are considered.

CONCLUSIONS

Services are needed at all ages in the Native American population. Youths and the elderly are at extreme risk of death. Working-age people are under pressures similar to those of the general population to support and care for both the young and the old. They are also as prone as anyone else to develop stress-related illnesses, including substance abuse. But some barriers to this population's accessing mental and other health services include their distrust of majority culture health service delivery models, evidenced by their high dropout rates, and the fact that the usual family therapy is impractical for traditionalists who are involved in extended, nonnuclear kinship systems (Ashbey et al., 1987).

Beck and Walters (1988) have suggested that Native Americans may have inhibitions that could prevent them from sharing their belief systems in counseling sessions because of prohibitions about discussing certain aspects of their religion, value system, or practices. It was not so long ago that Native American rituals and practices such as the Sun Dance were forbidden and people who violated these restrictions could be jailed (Mails, 1979). There is also a fear of assimilation by sharing and integrating with the nonnative population. Native people do not wish to lose their culture; rather, they wish to maintain and strengthen it. A Vietnam veteran of partial Cherokee ancestry related his experience. He was fair-skinned, and when asked what his denomination or religious preference was during a health assessment interview, he expressed himself in a manner that recognized the authority of the Great Spirit/Creator and a relationship with all living creatures. When questioned further, he stated that he considered himself Native American. He was told that he was lying or delusional. While he recovered from the insult, he expressed great distrust of the system (Anonymous interview, 1993). The health care system expects clients to adapt to it, but if Native American clients, urban Indians, half-breeds, or others who are not completely of the majority culture and value system are expected to use its services, the system will have to adapt to these clients to some degree (Tierney, 1991).

Certainly economic opportunities are an important factor in solving minority health care problems. While health care professionals may not be involved in vocational rehabilitation or habilitation, they must realize that lack of economic advantages are likely to be a part of any problem a Native American client may present. According to De Hoyos and colleagues (1986), when a society refuses to give any group the full opportunity to occupy rewarding roles, it arbitrarily isolates a portion of its own population from the mainstream. When economic rewards are unattainable, people develop a sense of hopelessness; therefore, alcoholism and other social ills may follow.

RECOMMENDATIONS

According to Nofz (1988), Native Americans are reluctant to self-disclose, especially if the social workers are nonnative. The preferred approach is task-centered group work that does not target the individual and that approximates what a "healer" in the traditional manner might do. According to Canda (1988), social workers of various religious backgrounds have successfully employed rituals similar to traditional Native American practices to help clients mark important life transitions and achieve crisis resolutions. Social workers who are Native American have called in a medicine person to conduct traditional ceremonies, where appropriate, for their clients.

Understanding nonverbal behavior is especially important when working with Native Americans, including Alaskans. For example, a group therapist working with Alaskan natives misread a female group participant's behavior. What he perceived as resistance to resolving feelings of grief by crying in the group setting was actually a fear of bringing shame on herself by crying in public (Richards & Oxereok, 1978).

According to Wilma Mankiller (1991), it is important to remember that there is no specific Native culture. There are more than 350 different tribal groups, and each has a distinct history, culture, and language. There are more commonalities than differences, but failure to recognize the differences is failure to accept the diversity that exists among groups within a racial or ethnic division.

Another recommendation is to give greater value to the religious and cultural beliefs of native people. By realizing the significance of indigenous beliefs and utilizing informal support networks, which are particularly strong among minority families and communities, social workers have discovered how to integrate native practices with their own professional techniques (Midgley, 1990). Practices such as the use of a sweat lodge in some alcohol treatment programs and inclusion of respected wise people or medicine people to help clients deal with crisis resolutions and important life transitions (Canda, 1988) are examples of culturally integrated practices.

Making an effort to develop trust between individuals and among groups cannot be too strongly recommended. Even professional caregivers have been known to label ethnically different clients as uncooperative when the real problem was a lack of understanding on both sides. Training programs for health care professionals might include a variety of experiences with individuals of ethnic diversity. It would be desirable to have both Native American faculty and students present in culturally diverse academic programs dealing with human services as well as programs related to American heritage and culture. By associating with native peoples on a daily basis, the nonnative faculty and students might come to accept them as real people rather than "pow-wow dancers" or interesting but pathetic remnants of a once proud people. Nonnative peoples could see that the Native American Indians are a part of the larger American heritage and culture, to be neither pitied nor envied. However, according to Kidwell (1991), there are few Native Americans with the credentials to teach on the college level, and that signals a dismal future to any expansion of ethnic study programs. In the Southwest, some colleges have Native American lecturers or speakers who serve as resource people without needing credentials (Ortega, 1989). A speaker who has no college training, is usually known to the outside community as an official or respected elder of the local tribe.

Showing respect for the individual client, whether Native American or from another ethnic group, is the most important trait a health care provider can acquire. Learning respectful gestures will go a long way toward lowering barriers. For example, older people of most minority groups should not be addressed by their first names, yet in hospitals and many public service areas people who are young enough to be the client's grandchild will immediately use the first name in addressing him or her. An employer of a household worker often calls the worker by her first name while the native employee continues to refer to the employer by her formal title. Anyone who is not on a friendly basis with an elder should ask permission before calling the elder "uncle" or "grandmother." This usage is a form of deep respect, but it is best for health care personnel to be aware of the customs of a particular tribe.

Healthcare providers should avoid stereotyping Native Americans as a people and as individuals. Otherwise, they may be blinded to the diversities within each tribal group (Brownlee, 1978). It takes time to get to know people who have lived with fear of the dominant society for their entire lifetimes and those of their grandparents. The peoples of the reservations come from an entirely different world, and those who have lived every day on the fringes of the dominant society may have bicultural beliefs and practices that they suspect are not acceptable to health care providers. It takes time and patience to create trust between people.

ACKNOWLEDGMENTS

Special thanks and most sincere appreciation are offered to Grandmother Carol Locust, Director of Training, Native American Research and Training Center, University of Arizona, Tucson. Dr. Locust took time from her busy schedule to review this work. Her suggestions and words of encouragement were invaluable. Many thanks are also given to all those who consented to have their words, accounts, and opinions quoted—to all my relations.

GLOSSARY

American Indians   Those people who inhabited what is now known as the Americas when Columbus arrived.

Ancestry   Family descent or lineage, or ancestors collectively.

Assimilation   The process of being absorbed or incorporated into a larger racial group, such as minorities being intermarried into the dominant society.

Barrio   Spanish term for suburb, often of poor people.

Ceremony/ceremonies   Formal act(s) established by custom as proper to a special occasion such as weddings, funerals, etc.

Chief   The leader or head of a group, clan, or tribe.

Clowns, Indian   People dressed in a silly manner who play jokes, with meaning, but who lighten the solemnity of a ceremony.

Council, Indian   A group of people, often representing different villages, or areas of a town on a reservation or in an urban setting. Its functions include social and cultural support.

Culture   The concepts, habits, skills, art, tools, and institutions of a group of people in a given period.

Bicultural   Having or utilizing concepts, habits, skills, arts, tools, and institutions of two different groups of people in overlapping periods or the same period of time.

Dance A social activity that may be recreational or religious. The Sun Dance is religious and private.

Dominant culture The culture practiced by the majority of the people in a country, superseding the cultures of minorities.

Elders Older persons, people of higher rank, ancestors.

Extinct Having no living descendant.

Ghetto A restricted area of a town where an ethnic or racial group of people is forced to live.

Giveaway A practice of sacrificing one's food or possessions to others more needy as a means of spiritual growth.

Great Mystery Great Spirit, God, Creator.

Harmony Balance or personal adjustment between desire or individual interests and the well-being of the group, such as the family, village, or tribe.

Healing The use of herbs, prayer, ceremonies, or personal influence to improve the well-being of another person.

Homogeneous The state of being identical because of similar race, family, or kind. American Indians are not homogeneous.

Hunters/trappers People who hunted and trapped animals and sold their skins for a living. In modern usage, hobbiests who copy those customs, dress in leathers, use muzzle-loader guns, and camp out at annual gatherings.

Medicine people Men or women who function as healers and wise people within their community.

Mestizo A term meaning of mixed race, especially of Indian and Spanish or Portuguese parentage.

Moon lodge A building or dwelling where women stay during their moon time, or menstrual period.

Pow-wow A social gathering where people dance, eat, and exchange gossip dating from the last gathering.

Rites of passage Ceremonies celebrating special occasions such as birth and name giving, puberty, etc.

Ritual Having the nature of a rite, such as ritual dances; a set form or system of rites or ceremonies.

Sacred That which is set aside and revered as holy or of God, also of religious rites and practices.

Sand painting A picture created in colored sand by a highly trained practioner that is intended to have healing properties.

Spirituality The quality, character, or nature of being spiritual rather than worldly in attitude, outlook, or behavior.

Sunrise ceremony Celebration when an Apache girl reaches puberty.

Sweat lodge A temporary building set aside for religious ceremonies of prayer and cleansing.

Tribe A group of related people, families, or clans descended from a common ancestor and living together as a community.

Tradition/traditionalist The oral handling down of stories, beliefs, and customs from one generation to another. One who adheres to and practices these beliefs and customs.

Sovereign nation A self-governing tribe of people recognized as an independent political authority within the borders of the United States.

Wannabees People who, being interested in a culture or ethnic group, find or invent ancestry of that group and affect the group's dress and mannerisms.

REFERENCES

Aaseng, N. (1992). *Navajo code talkers.* New York: Walker.

Altschuler, G. C. (1982). *Race, ethnicity and class in American social thought 1865–1919.* Arlington Heights, IL: Harlan Davidson.

American Association for Higher Education. (1991, March/April). Native Americans and higher education: New mood of optimism. *Change Magazine,* p. 27. Washington, DC: Heldref.

Ashbey, M. R., Gilcrist, L. D., & Miramontez, A. (1987, Winter). Group treatment for sexually abused American Indian adolescents. *Social Work with Groups, 10*(4), 21–32.

Atwood, M. D. (1991). *Spirit healing: Native American magic and medicine.* New York: Sterling.

Beck, P. V., & Walters, A. L. (1988). *The sacred ways of knowledge: Sources of life.* Tsaile (Navajo Nation), AZ: Navajo Community College Press.

Bennett, S. K., & Bigfoot-Sipes, D. S. (1991). American Indian and White college students' preferences for counselor characteristics. *Journal of Counseling Psychology, 38*(4), 440–445.

Block, M. R. (1978). Exiled Americans: The plight of American Indian aged in the United States. In D.E. Gelfand & A.J. Kutzik (Eds.), *Ethnicity and aging: Theory, research, and policy* (p. 188). New York: Springer.

Brown, J. E. (1982). *The spiritual legacy of the American Indian.* New York: Crossroad.

Brownlee, A. T. (1978). *Community, culture and care.* St. Louis: Mosby.

Bulterys, M. (1990, June). High incidence of sudden infant death syndrome among the Northern Indians and Alaska Natives compared with Southern Indians: Possible role of smoking. *Journal of Community Health 15*(3), 185–193.

Canda, E. R. (1988). Spirituality, religious diversity, and social work practice. *Social Casework: The Journal of Contemporary Social Work, 69*(4), 238–247.

De Hoyos, G., De Hoyos, A., & Anderson, C. B. (1986). Sociocultural dislocation: Beyond the dual perspective. *Social Work, 31*(1), 61–67.

Dippie, B. W. (1982). *White attitudes and U. S. Indian policy.* Middletown, CT: Wesleyan University Press.

Durning, A. T. (1991, November/December). Native Americans stand their ground. *World Watch,* p. 11. Washington, DC: World Watch Institute.

The Encyclopedia Americana. 15, 1–12. (1986). Danbury, CT: Grolier.

Fingerhut, L. A., & Makuc, D. M. (1992). Mortality among minority populations in the United States. *American Journal of Public Health, 82*(8), 1168–1170.

Foster, D. V. (1992, February). Treatment issues with American Indians. *NOFSW Newsletter,* pp. 4–5.

Garwood, A. N. (Ed.). (1987). *Almanac of the 50 States.* Wellesley Hills, MA: Information Publications.

Grossman, D. C., Milligan, B. C., & Deyo, R. A. (1991). Risk factors for suicide attempts among Navajo adolescents. *American Journal of Public Health, 81*(7), 870–873.

Hirschfelder, A. & Molin, P. (1992) *The encyclopedia of Native American religions.* New York: Facts on File.

Holappa, T. (1992). *American Indian educational research and consulting.* (Lecture). Washington, DC: ORBIS Associates.

Hsu, J. S. J., & Williams, S. D. (1991). Injury prevention awareness in an urban Native American population. *American Journal of Public Health, 81*(11), 1466–1468.

Itule, B. D. (1992). Growing up Apache. *Arizona Highways, 68*(9), 21–25.

Kidwell, C. S. (1991, March/April). The vanishing native reappears in the college curriculum. *Change Magazine,* pp. 19–23. Washington, DC: Heldref.

Mails, T. (1979). *Fools Crow.* Lincoln: University of Nebraska Press.

Mankiller, W. (1991). Education and Native Americans entering the twenty-first century on our own terms. *National Forum* (Phi Kappa Phi Journal), *71*(2), 5–6.

Mankiller, W. (1993). *Mankiller: A chief and her people.* New York: St Martin's Press.

Midgley, J. (1990). International social work: Learning from the third world. *Social Work, 35*(4), 295–300.

Nadar, R. (1973). American Indians: People without a future. *Myth and the American experience* (p. 427) Beverly Hills, CA: Glencoe.

Neumann, A. K., Mason, V., Chase, E., & Albaugh, B. (1991). Factors associated with success among Southern Cheyenne and Arapaho Indians. *Journal of Community Health, 16*(2), 103–115.

Nofz, M. P. (1988, February). Alcohol abuse and culturally marginal American Indians. *Social Casework: The Journal of Contemporary Social Work, 69*(2), 67–73.

Ortega, P. (1989) *Medicine man, seven clans, Apache Nation.* Lecture presented at the Bear Tribe Medicine Wheel Conference, Cincinnati, Ohio.

Richards, B., & Oxereok, C. (1978). Counseling Alaskan Natives. In J. McFadden (Ed.), *Transcultural counseling* (pp. 57–82) New York: Human Services Press.

Rodríguez, R. (1990, November). Mixed blood, Columbus's legacy: A world made mestizo. *Harper's Magazine,* pp. 47–56.

Steiger, B., & Steiger, S. (1991). *Indian wisdom and its guiding power.* West Chester, PA: Whitford.

Swan, J. A. (1990). *Sacred places.* Sante Fe, NM: Bear.

Tierney, W. G. (1991, March/April). Native voices in academe: strategies for empowerment. *Change Magazine,* pp. 36–39.

Ywahoo, D. (1987). *Voices of our ancestors: Cherokee teachings from the wisdom fire.* Boston: Shambhala.

SUGGESTED READINGS

American Heritage book of Indians. (1961). New York: American Heritage.

Erboes, E. (Ed.). (1984). *American Indian myths and legends.* New York: Rantheon.

Brown, V. (1975). *Great upon the mountain: The story of Crazy Horse, mystic and warrior.* New York: Macmillan.

Campbell, D. (1993). *Native American art and folklore.* Avenel, NJ: Crescent/Random House.

Courlander, H. (1971). *The fourth world of the Hopis.* New York: Crown.

Hofsinde, R. (1955). *The Indian's secret world.* New York: Morrow.

Hunt, W. B. (1991). *American Indian survival skills*. New York: Outdoor Life/Meredith.

Lincoln, K. & Slagle, A. L. (1987). *The good red road*. San Francisco: Harper and Row.

Marden, C. F., & Meyer, G. (1973). *Minorities in American society*. New York: Van Nostrand/Litton.

National Geographic Society (1992). *World of the American Indian* (Rev. ed.). Washington, DC: Author.

Utley, R. M. (1982). *The American Heritage history of the Indian wars*. New York: American Heritage.

Waldman, C. (1984). *Atlas of the North American Indian*. New York: Facts on File.

Washburn, W. (1964). *The Indian and the White man*. Garden City, NY: Anchor/Doubleday.

Washington, B. T. (1940). *The story of the Negro* (Vol 1.). New York: Peter Smith.

► 10

The Multicultural Challenge to Health Care

SHARY SCOTT RATLIFF

During a recent management orientation program at a metropolitan hospital, a newly hired engineer was perplexed by the announcement that the institution was preparing an aggressive educational initiative on "Managing Diversity." Why, he asked, was "diversity" such a big deal? Hadn't previous waves of immigrants blended virtually effortlessly into the American sea? What was so different about the current influx of people?

The question cannot be dismissed. Indeed, it underscores the critical significance of the issues raised in this book. Only an informed populace, an enlightened one, can design and support remedial and proactive structures, systems, and institutions responsive to the socioeconomic, educational, and psychophysical needs of our most vulnerable citizens. Yet, how many of us are aware of the full extent of atrocities perpetrated by the majority culture upon Native Americans? Or the Chinese? How many truly realize the ongoing suffering of African Americans, despite legal and social lip service to "equal rights"? Who can feel the helplessness of millions of Appalachians whose human dignity was stripped away as ruthlessly and cynically as their precious land? Too few majority Americans, especially those born after 1950, have any knowledge about the internment of Japanese Americans in concentration camps during World War II, about the confiscation of their property and the devastation of their lives while many of their sons fought bravely along-side White Americans.

Negative stereotypes about the Irish, Jews, Italians, Poles, Hungarians, and Russians prove that even White Europeans did not "blend in" without considerable prejudice and discrimination. These peoples did have a tremendous advantage, however, insofar as their pigmentation graced them with at least the potential to become "real Americans." Embedded both in the Naturalization Law of 1790 (Takaki, 1993) and in the collective unconscious of majority Americans is the presupposition that to be a U.S. citizen is to be White. So it is that Mexican Americans whose roots in South Texas grow back seven generations are mislabeled "aliens," and Chinese and Japanese Americans whose ancestors were building U.S. railroads over one hundred years ago are congratulated on how well they speak English! Such a dismal knowledge of our own history bodes ill even for multicultural *awareness* in the popular mind. Cultural *competence*, for most, is still a bridge too far to cross.

Yet awareness and competence for all professionals will become increasingly vital over the next three decades. Unlike previous immigrants, who swallowed their pride and masked their cultures, many of today's "hyphenated" Americans are choosing to celebrate their ethnic origins, joyously wearing the flowers born of their ancient roots. They have little interest in blending in with a majority culture that has written a tedious and fraudulent social script to validate its own so-called superiority. They are writing their own scripts in their native languages and are using traditional fabrics and foods. Ceremonies, rituals, and celebrations are being reborn among a generation that feels more responsibility than nostalgia, a sense of being the protecting godparents of values and symbols rapidly slipping from older memories. The development of the African-American Kwanzaa observance is but one example of this attempt to salvage and celebrate the packed-away pride of a people.

But even as suburban strip malls bloom with ethnic restaurants and international festivals bring the world to our home towns, the emerging reality of a *validated* multicultural society is engendering a powerful and paranoid backlash. The revitalization of White supremacist groups from Oregon to Louisiana raises grave concerns for those who thought the seeds of a major mindshift had taken at least some root in the 1960s. Ethnic cleansing in Bosnia and hate crimes in Germany seem a little closer to home when a Nigerian in Oregon is beaten to death by working-class "skinheads." How fragile and ephemeral tolerance is when competition for scarce resources hammers on an empty table!

The tortuous path from seemingly isolated instances of racially motivated violence to the lack of adequate, culturally competent health care for minorities becomes quite direct when we consider the genesis of power. As long as the democratic process is numerically controlled by culturally uninformed (or worse, culturally prejudiced) Whites, there will be little impetus to enact tax-burdening legislation to level the playing field for minorities. Charges of reverse discrimination already abound in both business and academe due to misuse and misunderstanding of affirmative action initiatives and alleged quotas for minorities. Few White political candidates will choose to put their necks in a noose for a population that cannot support them numerically, much less financially.

The pernicious downward spiral of political powerlessness, limited educational and employment opportunities, substandard living conditions, and home-wrecking hopelessness necessarily eventuates in high-risk behaviors and vulnerable health status. Politically and financially disadvantaged, minorities are nonetheless invited to pull themselves up by their own bootstraps.

HEALTH CARE FOR MINORITIES

A small and tentative grant here and there, the *noblesse oblige* of a wealthy private citizen, and the occasional guilt-driven funding by a city council are the usual avenues of support for neighborhood clinics responsive to the health needs of minorities. Underfunded, understaffed, and underequipped, such efforts gasp for every breath, never sure whether they will survive the next budget cut or grant cycle.

Alternatively, there are well-meaning outreach programs and projects of individual health-promoting associations and societies (e.g., cancer, diabetes, heart disease, hypertension) that want very much to provide timely interventions to minority groups. However, both their boards and their field workers are generally Whites who have little or no experience with any aspect of minority cultures.

During a recent consultation with such a group (which was extremely receptive to suggestions), the outreach committee members were concerned because minorities did not attend their "healthy cooking" demonstrations, did not send their children to the association's summer camp, and seemed polite but distant when approached by their White field workers. Their "target" populations were African Americans, Hispanics, Southeast Asian refugees, and Native Americans. Further discussion revealed that the cooking demonstrations were being held in an all-White part of the city and the recipes were based on traditionally White dietary preferences. The summer camp was 95 percent White, providing little psychological inclusion for minority children. In addition, the group had failed to consider lack of transportation to the camp, the impact on siblings who were ineligible because they were healthy, and cultural restrictions against allowing young children to be away from home with total strangers for days at a time. When field workers were sent to "interface" with minority leaders, the health care professionals frequently seemed authoritarian, condescending, impersonal, and more interested in the project than in the people. They had not attempted to identify local peer educators within the minority groups who might have facilitated the intervention initiative. The tragedy is that these organizations do want to help, and frequently they have the financial resources to make an impact. With appropriate education in cultural competence, their success rate would surely increase.

While neighborhood storefront clinics totter on the brink of collapse and single-disease-focused organizations struggle with cultural competence, metropolitan health care centers and hospitals have the responsibility—and the opportunity—of a lifetime. Although the last three decades have seen the demise of many hospitals across the country (from 7,123 in 1965 to 6,649 in 1990) (Hagland, 1992), larger medical care systems are holding their own due to diversification strategies that are increasingly focusing on home care and off-site outpatient facilities. For many hospitals, this is a survival response to the staggering surge in emergency department (ED) utilization over the past decade, with eighty-two million ED visits in 1980 and ninety-two million in 1990 (Hagland, 1992). Not only are staff and facilities stressed beyond all capabilities (some have resorted to "rolling brown-outs" to handle the load), but there are financial ramifications as well. Hagland (1992) has also indicated that patients admitted to the hospital through the ED "are more likely to have low incomes, to be uninsured or underinsured, and to use far more resources than those admitted in other ways" (p. 28). Demographics indicate that minority Americans are at a greater risk of being poor and of being uninsured (24 percent of African Americans and 33 percent of Hispanic Americans have no health insurance) (Friedman, 1991). Morbidity and mortality among minorities are sometimes three to four times as high as those of the majority population. With the prediction that minorities are on the brink of becoming cumulative majorities in several states (e.g., Texas and California), hospital systems must seek more efficient and cost-effective delivery systems. There are strong indications that this is already beginning to happen.

Financial and resource management demands alternatives to utilization of emergency departments for nonacute and primary care. According to *Hospitals and Health Networks* (Staff, 1993), "One of the certain outcomes of health care reform is a continuation of the shift from inpatient to outpatient treatment. In fact, new data show that 80 percent of a hospital's outpatient and emergency department procedures will most likely move to alternate delivery settings" (p. 52). In 1991, home health services "topped the list of diversification strategies" for the first time, according to Sabatino (1992, p. 50).

Among the new models of health care financing on the horizon, many advocate for a capitation system whereby hospitals are paid a set fee to care for all individuals in their catchment areas. Since inpatient and emergency care are much more expensive than outpatient and preventive care, the wise hospital administrator will do everything possible to promote wellness in the community.

It makes financial sense to treat a hypertensive adult or to immunize a baby in his or her own neighborhood rather than absorb the enormously expensive ED and/or inpatient costs resulting from lack of preventive care. If, in fact, this system prevails (and it appears that some version of it will), we will witness the greatest irony: The current disincentives to providing health care to minorities will become the very mobilizers driving outreach initiatives. We may see clean, modern, well-staffed and well-equipped clinics in the poorest of neighborhoods, in ghettos and barrios, in housing projects and pueblos, all funded by hospitals that are closing entire units of inpatient facilities.

In fact, this has already occurred in some areas. Parkland Memorial Hospital in Dallas has reduced ED visits from 178,000 in the mid-1980s to 148,000 in 1992 through the operation of an on-campus ambulatory center open from 7:00 A.M. to 11:00 P.M. or later that sees three hundred patients a day. Parkland also supports several community clinics near the worksites and residences of its clients. Both the University of Chicago and the Medical Center in Memphis have similar outreach clinics, the latter staffed by nurse practitioners (Hagland, 1992).

This sounds hopeful. However, both outreach and inpatient care providers will find themselves strangers in strange lands unless they become much more culturally competent. While minorities will frequently come to emergency departments when symptoms become too difficult to bear, visits to neighborhood clinics for preventive care are entirely optional and are rarely a cultural norm. Care providers will be required to invest considerable time educating clients about the wisdom of health maintenance. According to *Hospitals and Health Networks* (Staff, 1993), "If today's Medicaid, commercially insured, and uninsured populations are treated in a managed care environment, preventive medicine counseling will increase 87 percent—regardless of where the counseling takes place" (p. 52). At the same time, everyone involved in an outreach system, whether home based or clinic based, must become a serious student of the lifeworld of his or her clientele. For those clients who do require inpatient care, medical, nursing, and social service staff may find resistance, noncompliance, and unexpected readmissions if they mishandle patients' cultural needs. This adds to hospital expenses, which are not reimbursable if the capitation limit has been reached.

Just as business and industry are discovering the financial impact of mismanaging diversity in the workplace (47 percent of all U.S. businesses employing more than one hundred people had instituted diversity training programs by 1993) ("Training," Jan. 1994, p. 40), the health care industry is recognizing the value of honoring the diversity of its care staff and its clientele. As a cover article in *Hospitals* noted:

> *Hospitals . . . need to begin to think multiculturally, in terms of program design, services offered and actual contact with patients. New types of outreach will be necessary to acquaint immigrants with the health care system. Social workers, patient representatives, health educators and others—including physicians and nurses—will need language skills and cultural sensitivity in order to deal with these new patients. And, of course, discriminatory behavior must end. (Friedman, 1991, p. 40)*

Dana (1993) cited a 1986 study by J. H. Flaskerud that demonstrated that "culture-compatible services can result in increased utilization" of mental health facilities among African-American, Asian-American, Mexican-American, and mixed ethnic/racial populations in "four full-service, public, metropolitan mental health agencies":

> *A culture-compatible approach included therapists who shared the clients' culture, language or language style; use of family members in brief therapy; referrals to clergy and/or traditional healers; agency location in the client community; flexible hours/appointments; and involvement of consumers directly in determining, evaluating, and publicizing services. (Dana, 1993, p. 3)*

For hospitals in locations that historically have had little racial and ethnic diversity, such proactive initiatives have been nice options, but certainly have not been required for bottom-line success. On the other hand, hospitals that have been managing diversity for decades have charted the landscape and navigated it well. The birthing centers in Amish country, discussed in chapter 3, are splendid examples of highly functional and culturally comfortable accommodations for a very devout socioreligious people. St. Luke's Episcopal Hospital in Houston prints its menus in twenty-six different languages and allows delivering mothers to use acupuncture as anesthesia if that is their preference (Maurer, 1989). And why not? This is the crucial question that all health care and social service providers must ultimately confront.

CULTURAL COMPETENCE EDUCATION

What areas should the care provider seek to explore and understand? They are as numerous as the concepts we can name, ranging from the most basic of categories such as time and space to musical rhythms and the meanings of floral selections. It is probably safe to say that no nonnative of a culture will ever truly be "culturally literate." The positive side is that most natives of a culture do not expect this level of understanding and are deeply grateful for any such effort made by a nonnative. In general, they appreciate questions that provide opportunities for sharing their lifeworld.

A basic foundation for cultural competence must be sought in understanding the interface between the culture itself and the individual who is a member of that culture. There are many academic discussions about the nature of culture (if such a thing can be discussed in abstraction apart from real people) (Jordan & Swartz, 1990) and about the impact of culture upon personality development (Barnouw, 1985). However, it seems most realistic to recognize the interplay of culture and personality, each informing and modifying the other, with each individual representing an idiosyncratic moment within this process. By conceiving of this interface as a fluid process and each individual as a unique manifestation of it, we protect ourselves to some extent from creating stereotypical generalizations that can result in poor service to clients.

The personhood of the individual is impacted by the history of his or her people, including the past and present of the country of origin, critical factors surrounding the emigration of the ethnic group from that country, the circumstances that met them in the United States, and the history of their relationship with the majority U.S. population. The history of slavery for African Americans, for example, remains a vivid reality, the underlying premises of which continue to manifest in prejudice and discrimination in all areas of life. The horror of Pol Pot's genocidal regime in Cambodia has scarred refugees from that country for the rest of their lives. Vietnamese refugees in the United States realize that they are constant reminders of a lost war—a war that they also lost. Although the history is technically the same, the perspective is quite different.

The native language of the ethnic group may be the first language of the minority individual even though he or she may speak English as a second language with great fluency. If this is the case, the care provider should be aware that the foundational thought structures through which the client processes the world will likely be in the primary language, with English language interpretations only a rough equivalent of the original. Subtle shifts in meaning can create confusion, frustration, and even fear in the client or the client's family. On the other hand, second, third, and later generations of Chinese, Japanese, Korean, or Hispanic peoples may have been reared in homes where English was the only language spoken. They may rarely or never speak the language of their ancestral country, even if they know it—and many do not. Many a care provider has embarrassed such people by asking them where they learned English! Many second-generation children of refugees have learned to speak their native language at home but do not know how to read or write it. Some cultures actually speak two English-based languages with equal facility but use them differentially in various interfaces. Thus, an African American who may speak Ebonics in intracultural situations could speak mainstream "TV-news" English when interacting with Whites in the workplace. Appalachians who have achieved professional status outside of their home states may speak mainstream, unaccented English in the city and instantly revert to the cadences and accents of their families when they return home.

Beliefs and the values that spring from them provide a culture's basic assumptions about the world and the appropriate place of human beings in it. In a landmark study on value orientation, Kluckhohn and Strotdbeck (1961, cited in Barnouw, 1985) pointed out that all human societies have the same kinds of problems to solve and the same range of solutions. Many differences between societies and their cultures lie precisely in how these solutions are selected and judged effective. Cumulatively, these selections form the foundations for a world view, or a consensus about life's meaning. Kluckhohn and Strotdbeck suggested that there are five basic problems, each with three possible answers:

1. What is the innate nature of man? (Evil, neutral or mixture, or good);
2. What is the relation of man to nature? (Subjugated to nature, in harmony with nature, dominating over nature);
3. What is the nature of time orientation? (Past, present, future);
4. What is the modality of human activity? (Being, being-in-becoming, doing);
5. What is the modality of man's relationship to others? (Lineal, collateral, individualistic). (Barnouw, 1990, p. 190)

The role of religion, the significance of family, goal-orientation, elasticity or absoluteness of time, and the locus of control and responsibility (internal versus external) are both causes and effects of the answers chosen by a particular culture. The dominant U.S. majority orientation chooses individualism, a future time orientation, mastery over nature, doing, and belief in an evil but perfectible human nature (Barnouw, 1990). Most minority cultures, on the other hand, choose lineality or collaterality (a sense of the nuclear and extended family enduring and striving together through generations), a present time orientation, subjugation to or harmony with nature, being or being-in-becoming (except African-Americans, who choose "doing"), and a mixed or good human nature. These differences from the U.S. majority culture can cause serious misunderstandings in the areas of health and healing, partnering for health, commitments to appointments, priorities that place family and friends above personal advancement, and assessment of the minority client's self-esteem. As Dana (1993) has noted:

> *Our knowledge of self-concept stems almost entirely from research on Anglo Americans, individuals of the dominant culture in American society. The self for this population has firm boundaries that enclose what has been described as self-contained individualism, or egocentrism, characterized by personal control and a self-concept that excludes other persons. Until recently it was assumed by most social scientists that the self-concept of persons from other cultures could be defined similarly. One obvious result of this assumption was that persons from other cultures have typically appeared as deficient in self-esteem as indicated by personality measures. (p. 11)*

Religious beliefs may dictate food choices, clothing styles, customs of birthing and dying, etiquette in the sick room, use of modern conveniences, invasive procedures, organ donation/reception, use of blood products, certain diagnostic tests, gynecological procedures, spiritual influences on or control of sickness and healing, the wearing of protective devices or tatoos, and the need for prayers and rituals performed by various religious specialists. Although many hospitals have chapels or meditation rooms on site, most are self-consciously Christocentric, a feature not overlooked by Muslims, Jews, Buddhists, and Hindus.

Many hospitals could benefit from some sensitivity about holiday celebrations as well. If an outreach program in an ethnic neighborhood seeks to improve its cultural competence, the special celebrations of that minority should be highlighted with appropriate decorations and greetings. For example, Kwanzaa in an African-American community, Cinco de Mayo in a Hispanic neighborhood, Passover in a Jewish community, and New Year celebrations in Asian population centers would be supported enthusiastically by the clinic staff. Clinics with a large Native American clientele would need to be educated in the various traditional observances of particular tribes and nations.

All of these cultural components serve as the field out of which the individual emerges, but to equate the individual with the cultural field is to engage in the crudest form of stereotyping, depriving her or him of personhood. Interfacing with all of these background factors is the unique lifeworld of the individual. In what sort of family did he or she grow up? What were the parental roles and personalities? What was the family's economic status? Was substance abuse or physical abuse a concern in the home? What was the family's approach to health care and healing? How religious or spiritual was each of the family members? The educational ambitions and level achieved by the individual will also have a major impact on his or her evaluation of the cultural field. Contact and experience with the majority culture will either encourage additional interaction or reinforce suspicion and isolation from it. Contact itself may be dependent upon the location in which the family resided.

All of these experiences may have aroused a certain amount of dissonance with the background culture, forcing questions that challenge the ethnic loyalty of the individual. To the extent that the majority culture demands conformity, the individual may accept a degree of acculturation when forced to do so, subsequently reverting to the traditional culture as soon as possible. However, if the dissonance between the majority culture and the background culture resolves into a higher comfort level with the former, the individual may assimilate rather completely. It is along this interface between the background cultural influences and the individual's own private lifeworld that unique personhood develops. Nor is this a static phenomenon. As long as one continues to experience, examine, and judge, one is still a person-in-becoming, always subject to subtle or major mindshifts.

The lesson in all of this for health care and social service providers is simply that one cannot be sure who is walking through the door. Initially assessing the person as a member of a particular culture is an excellent place to begin, and serious study of that culture will be prerequisite to credibility and effectiveness. However, the assumption that this *person* is automatically going to fit the profile of that culture is ineffective and counterproductive. The skillful health care or social service provider will slowly and carefully draw the client into dialog about each of these areas until his or her individuality emerges clearly along the continuum. This takes time and thoughtfulness, but the effort is well worth the reward of becoming a trusted provider for the individual and his or her family and friends.

SOME ETHICAL CONCERNS

The interface of minorities and health care suggests some serious ethical concerns that may be exacerbated over time. Foremost among these issues are access to care, discrimination in quality of treatment, paternalism, informed consent, and respect for the whole person. As a discipline, ethics considers the bases for determining the moral rightness or wrongness of actions, and these bases flow consistently from a world view. Most Western systems of ethics postulate either *duty* or *beneficence* as the guiding principles for ethical decision making. Clearly, in a work of this type, it is important to note that there are ethical systems that have emerged from other world views that suggest rather different guiding principles. However, since the U.S. health care system as such is a product of an exclusively Western value orientation, these issues may be more productively discussed first within this framework.

From the perspective of applied social ethics, those who claim that society has a duty to provide health care (or other basic needs) for those who cannot afford it base this claim on the ground that, as members of a social order, we are obligated to provide for others the necessities that we would require for ourselves. Ethical theorist John Rawls (1971) uses an academic device whereby one would construct society and develop policy prior to knowing one's own socioeconomic, educational, and physical status within that society. This presumably assures maximizing one's own benefits regardless of one's ultimate situation. This and other systems based on social obligation predicate at least a modicum of protected rights for every member of society. If there are such rights, then there is an equal duty to assure their availability and accessibility to everyone.

However, those who claim that society has a *duty* to provide medical assistance that truly responds to the needs of minorities are often countered with the premise that *no one* has an intrinsic right to health care. Those who can afford it can purchase these services, but it is not incumbent upon society to guarantee health care to everyone. This position usually overlooks the fact that, from this same perspective, no one has an intrinsic right to freeway systems, police protection, safe drinking water, or any of the other costly amenities of advanced civilizations.

The "no intrinsic rights" theorists often foster an "atomistic" model of society wherein each individual is essentially an isolated, autonomous unit with no inherent relationship to any other individual. Their only commonality is the happenstance of contiguous physical location. If there is any outreach to another being, the motivation is an arbitrary and idiosyncratic act of fellow feeling or personal compassion rather than a sense of social responsibility. According to this conceptualization of society, there is no responsibility, much less duty, for individuals to concern themselves with the well-being of others.

Ethical systems grounded in the notion of beneficence often postulate that the action that brings the most benefit to the most people is the more ethical choice. On the face of it, this position would seem to favor whatever action the *majority* preferred, inasmuch as the outcome would presumably bring most benefit to the most people. Minority issues clearly could suffer under this so-called democratic viewpoint unless a secondary rule prohibited the majority from taking any action that would cause harm or jeopardize the well-being of a minority member.

Beneficence systems clearly conceive of society as a goal-oriented institution composed of individuals whose choices determine those goals for the entire population. As such, it would seem to be an improvement over an atomistic view of society. If the "cause no harm" rule is in place, the majority is precluded from actively exercising choices that create hardship for the minority. However, while this proviso apparently safeguards the status quo of minorities, there is no active advocacy for parity or remediation in this model, except insofar as the majority finds this ultimately beneficial for its own constituency. The minority population is not intentionally harmed, but negligence on the part of the majority creates de facto disparity and may activate a downward spiral in socioeconomic conditions.

An alternative conceptualization of society views its members as intersections, nexuses, in a network of interdependent relationships that cumulatively constitute the society. Anything that impacts one nexus ultimately impacts all of them; that is, if one end of the social ship has sustained damage, passengers at the other end are unwise to dismiss it as "their problem." This view acknowledges a responsibility to all members of the social network inasmuch as the welfare of some members is intimately connected with the welfare of all others, regardless of their socioeconomic position at any given time. This latter reading of social reality carries with it the implicit duty to render assistance to those in need, sometimes even at the price of temporary sacrifice of one's own surplus.

From a practical perspective, the "social nexus" view would argue for interdependent responsibility, perhaps citing environmental disasters as prime cases illustrating the impact of local situations on the entire society. One might also argue that the crisis of street crime in our cities might have been defused long ago if socioeconomic and educational initiatives had proactively addressed the challenges of inner city life. A health crisis of similar proportions looms on the horizon. Although there is a modest movement toward the social nexus view of society, there is by no means a consensus. Moreover, the willingness to share resources of all kinds weakens under the pressure of economic hardship. Until the ethics of social responsibility seeps deeply into the fabric of our country's values, systematic remedial initiatives will continue to be the most vulnerable targets on the budgetary cutting board. It appears clear that of the three views of social ethics briefly discussed here, the social nexus model will best respond to the problems facing minorities in their quest for parity in the health care system.

Access to Care

Not many years have passed since members of minority groups were blatantly denied access to health care, even emergency care, in White facilities. While the legal system has remedied this situation at least nominally, de facto discrimination continues in many areas. If hospitals and health clinics are located in neighborhoods that are difficult for minorities to reach or are psychologically uncomfortable for them, these hospitals may *claim* a posture of nondiscrimination while rarely responding to the needs of minority persons. If clinic hours are incompatible with work schedules, minority group members may be forced to lose work time and vital wages in order to meet their appointments. Lack of daytime child care assistance may prevent many women from coming to the clinic, even for important prenatal care. If insurance is prerequisite to any examination and treatment, many minority group members will not receive adequate health care. As noted before, large percentages of minority groups are inadequately insured.

The social nexus position would foster the development of interdisciplinary neighborhood-based clinics with sliding-scale payment systems and safety-net provisions for those with no expendable income for health care. Evening and weekend hours, on-site child care, and home health visits by bilingual or ethnically compatible health aides would be considered basic accommodations.

Quality of Care

The same dynamics impact quality and intensity of care. If preventive care is difficult to access, presentation for treatment may be delayed well into pathology. Surely maternal and infant mortality could be reduced if prenatal care were available in the right place and at the right time. Hypertension, kidney disease, heart disease, diabetes, and some cancers might also be significantly reduced through timely diagnosis and intervention. Accessing the health care system only after active disease is in process means more costly and time-intensive cases with less successful outcomes. Typically, the patient is chastised for waiting too long—a classic instance of blaming the victim. Premium technological and pharmaceutical treatment possibilities are out of the question for many minority group members who have little or no insurance and limited private resources.

Social nexus ethics will emphasize the responsibility of the health care industry to provide appropriate health education for minorities in schools, businesses, recreation centers, ethnic grocery stores, churches and temples, and other popular gathering places. Hospitals and clinics will provide preventive care at minimal cost. Quality-improvement data will indicate the level of care provided to members of minority groups compared to majority population patients with similar diagnostic profiles. Inequities will be reviewed and remediated.

Paternalism

The history of the United States to date documents the assumption of intellectual and moral superiority of Whites over persons of color. One of the effects of this putative superiority is a crippling paternalism that discounts the values, insights, perspectives, and inherent potential of much of this country's population. Even though this core assumption is increasingly challenged by some groups who will no longer participate as collusive victims, the roots of this world view as a whole run far too deep to be eliminated summarily. No dimension of U.S. culture has remained unaffected by this bias, and health care is a significant example of its impact.

However, the historically paternalistic position of physicians is giving way to a collaborative model of health care that gives some control to the client in his or her health management. Various treatment possibilities are presented more frequently as options rather than as commands. Decisions regarding life and death are becoming the province of the patient and family rather than that of the physician alone.

In brief, the physician is coming to be perceived as a person with his or her own value system and technical expertise who enters into a professional relationship with another person who perhaps has different values. While the technical expertise of the physician is of paramount importance in this relationship, the client's value perspective represents the personhood that is the basis of any relationship. This by no means suggests capitulation into ethical relativism in which every value system is considered as valid as every other. This does not have to be the interpretation. Rather, the entire situation must be value-weighted in the direction of the person who has the most at stake—in this case clearly the client, whose life may be on the line. Through discussion, education, and negotiation, a compromise position may be reached that brings the client's choices closer to those of the physician and vice versa. If, however, the physician cannot adjust for differential value-weighting, he or she should disengage from the case with referral to another provider who has less difficulty with the situation.

Within the framework of a social nexus ethic, the very nature of society is seen as dynamic and interactive, with variable value-weights constantly emerging from ever-changing contexts. Mediation and negotiation should be employed to optimize benefits for everyone in a particular context, but the primary stakeholders in it must be afforded value-weighted significance and agency.

Informed Consent

It is the ethical responsibility of all health care providers to ensure that a client has intelligible and complete data on which to base discussion of options and make decisions about his or her own care or that of an incompetent family member. This is difficult in the best of circumstances. However, some physicians may overlook indications that the client may have cultural, linguistic, or educational challenges in understanding medical terminology.

Such a situation does pose problems. Nonetheless, skillful bilingual and bicultural interpreters can and do make sense even of the most technical procedures and interventions. The task is to locate and educate these interpreters as peer advocates well in advance of needing their services. As an integral component of an interdisciplinary service network, these individuals can facilitate health care, social services, and mental health interventions, as well as public services such as fire and police protection. When appropriately informed, clients and their families may have more confidence in the health care system and be more likely to follow recommended homecare.

Only in a life-threatening emergency is it ever appropriate for a physician to initiate procedures on a human being without verified informed consent. If the central message of social nexus ethics is to recognize and honor the personhood of each individual in relation to all others, then informed consent is a fundamental right, regardless of the inconvenience presented by cultural, linguistic, or any other impediments. Moreover, by the proactive envelopment of peer advocates into the heart of the process, the network becomes stronger and healthier for everyone.

Respect for the Whole Person

"Why don't they just be like us?" "Well, they're *here* now; they need to learn to do things *our* way!" "If they can't even speak English, that's *their* problem." "Actually, people are all the same under the skin."

Such remarks have been heard repeatedly in the halls of medicine. Health care providers sometimes become exasperated by the challenges of multiculturalism, and in some cases, they simply deny them. The first three statements indicate a superiority bias toward majority culture and language that necessarily denigrates the personhood of the minority member. As discussed earlier, personhood includes all of one's racioethnic and personal history, language, values, folkways, traditions, beliefs, and practices. Social nexus ethics requires the affirmation of *all* persons as significant and valued, along with their unique perspectives. Forcing uniformity and conformity with the majority culture distorts the reality of society as it in fact is and discounts the realities of minority persons as irrelevant and inferior. Social nexus ethics insists that the network itself is a series of intersections of personal realities, no one of which is intrinsically superior to any other. Closer analysis often reveals that one's personal comfort zone is used as a barometer of cultural superiority; education about a particular culture can create a comfort zone that is much less threatened by "otherness."

Education itself, then, becomes an ethical issue. To what extent are health care providers morally responsible for learning about the cultures of minority groups? To the extent that they wish to provide optimum care to minority clients in general, such education is both a professional and a moral obligation. The changing demographics of the United States and emerging health care plans also argue for the prudence of achieving an effective level of cultural competence. But the most poignant and significant arguments come from the tragedies of real life.

In 1975, during the first wave of refugee resettlement from Southeast Asia, a Vietnamese father in California brought his desperately ill son to an emergency department for treatment of advanced influenza. In an effort to treat the child at home as the first line of defense, the family had used traditional Southeast Asian coin-rubbing on him to bring out the fever. This treatment creates highly regular Christmas-tree-like red marks radiating from the spine out along the interstices of the rib cage. The darker the marks become, the sicker the person is thought to be—hence the child's trip to the emergency department. Uninformed about this harmless and well-intentioned therapy, emergency department personnel contacted the police, who charged the father with child abuse and took him to jail. The child subsequently died due to complications from the flu. The father hanged himself in jail (Nong, 1976).

In Wisconsin, a Hmong family was accused of child abuse for treating a child with a traditional ointment that supposedly contained high levels of lead. When the police came to the door, the father first killed his wife and then turned the gun on himself, judging their deaths preferable to the shame of arrest (Lo Pao Vang, Personal communication, 1990). A little education in these highly sensitive cultural areas could well have saved both heartache and lives.

Education works both ways. Minority groups, especially those new to the United States and to Western systems, need time to discover and evaluate the properties of the dominant health care models. Should they choose to continue traditional curative techniques in parallel with cosmopolitan techniques, they will be able to do so with adequate information. Dominant-culture health care providers need time to study and appreciate the possible benefits of traditional healing arts, as well as the myriad dimensions of other lifeworlds. Many physicians, nurses, social workers, allied health professionals, and educators are discovering whole worlds of knowledge and experience and are gladly embracing them in lieu of myopic parochialism. In the multicultural reality of the twenty-first century, these individuals will be key intersections in the social nexus and champions of a new day in ethical understanding.

REFERENCES

Barnouw, V. (1985). *Culture and personality* (4th ed). Homewood, IL: Dorsey.

Dana, R. H. (1993). *Multicultural assessment perspectives for professional psychology*. Needham Heights, MA: Allyn and Bacon.

Friedman, E. (1991, April 5). Health care's changing face: The demographics of the 21st century. *Hospitals*, pp. 36–40.

Hagland, M. M. (1992, February 20) The sagging safety net: Emergency departments on the brink of crisis. *Hospitals*, pp. 26–32.

Jordan, D. K., & Swartz, M. J. (Eds.). (1990). *Personality and the cultural construction of society*. Tuscaloosa: The University of Alabama Press.

Maurer, D. (1989, Fall/Winter). Take two aspirin, break an egg under the bed, and call me in the morning. *HQ*, pp. 2–5.

Nong, T. A. (1976). Pseudo-battered child syndrome. *Journal of the American Medical Association*, 623, 2288.

Rawls, J. (1971). *A theory of justice*. Cambridge, MA: Harvard University Press.

Rossett, A., & Bickham, T. (1994, January). Diversity training, hope, faith and cynicism. *Training*, pp. 40–46.

Sabatino, F. (1992, January 5). Home health: PPOs top diversification options. *Hospitals*, p. 48.

Staff. (1993, July 20). Datawatch. *Hospitals and Health Network*.

Takaki, R. (1993). *A different mirror: A history of multicultural America*. Boston: Little, Brown.

SUGGESTED READINGS

Chan, S. (1991). *Asian Americans: An interpretive history.* Boston: Twayne.

Cornelius, L. J. (1991). Access to medical care for Black Americans with an episode of illness. *Journal of the National Medical Association, 83*(7), 617–626.

Cortese, A. (1990). *Ethnic ethics: The restructuring of moral theory.* Albany: State University of New York Press.

Dewey, J. (1958). *Experience and nature.* New York: Dover.

Festinger, L. (1957). *A theory of cognitive dissonance.* Stanford, CA: Stanford University Press.

Fisher, A. A. (1984). Coin dermatitis. *Cutis, 33*(6), 530.

Gioseffi, D. (1993). *On prejudice: A global perspective.* New York: Anchor Books/Doubleday.

Johnson, J. (1992, November 20). Economic forces drive collaboration push. *Hospitals,* p. 38.

May, L., & Sharratt, S. C. (Eds.). (1994). *Applied ethics: A multicultural approach.* Englewood Cliffs, NJ: Prentice Hall.

Outpatient procedures. (1993, July 20). *Hospitals and Health Networks,* p. 52.

Roberts, J.R. (1988). Beware: Vietnamese coin rubbing. (Letter to the Editor.) *Annals of Emergency Medicine, 17*(4), 384.

Tracking the long-term growth in outpatient care. (1991, December 5). *Hospitals,* p. 16.

Whitaker, B. (1984). *Minorities: A question of human rights?* New York: Pergamon.

Annotated Multicultural Bibliography by Health Care Profession

HEALTH EDUCATION

Adeyanju, M., Tricker, R., & Spencer, R. (1989/1990). Comparison of health status of international and American university students: Implications for health education. *International Quarterly of Community Health Education, 10*(2), 145–166.

These authors examine the differences between male and female international and American university students relative to their self-perceived health status, health attitudes, behaviors, and locus of control. Results indicate that sociocultural stressors may influence both groups' health status and care.

Amaro, H., Russo, N., & Parés-Avila, J. (1987). Contemporary research on Hispanic women: A selected bibliography of the social science literature. *Psychology of Women Quarterly, 11*(4), 523–532.

Objectives of the authors are to facilitate the integration of material on Hispanic women into the curriculum, promote and disseminate research on the psychology of Hispanic women, and recognize the contributions of early researchers of this neglected group.

Bateman, M. J., Pauley, D., & Woods, M. (1991). *Facing the world: An independent living/pre-employment curriculum for refugee youths.* Richmond, VA: Catholic Charities.

This document contains a curriculum guide focusing on both independent living skills and job readiness skills.

183

Clark, H. (1989, October). *Native perspectives on childbearing and health.* Paper presented at the National Symposium on Aboriginal Women of Canada: Past, Present, and Future, Lethbridge, Alberta, Canada.

This ethnographic study sought to understand, from the native perspective, the traditional childbearing values and practices of Coast Salish peoples and the difficulties in maintaining these in a society that is not oriented to native values and practices.

Ghazizadeh, M. (1992). Islamic health sciences: A model for health education and promotion. *Journal of Health Education, 23*(4), 227–231.

Because the concept of Islamic health sciences is unfamiliar to most professionals, the article reviews its history, focusing on physician–patient relationships, dental health, diet and nutrition, sexual health, reproduction, and boundaries for sexual behavior. The author recommends that health professionals recognize these issues when considering health education and promotion programs.

Jalan, R. (1992). Teaching minds, healing bodies: A Canadian college encourages students to enter health careers by emphasizing math and science skills. *Tribal College: Journal of American Indian Higher Education, 3*(3), 16–18.

This article describes Saskatchewan Indian Federated College's preprofessional, a university-level science program and its focus on building math and science skills and on Indian culture, traditional medicine, current and future health care needs, and the goals of Indian people.

King, L. (1982). Professional preparation: Multicultural health beliefs in action. *Health Education, 13*(5), 24–25.

A course dealing with health beliefs was developed. An ethnically diverse class visited different cultural settings to study beliefs about religion, nutrition, folk medicine, and other customs affecting health practices.

Knaub, P. K., & Anderson, K. (1987). Measuring conception and pregnancy myths. *Journal of Home Economics, 79*(10–13), 54.

To establish whether contemporary women accept or reject myths relative to conception and pregnancy, two groups of women (pregnant and never pregnant) were surveyed on sixty related items. Scores for the two groups did not differ significantly; however, the advent of pregnancy does appear to improve pregnancy knowledge.

Lamarine, R. (1989). The dilemma of Native American health. *Health Education, 20*(5), 15–18.

This article relates the poor health status of Native Americans to low self-esteem, inadequate formal education, poverty, and a traditional value system that has been ignored or disparaged by White society. Recommendations for health education are made.

Laveist, T. (1993). Segregation, poverty and empowerment: Health consequences for African Americans. *Millbank Quarterly, 71*(1), 41–64.

Multivariate analysis in this study, including indices of racial residential segregation, poverty, and black political empowerment, shows that the association between poverty and infant mortality is stronger for Whites than for Blacks.

Moody, L., & Laurent, M. (1984). Promoting health through the use of storytelling. *Health Education, 15*(1), 8–10, 12.

Storytelling can be used to motivate people toward good helath behaviors. When Seminole Indians were told health-related folktales, they became more aware of health problems. Suggestions for developing stories and questions are listed along with recommendations and conclusions.

Patterson, D. (1990). Gaining access to community resources: Breaking the cycle of adolescent pregnancy. *Journal of Health Care for the Poor and Underserved, 1*(1), 147–149.

Adolescent pregnancy results from a combination of factors, including feelings of hopelessness, poor education, and the effects of racism. This article reiterates findings that preg- nancy prevention programs should be sensitive to the target group culture, include other family members, and reach males as well as females.

Randolph, S., & Banks, H. D. (1993). Making a way out of no way: The promise of Africentric approaches to HIV prevention. *Journal of Black Psychology, 19*(2), 204–214.

This article discusses ways in which selected factors limit human immunodeficiency virus prevention efforts in African-American communities, focusing on the stigma associated with acquired immune deficiency syndrome, reliance on traditional models of health, and the lack of funding for needed services and research.

Stein, H., & Hill, R. (1977). The limits of ethnicity. *American Scholar, 46*(2), 181–189.

A description and analysis are presented of the identity, ideology, and polity of the New Ethnicity or the White Ethnic Movement. The Age of Pluralism is seen as succeeding the Age of Integration, with the metaphor of the static "mosaic" replacing that of the dynamic Melting Pot-American Dream imagery.

MEDICINE

Ackerman, A. (1983, June). *Lead oxides used in the treatment of empacho.* Paper presented at the U.S./Mexico Cross Border Health Association Meeting, Albuquerque, New Mexico.

Many Mexican Americans regard "Azarcon" and "Greta" as desired medical treatments for empacho, a perceived intestinal blockage. The folk medicines, available in Mexico but not in the United States, can cause lead poisoning, which can result in brain swelling, coma, permanent mental retardation, and death.

Ahmad, W. I. U. (1992). The maligned healer: The hakim and western medicine. *New Community, 18*(4), 521–536.

Concerns about Eastern medicine are explored, examining such issues as the hakim's education and training, treatment regimens, concepts of health and illness prevalent in the Asian communities and their relevance to the choice of practitioner, and implications for health.

Bates, V. E. (1981, August). *Traditional healing and Western health care: A case against formal integration.* Paper presented at the Annual Convention of the American Psychological Association, Los Angeles, California.

Based on selected readings of the literature on medical anthropology and the sociology of modern and traditional system integration in other societies, this paper argues that state heteronomy is patently contraindicated, yet inevitable, should the funding and power structure behind Western health care systems be formally integrated with the traditional American Indian healing system. The paper attempts to reflect strengths in the traditional healing system and discusses nonmedical interventions and the destructive aspects of large-scale educational efforts to incorporate the traditional into the modern system.

Coreil, J. (1983). Parallel structures in professional and folk health care: A model applied to rural Haiti. *Culture, Medicine and Psychiatry, 7*(2), 131–151.

Professional and folk sectors of pluralistic health care systems share certain structural features that in some respects have equal or greater importance than obvious differences. A model based on the concepts of primary, secondary, and tertiary care is adapted to an analysis of both folk and professional domains of the rural Haitian health care system.

Erzinger, S. (1991). Communication between Spanish-speaking patients and their doctors in medical encounters. *Culture, Medicine and Psychiatry, 15*(1), 91–110.

This study examines the interaction of language and culture in medical encounters between Spanish-speaking Latino patients and their doctors, who have a range of Spanish language ability and a variety of cultural backgrounds. Data illustrate how language and culture interact in accomplishing communicative tasks as doctors attend Spanish-speaking patients.

Farrell, S., Kohl, H., & Rogers, T. (1987). The independent effect of ehtnicity on cardiovascular fitness. *Human Biology, 59*(4), 657–666.

The authors completed an examination of differences in fitness-related variables due to ethnicity among teachers.

Heggenhougen, H., & Shore, L. (1986). Cultural components of behavioural epidemiology: Implications for primary health care. *Social Science and Medicine, 22*(11), 1235–1245.

The association of culturally linked behavior and epidemiology is discussed to determine whether patterns of disease are significantly related to cultural sets of normative beliefs and behavior.

Kundstadter, P. (1980). Medical ethics in cross-cultural ànd multi-cultural perspectives. *Social Science and Medicine, 14B*(4), 289–296.

The ethical implications of medical pluralism have been little studied in Western coutnries, and not at all in non-Western countries, yet ethical differences reflecting cultural values must be considered in international health programs and policies, where Western innovations will increasingly be adapted to the medical needs of non-Western societies.

Linzer, N. (1986). The obligations of adult children to aged parents: A view from Jewish tradition. *Journal of Aging and Judaism, 1*(1), 34–48.

Pressures on adult children caught between responsibility for their elderly parents and for their young children are discussed, and limitations of filial responsibility for sick parents are offered.

Mardiros, M. (1989). Conception of childhood disability among Mexican-

American parents. *Medical Anthropology, 12*(1), 55–68.

This article examines the responses of Mexican-American parents to their child's physical or mental disability. Data show that eliciting culturally relevant information from parents is essential in promoting the well-being of parents and children.

McGlynn, F. (Ed.). (1984). Health care in the Caribbean and Central America. *Studies in Third World Societies, 30,* 166.

This publication examines a range of public health issues in the Caribbean Basin including conditions responsible for the transmission of disease, folk palliatives, and factors affecting preventive and curative health services on the national level. Comparisons are also made among the various Caribbean countries.

Palinkas, L. (1987). A longitudinal study of ethnicity and disease incidence. *Medical Anthropology Quarterly (New Series), 1*(1), 85–108.

The results of a prospective study of ethnic group differences in rates of hospitalization for all diseases and injuries among a cohort of U.S. Navy enlisted men are examined.

Roberts, R. (1984). *Ethnicity and health: Mexican Americans. A guide for health care providers.* Bethesda MD: National Fund for Medical Education, National Institute Of Mental Health.

Several characteristics of and perspectives on how Mexican Americans regard health care are presented for health care providers. Following a brief discussion of culture and health, the guide describes the traditional and modern value orientations of Hispanics and the external forces that contribute to their adoption.

Saver, J., & Denlinger, S. (1985). Which doctor is not a witch doctor? *Advances, 2*(1) 20–30.

This article reports on a seminar in which participants examined the interplay of mind and body in disease, providing a possibly unique glimpse of medical students and educators struggling to comprehend more fully how the mind may affect health and illness.

NURSING

Alonzo, A. A. (1985). Health as situational adaption: A social psychological perspective. *Social Science and Medicine, 21*(12), 1341–1344.

This study explores a relational conception of health, the central importance of the socially defined situation for health and adaptation, and the limits of medicine and holism in intervening in problems of adaptation, and it suggests a situational approach to the study of health and adaptation.

Berkanovic, E., & Telesky, C. (1985). Mexican-American, Black-American and White-American differences in reporting illnesses, disability and physician visits for illnesses. *Social Science and Medicine, 20*(6), 567–77.

This article presents data on the reporting of illnesses, disability due to illnesses, and the decision to seek medical attention for illnesses among a representative sample of Mexican Americans, Black Americans and White Americans. Speculations are offered regarding the meaning and historical sources of the differences observed.

Buckwalter, K. C., Abraham, I. L., Smith, M., & Smullen, D. E. (1993). Nursing outreach to rural elderly people who are mentally ill. *Hospital and Community Psychiatry, 44*(9), 821–823.

This article describes outreach models of care designed to provide services to rural elderly residents who are mentally ill. Although the models differ in some important respects, both are multidisciplinary, emphasize geographical appropriateness of services, promote utilization of existing community resources, coordinate diverse services, and offer supportive programs such as those for caregivers.

Champion, V., Austin, J., & Tzeng, O. C. (1987). Cross-cultural comparison of images of nurses and physicians. *International Nursing Review, 34*(2), 43–8.

This study investigates attitudes related to the image of nurses and physicians across thirty cultures. The author contends that nurses' ability to influence health care decision making may be limited if they are viewed as powerless, and they must address this deficit in their public image.

Champion, V. L., Austin, J. K., & Tzeng, O. C. S. (1990). Relationship between cross-cultural health attitudes and community health indicators. *Public Health Nursing, 7*(4), 243–50.

The purpose of the study was to investigate the relationship between attitudes toward health and indexes of community health. Positive relationships were found between public health expenditures and nurses, indicating that in countries with more expenditures for community and public

health, attitudes toward nurses were more positive.

DeSantis, L. (1989). Health care orientations of Cuban and Haitian immigrant mothers: Implications for health care professionals. *Medical Anthropology, 12*(1), 69–89.

Data from Cuban and Haitian immigrant mothers on their beliefs and practices as parents in relation to child socialization and health illustrate that the process of determining culture-specific care is basically the same for any individual.

Eliason, M. J., & Randall, C. E. (1991). Lesbian phobia in nursing students. *Western Journal of Nursing Research, 13*(3), 363–374.

The author investigated female undergraduate nursing students' attitudes toward lesbians, particularly in relation to age, sex-role identity, and familiarity with lesbian life-styles. Lesbian phobia was common among subjects, and 50 percent of them indicated that lesbian life-styles were not acceptable. Suggestions are given for inclusion of lesbian culture in nursing education.

Flaskerud, J. H. (1990). Matching client and therapist ethnicity, language, and gender: A review of research. *Issues in Mental Health Nursing, 11*(4), 321–336.

The purpose of this article is to examine whether therapy process and outcome are influenced by a client–therapist ethnicity, language, or gender match.

Ganong, L. H., Coleman, M., & Riley, C. (1988). Nursing students' stereotypes of married and unmarried pregnant clients. *Research in Nursing and Health, 11*(5), 333–342.

The authors investigated the effects of information about a pregnant client's marital status on nursing students' initial perceptions of the client, attributions of group stereotypes to the client, predictions of client behavior, data sought, and verbal responses toward the client. Results indicate that married clients were more positively evaluated than the unmarried clients. Perceptions were consistent with cultural stereotypes.

Giger, J. N. (1992). Black American folk medicine health care beliefs: Implication for nursing plans of care. *ABNF Journal, 3*(2), 42–46.

Even in this age of information, some African Americans equate good health with luck or success. An illness or disease, viewed as undesirable, may be equated with bad luck, chance, fate, poverty, domestic turmoil, or unemployment, and in such cases Black Americans will consult a physician only after attempts with home remedies have failed. According to the author, it is important that the nurse, when working with Black patients, remember that when a particular patient enters the traditional biomedical health care delivery system it is best to assume that all known and available cultural home remedies have been tried. It is also essential that the nurse determine whether these home remedies will interact or interfere with orthodox medical approaches.

Harel, Z. (1990). Ethnicity and aging: Implications for the Jewish community. *Contemporary Jewry, 11*(2), 77–91.

This article presents an overview of the theoretical and empirical literature on the effects of ethnicity in the lives of older Jewish persons. Implications for the planning and delivery of health and human services are discussed.

Huff, C. (1990, November). *Pediatric health fairs: One approach to the health needs of Appalachian children.* Paper presented at the Fifth Conference on Appalachia, Lexington, Kentucky.

An assessment of the health education needs of children resulted in the initiation of a pediatric health fair, which helped meet educational goals and helped establish communication between the school and community.

Kavanagh, K. H. (1991). Invisibility and selective avoidance: Gender and ethnicity in psychiatry and psychiatric nursing staff interaction. *Culture, Medicine and Psychiatry, 15*(2), 245–274.

The author of this article analyzes institutionalized inequity and discrimination in the forms of sexism and racism in a medical center's department of psychiatry. Despite recognition of the roles that culture and gender play in care and treatment of patients, psychiatric and mental health professionals tended to avoid critical examination of their own and their coworkers' ethnicity and gender as those characteristics influenced life experiences, occupational roles and status, and hierarchical relationships.

Laing, M. (1993). Gossip: Does it play a role in the socialization of nurses? *IMAGE: Journal of Nursing Scholarship, 25*(1), 37–43.

This article discusses gossip from historical, analytical, and feminist perspectives and describes the manner in which gossip contributes to the socialization of nurses to their professional role and to their work culture. It is argued that despite its generally negative reputation, gossip is a significant genre of communication in every society. A major component of professional socialization is internalization of the norms and values of the work culture. As a social process, gossip strengthens the assumptions of group members regarding their professional ideology.

Lightfoot, K. H. (1989). Rites of purification and their effects: Some psychological aspects of female genital circumcision and infibulation (Pharaonic circumcision) in an Afro-Arab Islamic society (Sudan). *Journal of Psychology and Human Sexuality, 2*(2), 79–91.

Pharaonic circumcision is a culturally embedded practice interwoven with patrilineage, family honor, and social position. It is clung to tenaciously by both sexes, although its long-term effects are detrimental to the health of girls and women and thereby the well-being of the entire family. The adverse psychological effects of this practice on women are mitigated by a strong conviction that its performance purifies and ennobles them.

Lipson, J. G., & Meleis, A. I. (1989). Methodological issues in research with immigrants. *Medical Anthropology, 12*(1), 103–115.

Three strategies are described that can help researchers work with the issues of how informants present themselves, answer in accordance to what they perceive that interviewers expect, and choose what and what not to divulge.

Maroney, D., & Golub, S. (1992). Nurses' attitudes toward obese persons and certain ethnic groups. *Perceptual and Motor Skills, 75*(2), 387–391.

A study on nurses' attitudes toward obese persons reflected that nurses who showed more negative attitudes toward obese persons also expressed more ethnic prejudices. A surprising finding was a new target of ethnic prejudice: the Caucasian majority.

Minrath, M. (1985). Breaking the race barrier. *Journal of Psychosocial Nursing and Mental Health Services, 23*(8), 19–20, 22–24.

Only when therapists have come to some resolution of their own feelings about the plight of ethnic minorities in this country can they develop acumen in interracial practice. The author of the article argues that although the therapeutic skills applied in psychotherapy with ethnic minorities are in no way different from overall therapeutic skills, certain techniques may be especially useful in interracial practice.

O'Rourke, M. (1986). The influence of social, demographic, employment, and health factors on the psychological well-being of employed women. *Issues in Mental Health Nursing, 8*(2), 121–141.

The author studied the relationship between social, demographic, employment, and health characteristics and psychological well-being in a selected sample of generally healthy, university-employed women. No significant relationships were found between psychological well-being and ethnicity.

Pachter, L. M. (1994). Culture and clinical care: Folk illness beliefs and behaviors and their implications for health care delivery. *Journal of the*

American Medical Association, 271(9), 690–694.

This article presents an approach to the evaluation of patient-held beliefs and behaviors that may not be concordant with those of biomedicine. Clinical issues surrounding folk beliefs and behaviors are discussed in a culturally sensitive way.

Press, I. (1978). Urban folk medicine: A functional overview. *American Anthropologist, 80*(1), 71–84.

Socioeconomic functions of folk disease and folk medicine are examined in terms of their response to urban socioeconomic characteristics. Such practices appear to serve functions of acculturation, guilt displacement resulting from failure to achieve, and subgroup identity maintenance, among others.

Rapp, R. (1993). Amniocentesis in sociocultural perspective. *Journal of Genetic Counseling, 2*(3), 183–196.

This article reports on an anthropological investigation of the social impact and cultural meaning of amniocentesis illustrating how class differences, as well as sociocultural diversity, deeply affect pregnant women's acceptance, rejection, and interpretation of prenatal testing.

Reyes-Acosta, V. (1985). Folk illnesses reported to physicians in the Lower Rio Grande Valley: A binational comparison. *Ethnology, 24*(3), 229–236.

This article contains an examination of self-report illness behavior associated with folk illnesses common to the Hispano-American folk medicine tradition.

Rodríguez, R. (1993). Violence in transience: Nursing care of battered migrant women. *Clinical Issues in Perinatal and Women's Health Nursing, 4*(3), 437–440.

Poverty, language, and cultural differences between farmworker women and health care providers present substantial barriers to women obtaining access to the health care system. These differences are especially important in instances of domestic violence. Strategies for working with migrant battered women are offered.

Sebej, F. (1989). Psychological risk factors of coronary heart diseases as culture-related phenomena. *Studia Psychologica, 31*(4), 259–269.

This article reviews the published results of meta-analytical studies of Type A behavior patterns. A hypothesis called *psychological risk factors of cardiovascular diseases* is proposed, that is strongly culture dependent. Traits and states of culture are also proposed that could contribute to the development of coronary-prone personality and to coronary health-endangering life situations.

Sheppard, M. (1992). Contact and collaboration with general practitioners: A comparison of social workers and community psychiatric nurses. *British Journal of Social Work, 22*(4), 419–436.

This study compares communication and collaboration between social workers and general practitioners (GPs) with that between community psychiatric nurses (CPNs) and general practitioners.

Stein, J. A., Fox, S. A., & Murata, P. J. (1991). The influence of ethnicity, socioeconomic status, and psychological barriers on use of mammography. *Journal of Health and Social Behavior, 32*(2), 101–113.

This study assessed the relative influence of psychological barriers, socioeconomic status, and ethnic differences in mammography use for a community sample of White, Black, and Hispanic women.

Stevenson, T. (1985–1986). A workshop in transcultural nursing. *Community College Review, 13*(3), 40–46.

This article describes an experimental workshop on the relationship between health and culture.

Stumpf, S. H., & Bass, K. (1992). Cross cultural communication to help physician assistants provide unbiased health care. *Public Health Reports, 107*(1), 113–115.

Teaching cross-cultural communication typically involves instruction in differences between groups. The authors present a model ("Differences + Discomforts = Discoveries") that inhibits factionalizing and promotes depth of knowledge about underserved groups.

Tellis-Nayak, V, & Tellis-Nayak, M. (1989). Quality of care and the burden of two cultures: When the world of nurse's aide enters the world of the nursing home. *The Gerontologist, 29*(3), 307–313.

Using ethnographic data, the study reported in this article examined the two worlds of the nurse's aide: the world in which she lives and the world in which she works. Because the institutional culture of the nursing home often adds to the adversity of their personal lives, nurse's aides move between the two mileaus in a self-perpetuating negative cycle.

Watson, E., & Evans, S. J. (1986). An example of cross-cultural measurement of psychological symptoms in postpartum mothers. *Social Science and Medicine, 23*(9), 869–874.

As part of a longitudinal study of child health services usage, psychiatric morbidity was assessed across cultures in three groups of mothers. Results suggest that it is possible to compare psychiatric morbidity across cultures. In addition, there seemed to be little difference in the psychological symptoms experienced in the year following their infants' birth in the varying cultures.

Weitzel, M. H., & Waller, P. (1990). Predictive factors for health-promotive behaviors in White, Hispanic, and Black blue-collar workers. *Family and Community Health, 13*(1), 23–34.

The authors studied White, Hispanic, and Black blue-collar workers to determine whether demographic and cognitive-perceptual factors predicted health-promoting behaviors.

Westbrook, M., Legge, V., & Pennay, M. (1993). Attitudes towards disabilities in a multicultural society. *Social Science and Medicine, 36*(5), 615–623.

Chinese, Italian, German, Greek, Arabic, and Anglo-Australian communities are used to evaluate their attitudes toward disability groups. Implications for people with disabilities and health practitioners in multicultural societies are discussed.

NUTRITION

Balsam, A. L., Poe, D. M., & Bottum, C. (1992). Food habits and nutritional knowledge of Portuguese participants in an elderly nutrition program. *Journal of Nutrition for the Elderly, 12*(1), 33–42.

The authors developed a special nutrition program to provide culturally appropriate lunches, followed by socialization activities for Portuguese elderly.

DeMars, P. (1992). An occupational therapy life skills curriculum model for a Native American tribe: A health promotion program based on ethnographic field research. *American Journal of Occupational Therapy, 46*(8), 727–736.

This article describes the development of a series of life skills and prevocational programs for Native Americans, focusing on the educational program philosophy, theory base, and role of occupational therapy in program development.

Food and Nutrition Service. (1984). *Nutrition education for Native Americans: A guide for nutrition educators*. Washington, DC: U.S. Department of Agriculture.

Written for professionals working with food assistance and other programs with a nutrition component, this guide is intended to aid in understanding the cultural characteristics and basic health and diet-related problems of Native Americans and to promote more effective nutrition counseling and community nutrition education.

Guarnaccia, P. J., Angel, R., & Worobey, J. L. (1989). The factor structure of the CES-D in the Hispanic health and nutrition examination survey: The influences of ethnicity, gender and language. *Social Science and Medicine, 29*(1), 85–94

These authors examined the factor structure of the Center for Epidemiologic Studies-Depression Scale (CES-D) in the Hispanic Health and Nutrition Examination Survey (Hispanic HANES). Significant intragroup differences were found among Mexican Americans, Puerto Ricans,

and Cuban Americans, which were strongly influenced by the gender of the respondent and the language in which the person was interviewed.

Kendall, L. (1987). Cold wombs in balmy Honolulu: Ethnogynecology among Korean immigrants. Special issue: Hot-cold food and medical theories: Cross-cultural perspectives. *Social Science and Medicine, 25*(4), 367–376.

The author addresses *naeng* in relation to the interlayering of information and experience that shapes a Korean woman's sense of illness or well-being when she describes an intimate condition as *naeng*. Various dimensions relevant to health care emerge. It is argued that a definition of cold wombs as folk illness would not explain the particular anxieties that *naeng* sufferers bring to a clinic.

Launer, L. J., & Habicht, J. P. (1989). Concepts about infant health, growth, and weaning: A comparison between nutritional scientists and Madurese mothers. *Social Science and Medicine, 29*(1), 13–22.

This study compared the views of nutritional scientists and mothers in Indonesia on (1) health and disease and (2) the relationship of foods to the concepts of state of health, infancy, and growth. Findings are discussed with regard to the relation between cultural ideas, feeding practice, and health outcomes.

Schilling, B., & Brannon, E. (1986). *Cross-cultural counseling: A guide for nutrition and health counselors*. Washington, DC: U.S. Department of Agriculture; U.S. Department of Health and Human Services.

This guide promotes awareness of cross-cultural counseling problems and provides information for counseling clients with different beliefs, customs, and behaviors related to food and health.

PSYCHOLOGY AND PSYCHIATRY

Berlin, I. (1987). Effects of changing Native American cultures on child development. *Journal of Community Psychology, 15*(3), 299–306.

This article discusses the critical developmental problems that exist for children in many American Indian reservations, including child abuse and neglect, substance abuse, depression, and nonlearning in schools.

Bond, M. (1991). Chinese values and health: A cultural-level examination. *Psychology and Health, 5*(2), 137–152.

This country-level analysis revealed relationships between value dimension theories about cultural emphases on individualism and on material success.

Carden, A., & Feicht, R. (1991). Homesickness among American and Turkish college students. *Journal of Cross Cultural Psychology, 22*(3), 418–428.

This article explores the cultural differences in the degree of homesickness. The mean homesickness rating of the American sample studied by the authors was significantly less than the mean homesickness rating of a Turkish sample.

Cheng, L. Y., & Lo, H. T. (1991). On the advantages of cross-culture psychotherapy: the minority therapist/mainstream patient dyad. *Psychiatry, 54*(4), 386–396.

The personal quality of the therapist is a key element in therapy. Advantages discussed include language independence, culture independence, positive transference, and analogous experiences.

Fernando, S. (1992). Racism and the health of ethnic minorities. *International Migration, 30,* 87–101.

Recognition of how racism is embedded in both the tradition and professional practice of psychiatry is a sine qua non condition to provision of appropriate health services for everyone.

Fraser, M. W., & Pecora, P. J. (1985). Psychological adaptation among Indochinese refugees. *Journal of Applied Social Sciences, 10*(1), 20–39.

The authors examined common mental health needs among Indo-Chinese refugees and assessed the effectiveness of programs and services in promoting self-sufficiency. Clinical strategies are suggested in light of resettlement policies and refugees' views toward mental health services.

Furnham, A., & Shiekh, S. (1993). Gender, generational and social support correlates of mental health in Asian immigrants. *International Journal of Social Psychiatry, 39*(1), 22–33.

The authors interviewed female and male Asian immigrants, mainly from India and Pakistan, concerning their psychological adjustment to life in the United Kingdom. Social support networks contributed to or allayed psychological stress in different ways for immigrants. Results indicate that female immigrants have a harder time adjusting and that second-generation immigrants experience more psychological distress than first-generation immigrants.

Gorkin, M. (1986). Countertransference in cross-cultural psychotherapy: The example of Jewish therapist and Arab patient. *Psychiatry, 49*(1), 69–79.

The focus of this article is on some of the countertransference issues in cross-cultural psychotherapy, with reference to one specific, and in some ways unique, therapist–patient dyad: the Jewish (Israeli) therapist and the Arab patient. The author explores some of the more typical and troublesome countertransference issues that often occur in this particular example of cross-cultural psychotherapy.

Grieve, N., Rosenthal, D., & Cavallo, A. (1988). Self-esteem and sex-role attitudes: A comparison of Italian- and Anglo-Australian adolescent girls. *Psychology of Women Quarterly, 12*(2), 175–189.

Italian-Australian and Anglo-Austrialian girls were compared on self-esteem and on measures associated with sex roles, including attitudes toward sex-role differentiation in the family and the culture.

Karanci, N. (1986). Causal attributions for psychological illness among Turkish psychiatric in-patients and their relationships with hope. *International Journal of Social Psychiatry, 32*(4), 3–12.

The author emphasizes the non-Western familial and cultural traits and attributions that must be considered when working in psychiatric departments in Turkey.

Nakano, K. (1991). Coping strategies and psychological symptoms in a Japanese sample. *Journal of Clinical Psychology, 47*(3), 346–350.

The role of coping strategies as moderators in the relationship between hassles and psychological/physical well-being was investigated by the author. Results indicated that the role of coping strategies did not appear to be influenced by the Japanese cultural environment.

Nilchaikovit, T., Hill, J. M., & Holland J. C. (1993). The effects of culture on illness behavior and medical care. Asian and American differences. *General Hospital Psychiatry, 15*(1), 41–50.

This paper examines the effects of culture on illness behavior and medical care by contrasting the differences between American and Asian cultures.

Office of Ethnic Minority Affairs. (1993). Guidelines for providers of psychological services to ethnic, linguistic, and culturally diverse populations. *American Psychologist, 48*(1), 45–48.

This article presents guidelines formulated by the American Psychological Association to provide psychological service providers with the requisite skills for multicultural assessment and intervention and to assist them in understanding the role that culture and ethnicity/race play in the sociopsychological and economic development of culturally diverse populations.

Powell, G., Wyatt, G., & Bass, B. (1983). Mental health professionals' views of Afro-American family life and sexuality. *Journal of Sex and Marital Therapy, 9*(1), 51–66.

Significant differences are found among southern California mental health professionals in an analysis of their responses in the areas of family life patterns and marital relationships and sexual values and behavior as described in the Survey of Afro-American Behavior.

Scott, W., Scott, R., Boehnke, K., & Cheng, S. (1991). Children's personality as a function of family relations within and between cultures. *Journal of Cross Cultural Psychology, 22*(2), 182–208.

The degree to which cultural differences in children's personalities could be explained by the culturally characteristic patterns of family relations to which they were exposed is examined in this article.

Shek, D. (1989). Sex differences in the psychological well-being of Chinese adolescents. *Journal of Psychology, 123*(4), 405–412.

This author assesses sex differences in the psychological well-being of Chinese students. Findings suggest that, in the Chinese culture, sex differences in mental health begin to appear in adolescence.

Shokoohi-Yekta, M., & Retish, P. (1991). Attitudes of Chinese and American male students towards mental illness. *International Journal of Social Psychiatry, 37*(3), 192–200.

The authors compared the attitudes of Chinese and American male graduate students toward mental illness. Significant between-group differences were found.

Thorpe, K., Dragonas, T., & Golding, J. (1992). The effects of psychosocial factors on the mother's emotional well-being during early parenthood: A cross-cultural study of Britain and Greece. *Journal of Reproductive and Infant Psychology, 10*(4), 205–217.

This article examines the effect of psychosocial factors on the emotional well-being of Greek and British mothers and their partners following childbirth. Social support and life events predicted postnatal depression in both cultures.

Trimble, J. E. (1990). Application of psychological knowledge for American Indians and Alaska Natives. *Journal of Training and Practice in Professional Psychology, 4*(1), 45–63.

The article discusses Native American and Alaska Native mental health and alcohol and drug abuse and training of Native American psychologists in the context of the discipline of psychology.

Vega, W. (1992). Theoretical and pragmatic implications of cultural diversity for community research. *American Journal of Community Psychology, 20*(3), 375–391.

In conducting applied research with subgroups from varying cultural backgrounds, certain issues are commonly encountered but often overlooked. Recommendations for overcoming limitations are advanced, emphasizing the need for better relations between university and community.

Wade, J. (1993). Institutional racism: An analysis of the mental health system. *American Journal of Orthopsychiatry, 63*(4), 536–544.

Institutional racism is defined, and its conceptual application to the institution of psychiatry and the mental health system is described.

SOCIAL WORK

Aponte, H. J. (1991). Training on the person of the therapist for work with the poor and minorities. *Journal of Independent Social Work, 5*(3/4), 23–39.

This article focuses on a model for training the person of the therapist who works with low income and minority families. It describes a training model for professionals who already have graduate degrees and want to learn family therapy as it relates to working with multicultural poor, underorganized families. The author presents a framework for training and shows how he has students face their own biases and personal issues in working with this population.

Ball, R. (1993). Children and marital happiness of Black Americans. *Journal of Comparative Family Studies, 24*(2), 203–218.

Data showed that the presence of minor children in the home was associated with lower marital happiness for Black wives.

Bartlett, R. (1974). Ethnicity, professionalism, and Black paternalism: Implications for social welfare services. *Journal of Sociology and Social Welfare, 1*(3), 101–111.

The mid-1960s ushered in the widespread use of indigenous nonprofessionals as a source of new manpower in health, education, and welfare fields, forming a bridge between the client system and the social agency. This research was conducted in a Black ghetto serviced by a Black-staffed community action agency, and the results suggest that a Black professional collective-oriented self-concept is an antidote to Black paternalism.

Chafetz, J., Sampson, P., Beck, P., & West, J. (1974). A study of homosexual women. *Social Work, 19*(6), 714–723.

Existing literature is reviewed, and the conclusion is drawn that almost all research concerning homosexual women is seriously marred by questionable sampling techniques and a normatively based pscyhological approach that reflects prejudice against both women and homosexuals.

Fandetti, D., & Goldmeier, J. (1988). Social workers as culture mediators in health care settings. *Health and Social Work, 13*(3), 171–179.

This article highlights ethnicity as an important factor in assessment and intervention and emphasizes the importance of making social workers aware of the multiple levels involved. Although micro-level assessment, that is, assessment of the identified patient in a health care setting, is a familiar process to social workers, ethnic assessment should not be limited to this level but should be expanded to include inquiries into mezzo and macro levels as well.

Glassman, U. (1991). The social work group and its distinct healing qualities in the health care setting. *Health and Social Work, 16*(3), 203–212.

This article describes how the humanistic values and democratic norms fundamental to social group work are operationalized in groups in the medical setting. The author delineates numerous values and norms and identifies and describes the uses of practice interventions in health care groups.

Gómez, E., & Becker, R. E. (1985). Comparisons between the perceptions of human service workers and Chicano clients in assessments. *Social Thought, 11*(3), 40–48.

A study examined the extent of agreement between social workers and Chicano clients regarding initial assessments and changes in the severity of the problems. Findings revealed that workers perceived clients' complaints as more severe at initial assessment and as changing less in severity than did clients. This lack of congruence was explained by differences between the professional culture of human service workers and the ethnic culture of clients.

Gould, K. (1985). A minority-feminist perspective on child welfare issues. *Child Welfare, 64*(3), 291–305.

The author of this article argues that a minority-feminist perspective on child welfare issues differs from a minority perspective on feminist issues of child welfare in terms of priorities. Illustrations for these ideas are provided from different areas of child welfare practice. The focus is on the contribution of the minority-feminist viewpoint in shaping child welfare practice and policy.

Jayaratne, S, Gant, L. M., Brabson, H. V., Nagda, B. A., Singh, A. K., & Chess, W. A. (1992). Worker perceptions of effectiveness and minority-relevant education as a function of worker and client ethnicity. *Journal of Teaching in Social Work, 6*(1), 93–116.

This study explores the relationship between perceived effectiveness of services delivered to minority clients and the usefulness of education in the delivery of services. The results indicate a stronger correlation between effectiveness and educational adequacy for the Caucasian sample compared to the minority sample. The data also suggest that the proportion of minority clients in a worker's caseload results in differential perceptions of understanding of client problems and the presence of value conflicts.

Juliá, M. (1992). Infant mortality and racially and culturally sensitive care: Problem and prospect for social workers. *Journal of Multicultural Social Work, 2*(4), 59–73.

This article discusses neonatal mortality or death that occurs during the first twenty-eight days of life. It reviews the problem and presents a synopsis of initiatives that have been taken to reconsider and revive, from a social work perspective, the person–environment concern, focus, and commitment to reduce infant mortality, especially among Blacks and other racial/ethnic minorities.

McLaughlin, M., & Balch, P. (1980). Effects of client–therapist ethnic homophily on therapists' judgments. *American Journal of Community Psychology, 8*(2), 243–252.

This article reports on a study aimed at examing attitudes toward clients identified as Chicano and studying the homophily effect regarding ethnicity. Findings provided no support for the view that there are therapist-related differences in client perception, recommendations for treatment, or client acceptance for treatment relative to client–therapist ethnic matching. Discussion focuses on the possibility that ethnicity may operate differently from social class on the therapeutic interaction and on the need to extend this research to indigenous paraprofessional therapist populations.

Mokuau, N. (1987). Social workers' perceptions of counseling effectiveness for Asian American clients. *Social Work, 32*(4), 331–335.

A four-way factorial design was used to examine the impact of four independent variables on social workers' perceptions of effectiveness: (1) ethnicity of the social work respondent—White or Asian; (2) ethnicity of the social worker on the audiotape—White or Asian; (3) counseling style—directive or nondirective; and (4) presenting problem—ethnic or nonethnic. The findings did not support the contention that White and Asian respondents have different perceptions of counseling effectiveness attributable to their different cultural backgrounds: White and Asian social workers appeared to agree on the effectiveness of the nondirective counseling style for Asian clients.

Montalvo, F., Lasater, T., & Valdez, N. (1982). Training child welfare workers for cultural awareness: The culture simulator technique. *Child Welfare, 61*(6), 341–352.

These authors argue that developing effective methods of training child welfare workers about cultural values and beliefs would provide an interim step toward improving child welfare services to the Hispanic family and community. The traditional values discussed apply to various groups, and the technique is adaptable to other ethnic groups and fields of practice.

Morris, L., & Morris, J. (1981). Preparing human service workers for practice in boom communities. *Human Services in the Rural Environment, 6*(1), 22–28.

The author argues that human service workers can be trained for effective practice in rapidly growing communities through the use of simulations that emphasize the complex social, economic, and cultural changes that accompany the boom–bust process. Skills emphasized in simulation training include (1) assessment of the multiple changes accompanying rapid economic growth, (2) network building and maintenance, (3) awareness of value diversity associated with the problem of boom-town bifurcation, and (4) analysis of differential costs and benefits of rapid growth for various groups in the rural community.

Ryan, A., & Henricks, C. (1989). Culture and communication: Supervising the

Asian and Hispanic social worker. *The Clinical Supervisor, 7*(1), 27–40.

Saldov, M. (1991). The ethnic elderly: Communication barriers to health care. *Canadian Social Work Review, 8*(2), 269–277.

It is argued here that Canada's ethnic elderly, individuals aged 65 and over who speak neither English nor French, are isolated from the mainstream of North American society. Serious communication problems with this group in the context of delivery of social and health services lead to deficient treatment, extended hospital stays, unnecessary testing, premature discharge, and problematic follow-up.

Stevenson, K., Cheung, K., & Leung, P. (1992). A new approach to training child protective service workers for ethnically sensitive practice. *Child Welfare, 71*(4), 291–305.

A three-dimensional approach to ethnic sensitivity is presented as one of the critical components in the broader context of cultural sensitivity for child protective services training and evaluation. Training exercises using this approach and a systematic questioning method are recommended.

THEOLOGY

Chalfant, H. P., Heller, P., Roberts, A., Briones, D., Aguirre-Hochbaum, S., & Farr, W. (1990). The clergy as a resource for those encountering psychological distress. *Review of Religious Research, 31*(3), 305–313.

Findings concur with previous national studies showing that the clergy are the most popular source of counseling. This popularity is not significantly affected by religious affiliation, but ethnicity does influence the choice of clergy for help with a personal problem.

Neff, J. A., & Hoppe, S. K. (1993). Race/ethnicity, acculturation, and psychological distress: Fatalism and religiosity as cultural resources. *Journal of Community Psychology, 21*(1), 3–20.

The authors contend that the interplay of acculturation, fatalism, and religiosity supports a complex model of acculturation, emphasizing the consistency of attitudinal elements and language use as facilitators or inhibitors of assimilation into Anglo culture.

Ridley, C. R. (1986). Cross-cultural counseling in theological context. *Journal of Psychology and Theology, 14*(4), 288–297.

Cross-cultural issues have been neglected in the Christian psychology literature. In response to this neglect, the author examines Western cultural assumptions and four salient cross-cultural counseling themes: conceptions of mental health, goals of treatment, techniques of treatment, and roles of therapeutic participants.

Ullman, C. (1988). Psychological well-being among converts in traditional and nontraditional religious groups. *Psychiatry, 51*(3), 312–322.

The author evaluated the psychological well-being of converts to reli-

gious groups foreign to Western culture in comparison with that of converts to mainstream religious groups. Results suggest a sudden upsurge of turmoil often triggered by a specific stressor as a more frequent antecedent to conversion among Jewish and Catholic subjects and a picture of chronic character difficulties as more frequent among other religious groups.

Veatch, R. (1979). Just social institutions and the right to health care. *Journal of Medicine and Philosophy, 4*(2), 170–173.

Health care facilities must be evaluated on a moral, just basis; for them not to provide high-priority services because of arbitrary resource allocation would be in violation of the most basic social code.

Weiss, A., & Mendoza, R. (1990). Effects of acculturation into the Hare Krishna movement on mental health and personality. *Journal for the Scientific Study of Religion, 29*(2), 173–184.

Mental health and personality as a result of acculturation experiences in the Hare Krishna movement were studied. Results of the study indicate that personality traits were mostly invariant with acculturation, and those traits on which the Hare Krishnas differed from the norm group may be prerequisite to membership rather than being its consequences.

Biographical Sketches of Authors

MARÍA C. JULIÁ

María Juliá is an associate professor at The Ohio State University College of Social Work, where she also received her doctorate. Previous to joining the OSU faculty, she served as a social work consultant for both the Ohio and Puerto Rico health departments. Dr. Juliá is actively involved in over a dozen professional and citizens' task forces, committees, and boards, where she volunteers her time for various maternal and child health issues. She provides volunteer professional services to various state, national, and international organizations as well. All of these professional activities have provided much of the data and experiences for her numerous presentations and publications in the area of maternal and child health and international social development. Her interest in women's health has gradually expanded into issues of women in international social development.

HILDA BURGOS-OCASIO

Hilda Burgos-Ocasio is a Ph.D. graduate from The Ohio State University, College of Social Work. She was born and raised in Puerto Rico and received her master's degree in social work from St. Louis University. She has extensive professional experience in the area of child abuse and neglect, especially with Hispanic families. Dr. Burgos-Ocasio's current research is in the area of maternal substance abuse and child drug exposure.

ELIZABETH L. CHUNG

Elizabeth L. Chung is on the staff of the Ohio Commission on Minority Health. She migrated to the United States from Hong Kong in the early 1970s and began her work in the field of public health. She earned a B.S. in nutrition science from the University of Hawaii and an M.S. in public health nutrition from Pennsylvania State University. She is a registered dietitian and is licensed in the state of Ohio. She is actively serving on various committees both at the local and the state level, advocating to improve the well-being of the Asian community, and has held responsible positions in administrative dietetics as well as program planning and development in community-based projects. She has provided numerous presentations, cross-cultural training, and publications related to Asian health and dietary practices. Her strong commitment to public health issues entails numerous hours of service to civic and professional activities. She has been acknowledged as the recipient of numerous awards for her community work.

KAREN V. HARPER

Karen V. Harper is dean of the School of Social Work, West Virginia University. Her research focuses on children and families, women, higher education administration, rural and Appalachian people, and adoption issues and is published in a number of professional human service journals. Dr. Harper directed the master's program and chaired the social administration curriculum in the College of Social Work, The Ohio State University, where she taught social work practice, child welfare, and social administration. A native of Appalachia, Dr. Harper has worked in health care in the region. Committed to multicultural social work practice and service delivery, she has contributed to the development of practice with Appalachian families who have experienced poverty, rural-to-urban migration, and loss of self-esteem and meaning of daily life, particularly losses related to relocation in searching for employment and resources.

ANAHID DERVARTANIAN KULWICKI

Anahid DerVartanian Kulwicki is an associate professor at Oakland University School of Nursing. She is also the director of health research at the Arab Community Center for Economic and Social Services. Dr. Kulwicki received the bachelor's degree in nursing from the American University of Beirut and her master's and doctorate from the Indiana School of Nursing.

SHARY SCOTT RATLIFF

Shary Scott Ratliff credits her own "hidden minority" status as an Appalachian with her lifelong interest in the dynamics of cultural understanding. As a hospital educator, a college professor of world religions, ethics, and philosophy, and the founder and president of the Cambodian Humanitarian Foundation, she brings an interdisciplinary perspective to the issues of cultural diversity and interpersonal connectedness. Dr. Ratliff is also a "Managing Diversity" trainer and a private consultant on intercultural issues in the area of health care.

MARÍA J. ROBBINS

María J. Robbins received her B.A. from Marshall University, Huntington, West Virginia, in languages and education and her master's degree in education from Wright State University, Dayton, Ohio, in counseling and is a licensed professional counselor. She was a National Defense Fellow in Languages for two years at the University of Pittsburgh. She has served as an adjunct instructor with Capital University Without Walls and is a guest lecturer at Antioch University, Yellow Springs, Ohio. She is a commissioner on the State of Ohio Commission of Minority Health and a member of the Committee on Minority Mental Health Concerns. She has lectured throughout the state of Ohio on Native American concerns and issues. Her ethnic background includes the lineage of Blackfoot Indian of the Algonquin stock and Appalachia Cherokee. She follows the "Wise Woman path" rather than that of the warrior.

DARYLE SPERO

Daryle Spero is a registered nurse, is certified by the International Childbirth Education Association as a childbirth educator, and is the mother of four children. She works at the Mount Sinai Medical Center of Cleveland and its affiliate, the Maternity Matters Center, as a perinatal educator. Her responsibilities include all aspects of the perinatal period—early pregnancy, labor and delivery, the postpartum period, infant care, and parenting classes. Previously, she worked as an R.N. in renal and gastrointestinal diseases at Mount Sinai Medical Center and at the Cleveland Clinic Foundation. She received her R.N. and associate of arts and associate of science degrees at Cuyahoga Community College. She is currently completing her B.A. in Psychology at Case Western Reserve University.

GRETCHEN H. WALTMAN

Gretchen H. Waltman is a self-employed social work consultant and trainer and an approved continuing education provider for the Ohio Counselor and Social Worker Board. She has a master's degree in social work from The Ohio State University and has been an adjunct instructor for the university. Her clinical experience includes medical, family and children's services, and psychiatric settings. Consultation services include a small rural hospital and an outpatient medical rehabilitation center.

Having lived among the Amish in Holmes and Tuscarawas Counties most of her life, she has a unique opportunity to observe the Amish culture and life-style and has business and personal relationships with Amish people. She conducts workshops on the Amish to assist health care and human service professionals to understand and appreciate the strengths and special needs of the Amish population.

GRETA BERRY WINBUSH

Greta Berry Winbush is an assistant professor in the College of Social Work, The Ohio State University, teaching courses in aging policy and practice and race and ethnic perspectives. After doctoral work in gerontology, she worked with the Ohio Department of Aging on state-level aging policy and with the California legislative program for supportive services to family caregivers of brain-impaired adults. Dr. Winbush has conducted research and written articles on family caregiving, community-based service delivery to older adults, and minority mental health issues.

Index